MICA PRESS

VOICES FROM THE UNDERGROUND: —VOLUME 2 A DIRECTORY OF SOURCES AND RESOURCES ON THE VIETNAM ERA UNDERGROUND PRESS

Edited by Ken Wachsberger
with Foreword by
Sanford Berman

ALTERNATIVE CATALOGING IN PUBLICATION DATA

Wachsberger, Ken, 1949- editor.
    Voices from the underground. Tempe, AZ: Mica's Press

        2 volumes.
        PARTIAL CONTENTS: volume 1: Insider histories of the Vietnam era underground press; with forewords by William M. Kunstler and Abe Peck. -volume 2: A directory of sources and resources on the Vietnam era underground press; with foreword by Sanford Berman.

        1. Alternative press—History and criticism. 2. Alternative press editors—Personal narratives. 3. Counterculture—Personal narratives. 4. Counterculture—Periodicals—History and criticism. 5. Alternative press—Bibliography. 6. Libraries—Special collections—Alternative press—Directories. 7. Acquisition of alternative press publications. 8. The Sixties—Personal narratives. 9. Vietnam War, 1961-1975—Protest movements—Personal narratives. 10. The Sixties—Periodicals—History and criticism. 11. Vietnam War, 1961-1975—Protest movements—Periodicals—History and criticism. I. Mica's Press. II. Title: Underground voices. III. Title: Insider histories of the Vietnam era underground press. IV. Title: The Vietnam era underground press. V. Title: A directory of sources and resources on the Vietnam era underground press. VI. Kunstler, William M., 1919- Foreword. VII. Peck, Abe, 1945- Foreword. VIII. Berman, Sanford, 1933- Foreword. IX. Title.

070.4509 or 301.2309   92-082780

ISBN: 187946101-3 (Volume 1)
      187946102-1 (Volume 2)
      187946103-X (Collection)

Both volumes are 8 1/2" x 11", softbound, Smyth sewn, with alkaline paper. The paper used in this publication meets the minimum requirements of American National Standards Institute for information sciences—permanence of paper for printed library materials, ANSI Z39.48-1984.   ∞

Cover by Merilea.

Manufactured in the United States of America.

Mica's Press
Box 25544—Library Lane

Other books by Ken Wachsberger:

Beercans on the Side of the Road: The Story of Henry the Hitchhiker. Ann Arbor, MI: Azenphony Press, 1988. Paper $8.95. ISBN 0-945531-00-1.

The Last Selection: A Child's Journey through the Holocaust, with Golda Szachter Kalib and Sylvan Kalib. Amherst, MA: The University of Massachusetts Press, 1991. Cloth $29.95. ISBN 0-87023-758-6.

Both books can be ordered from:

Azenphony Press
PO Box 15152
Ann Arbor, MI 48106

"...skillful editing and a welcome range of voices in the chorus. *Voices from the Underground* includes writers not just from big-city papers on either coast, but from small towns, military bases, even the prisons. Especially prominent are some of the feminist and gay writers who created a revolution within a revolution."

—**Abe Peck**, author of *Uncovering the Sixties: The Life and Times of the Underground Press* and professor of journalism at Northwestern University, from foreword to *Voices from the Underground: Insider Histories of the Vietnam Era Underground Press*

"[*Voices from the Underground*] furnishes the tools for students, librarians, historians, sixties' veterans, and latter-day activists and journalists to variously identify, access, use, understand, appreciate, and perhaps be energized by that still vibrant, icon-toppling, uninhibited, and hopeful corpus of newsprint called the 'underground press.'"

—**Sanford Berman**, head cataloger at the Hennepin County Library, Minnetonka, Minnesota and co-editor of *Alternative Library Literature*, from foreword to *Voices from the Underground: A Directory of Resources and Sources on the Vietnam Era Underground Press*

"*Voices from the Underground* allows 'the people who were there' to document the role of the underground and countercultural press in the development of political consciousness in the 1960s and 70s. In their own words and styles, editors and writers offer insights that scholars and students will find indispensable to the next wave of analytical writing on this important period. This is *the* volume for scholars who want to teach their students about the sixties and the underground press."

—**Barbara L. Tischler**, assistant dean of student affairs, Columbia University School of General Studies, and editor of *Perspectives on the Sixties*

"At a time when some 70 percent of Americans get all their news from network TV, with its constant diet of power elite supplied 'sound bites,' and when Third World bashing, at home and abroad, has become endemic, it is most appropriate that attention be drawn to the very vital role played by the underground and alternative press in the 60s and 70s....*Voices from the Underground* is an important guide and an inspiration for young journalism students and others who recognize the need for a media of integrity, commitment, depth, and truth; a media committed to the propagation of universal human value."

—**David G. Du Bois**, president, W.E.B. Du Bois Foundation, and visiting professor of journalism/Afro American studies, University of Massachusetts

"*Voices* is an important contribution to the history of contemporary dissent in America. Librarians should promote wide use of this insightful and unique publication."
—**Bill Katz**, editor, *Magazines for Libraries*

"The period of the late sixties and early seventies was a high water mark for American journalism. For the first time in American history, the vision of Justices Holmes and Brandeis blossomed and bore fruit. A multitude of voices, the essence of democracy, resounded through the land providing a compelling alternative against the stifling banality of the establishment press. What this nation had during the Vietnam War was exactly what the founding fathers understood the press to be all about when they wrote the First Amendment. You are to be congratulated on making a significant contribution to American journalism. I recommend that anyone who truly cares about the nation's press buy a copy and explore with your writers what journalism was really like when the alternative press flourished."
—**Art Levin**, chair, department of journalism, Butler University

"The true brief shining moment in American press history was the 1960s' voices of liberation as reflected in the grassroots press of the day. Ken Wachsberger has brought together a collection of outstanding memoirs of that age in *Voices from the Underground*: all the more important today when the shining has tarnished and the word 'liberation' is lost in the wind."
—**Barbara Grier**, author of *The Lesbian in Literature*, CEO of Naiad Press, and former editor/publisher of *The Ladder*

"This is indeed an important collection of underground press histories, and it does come with the right forewords and advance endorsements."
—**Editor**, Carol Publishing Group

"...an impressive piece of scholarship...."
—**Editor**, Little, Brown and Company Publishers

"Thank you for submitting Ken Wachsberger's impressive *Voices from the Underground*. I've hesitated to return it to you because I was busy reading it—it's a wonderful, authoritative, and much needed collection...I'm genuinely sorry that we will have to decline it. I am sure the book will do very well...Good luck!"
—**Editor**, Thunder's Mouth Press

"...couldn't put it down...extraordinary book...rave rejection...."
—**Editor**, Pantheon Books

* COLLECTIVE DEDICATION *

Contributors to this two-volume set of *Voices from the Underground* pay tribute to Tom Paine, whose *Common Sense* would not have been syndicated in England; to Upton Sinclair and other turn-of-the-century muckrakers, whose pens forced changes in labeling laws, child labor laws, and other issues that primarily affected poor people; and to all the other dissident pens throughout world history who gave us our tradition of independent reporting and analysis.

We pay further tribute to non-newspaper forms of media that complemented the underground press during the sixties, including FM-radio, poster art, and underground comix; and to underground papers that were published in Canada, France, Germany, England, China, and all over the world. Comparable books to *Voices from the Underground* that cover those topics remain to be written.

In addition, contributors have collectively dedicated *Voices from the Underground* to the following personal inspirations: David Joel and Carrie Suzanne, who hopefully will read this book someday, I.F. Stone, Abbie Hoffman, Huey P. Newton, Judy Grahn, Reed Baird, Marshall Bloom, Libby Gregory, Tom Forcade, every gay and lesbian who came out before there was a movement, Fredy Perlman, Marshall McLuhan, Russ Benedict, Emily, Zoltan Ferency, Steve Peake, Uncle Ho, John Lennon and Phil Ochs and the many other musicians and songwriters who attempted to capture the spirit of the time and whose work provided both the soundtrack and often the inspiration for our efforts in the media and the larger political movement, Mary Ellen, Myra, Annette, Max Scherr, Angela Davis, Allen Katzman, Myra Wolfgang, Clara Fraser, the Beat writers who preceded us and whose poetry and prose opened the paths to our free expression, Michael Patrick Madden, Jennifer Brooke Stanton Webb and the new generation of feminism, Scottie Remington, Richard Durham, Reinaldo Arenas, Charles P. Howard, Ti-Grace Atkinson, Elijah Muhammad, Malcolm X, Ron Ausburn, Christy and Joyce, Richie Havens and Country Joe, Sharlane, Charity, and Magda Grant, Meridel LeSueur, Agnes Tuttle, and the many prisoners whose signed articles guaranteed them gassings, beatings, endless time in solitary confinement, and sometimes death.

Finally, we dedicate the book to:

- our intergenerational peers—those students of today who are the age now that we were then, and who grew to political awareness during the Reagan years but didn't buy his explanations and interpretations;

- those heroic alternative newspapers of today that carry on the tradition of investigative journalism without being snowed under with record and movie reviews; and

- the National Writers Union (873 Broadway, Suite 203, New York, NY 10003-1209; 212-254-0279), whose leaders emerged from the underground press and whose victories are the victories of all independent writers.

TABLE OF CONTENTS FOR VOLUME 2

*Voices from the Underground: A Directory of Sources and Resources
on the Vietnam Era Underground Press*

        by Anne E. Zald and Cathy Seitz Whitaker. With sidebars from Peggy D'Adamo, Liz O'Lexa, and Sanford Berman
                Although there never was a truly "underground" press during the Vietnam era, there was indeed a radical voice raised throughout the United States to challenge First Amendment limits and the government's unwillingness to handle dissent in the media. Today, the subject of the underground press is folklore, as veterans and fascinated onlookers continue to embrace its memory, even while critically evaluating it. Books, articles, master's theses, and doctoral dissertations have compared and contrasted the underground press to the mainstream press, spotlighted individuals from the underground press, and documented government harassment of the underground press. Anthologies have brought together its best writings. In this article, Zald and Whitaker present the most in-depth and substantive annotated bibliography available on this fascinating and important topic. In sidebars, Peggy D'Adamo and Liz O'Lexa introduce readers to the Alternative Press Center and Sanford Berman offers his own annotated bibliography for libraries that want to expand their own collections of alternative materials.

        by Ellen E. Embardo
                Librarians are the original packrats, and the Vietnam era was a packrat librarian's dream period. Collectible materials that originated then, in the form of books, underground newspapers, bumperstickers, buttons, flyers, posters, films, and unpublished notes, were as colorful, inspiring, and intellectually stimulating as any our country's brief history has created. In 1982, Scarecrow Press published *Alternative Materials in Libraries*. One chapter, by Patricia Case, proved immensely useful as a reference tool for identifying many of these special collections libraries throughout the United States and Canada. In this article, Embardo updates and expands that directory, which appears in three parts. One listing, devoted to gay and lesbian special collections libraries, expands Cal Gough's 1989 "Gay/Lesbian Archives and Libraries in North America."

        by Daniel C. Tsang
                Why should one attempt to preserve the underground or alternative press in microform? According to Tsang, there are several reasons, including the longer life expectancy the process offers to materials, reduced storage space requirements for libraries, less wear and tear caused by users, and reduced risk of loss through fire, damage, or theft. In addition, of course, for researchers ease of access can be facilitated. In this article, Tsang presents an overview of several important microfilming projects to date, including the problems they have faced and the challenges they have overcome. He concludes with comprehensive or selected listings of seven collections in microform. An eighth appendix is of underground press anthologies or reprint editions.

PUBLISHER'S NOTES

Joseph W. Grant

The courage *Voices from the Underground* celebrates is ancient. That it details the times of our lives is happenstance. Walls of terrible, selfish wrong were splattered by the writers included here—writers who fought this fight with words and actions. Their assault weakened the walls of exclusion and secrecy that government had erected and exposed its military machinations.

My part is small. My contribution, as detailed in the final chapters concerning the *Penal Digest International (PDI)*, is properly placed. Imprisonment and isolation are a last resort of the tyrant. My nobility was after the fact. I came late to the party, as a voice from the dungeon.

Twenty years later, when Ken Wachsberger asked me to write the *PDI*'s history for *Voices*, I was a different person. The *Penal Digest International* had become the *Prisoners Digest International* and had long since passed, in modern forms and under different names, to intensely ardent young women and men. I was by then suffering other lonely efforts under the ever-watchful eyes of a wife, whose intellect and field of study I greatly admire, and a college-bound daughter. At first I thought the publication of my old voice might finally enable me to explain myself to them. It was ego. I felt the pain of this reconstructed dissonance in purely personal terms. I did not see myself as one small part of a larger portrait.

Ken, on the other hand, believed that the other contributors and I were sitting on information of immense social value, especially to the younger

Grant is an artist, writer, and graphic designer living with his best friend and their daughter in the Southwest. His documentaries on El Salvador ("Prisons and Prisons: El Salvador") and author Meridel LeSueur ("Women in the Breadlines" and "The Iowa Tour") have been shown on the Time/Life and other cable networks. He believes that never before in our history has there been a greater need for the *PDI* to be publishing and providing a means for prisoners and people in the free world to communicate. He is open to suggestions.

generation of scholars and creative dissidents he calls "our intergenerational peers," who have learned about the sixties and the Vietnam era from the people we opposed then—many of whom cheered as our heads were busted and we were thrown into jail for exercising our constitutional rights to free speech and assembly.

While the writing of the *PDI*'s biography was occupying me obsessively, the original publisher withdrew from the project, citing a bad economy as the main reason and the possibility of libel as another. By the time my article was finished, Ken had found a New York agent and the manuscript was making the rounds of major publishing houses.

Ken and I talked at night long-distance. He read me the letters of rejection. The editors who wrote them were saying "No" in a wind of admiration: "an impressive piece of scholarship," said one; "much needed collection," said another; and a third—"couldn't put it down...extraordinary book...rave rejection...."

They wrote with praise and turned-away eyes as they said "No" in the "I-can't-afford-it" voice of the meek.

They were wrong, of course. For in the same way that we needed to hear history's voices from the underground that had witnessed against slavery and the Holocaust and the incidents at Wounded Knee, we must now hear these Vietnam era *Voices from the Underground*.

One night, long after these books should already have been in libraries and bookstores, after another of those midnight conversations with Ken, it finally dawned on me that I could not limit my participation to that of contributor and observer. And so again, late to the party, and worried about the insidious forms censorship—including self-censorship—continues to take in the nineties, I have become a publisher.

The voices you are privileged to read here are those of my sisters and brothers, brought together to share their dreams as well as their anger and frustration, their beatings and arrests, their triumphs and failures, and their lessons.

It's been an adventure and a challenge creating Mica's Press for the *Voices from the Underground* series. As this new publishing house continues to evolve, I hope it will do justice to the efforts of the biographers and exemplify the kind of sharing and acceptance that came of age within the underground movement of the Vietnam era. Founding and funding a publishing company is a story of its own—a story for another time.

For now, welcome to the underground of the Vietnam era and to a long overdue set of books. I hope these unimaginable experiences—these adventures—generate perilous thoughts, risky feelings, dangerous dreams, and the temptation for you to act on them.

Read them and decide. Then let your voice be heard.

MICA PRESS

FOREWORD

Sanford Berman

Maybe it was 1960. Maybe 1961. Anyway, someone I worked with in the acquisitions department at DC Public Library suggested I go to a poetry reading. Although I'd written much doggerel and some pretentious free verse myself, I don't think I'd ever actually been to a "reading." The poets I never heard of. The place was a dingy, dark hotel auditorium in downtown Washington. People—many of them grungy-looking—packed the small and smoky room even before the event started. Being the tie-wearing, white-shirted, clean-shaven assistant chief of a public library department and soon-to-graduate library school student (I'd enrolled in DCPL's "Work-study" program, which meant working for DCPL full-time and studying whenever I could), I wondered what in hell I was doing there and how quickly I could get out.

Until the event began. And then I knew—almost instantly—that I didn't want to be anywhere else. Four guys read their own works. And *what* I heard at once amazed, refreshed, and excited me, because what I heard was poetry about important things, about usually-suppressed feelings and topics, about anger and injustice and joy and being free, about fucked-up systems and shibboleths, about moral straitjackets and political insanity. And I heard it in the kind of voice that Whitman would have used in 1960: irreverent, real, unexpected, unrestrained, and singing. It was a poetry of emotions and criticism and hope and ideas expressed in a way that not only shattered convention but also made the words and messages much more

Berman is head cataloger at the Hennepin County Library (Minnetonka, Minnesota) and co-editor of the biennial anthology, *Alternative Library Literature* (McFarland). In 1989 he won the American Library Association's Equality Award.

accessible to a waiting and (metaphorically) starved audience.

Well, I readily became one of the hungry listeners to those shabby, tradition-busting, anti-Establishment troubadours. Their names? Allen Ginsberg. Leroi Jones (now Amiri Baraka). Gregory Corso. And Peter Orlovsky.

Fire marshals ended the program prematurely, but that evening's experience so profoundly affected me (although I confess to already having been powerfully influenced by reading Henry Miller in clandestine, Paris-printed paperbacks while a GI in Germany) that later, working as an army librarian in Europe, I managed (by means of genuinely "creative financing") to get whole anthologies of Beat writing as well as several issues of *City Lights Journal* into the libraries I supervised (which incidentally prompted a censorship attempt by a Southern Methodist chaplain who wore paratroop boots while conducting Sunday services). One month I also mounted a counter-top "Beat Lit." display featuring a photo of Allen at his shaggiest and most unkempt, not exactly the type of gung-ho role-model exhibit my civilian "brass" encouraged in barracks libraries.

And we did our *own* poetry readings at base service clubs. GIs and I shared work we had written ourselves, together with a large dose of Whitman, William Carlos Williams, Corso, Ginsberg, Garcia Lorca, Brecht, Yevtushenko, Lawrence Ferlinghetti, Vachel Lindsay, and Hans Magnus Enzensberger, among others.

Finally, in early 1966, we went the whole way. That February, *Yin Yang* appeared. "An independent journal of art, ideas, and imagination, published from time to time by Coleman Barracks Library" in Mannheim-Sandhofen, West Germany, it contained poems, graphics, plays, photos, and short stories, by me and about a dozen soldiers. GIs composed three-fourths of the editorial board. That first issue proved sufficiently candid, if not actually brash, "liberating," and un-military, that a Lt. Colonel visited me in the library office to report that "some people" thought it "subversive" and to deliver a not-so-veiled warning about publishing another number.

Even as he cautioned us, the master pages for the March issue rested quietly in an office drawer. (In fact, the "Good News" Colonel practically sat on them as he spoke.) Later they *became* the March issue, featuring splendid, mind-warping collages and photographs by Norman Morris (a truly inspired and utterly unique artist whose permanent legacy to Coleman Barracks was a totally-rearranged/redecorated display case) and Jim Caccavo (afterwards a celebrated war photographer and teacher), ironic poetry by Ed Badajos (within a few years to become a major surrealist cartoonist and author

of both *Filipino Food* and *Dick*!), and "unspeakable" verse like this excerpt from "Rotation to Freedom," by John S. Cunningham, who planned after discharge to attend college in Baltimore and get active in the Civil Rights movement:

There will be reason,
as well as purpose,
for the deeds I do.
No more asking, Why?
I'll get answers that make more sense
than "authority" or "jurisdiction"!
But, most important,
I'll be free.
Hallelujah!

Whether those two issues of *Yin Yang* influenced the later GI underground press, I don't know. But I happily nominate them as among the first of the genre.

Following my five-year stint in Europe, I returned to hometown Los Angeles for a year, employed as periodicals librarian in UCLA's research library. The "counterculture" flourished in and around Westwood during 1968. Head shops. Free Press Kazoos. Papa Bach's incredible bookstore-cum-activist-hangout. And the local underground press. Dominant, of course, was Art Kunkin's *Los Angeles Free Press*, to which—three years later, while in-between overseas jobs—I contributed "Libraries To the People!," a "rabble-rousing," patron-empowering rant.

But the *Freep* wasn't the only underground rag in town. Another was *Open City*, which made the colossal "mistake" of crucifying the local constabulary for their many and brutal misdeeds. (The Rodney King incident didn't happen in an historical vacuum.) In retaliation, the district attorney charged *Open City* with obscenity. That's right, *obscenity*. No charges directly for blowing the whistle on the cops, but rather a trumped-up rap for printing a music ad showing a nude rock group in wholly unmoving, stonelike, static postures. That the graphic was laughably *un*obscene, in fact a parody of "obscenity," should have been obvious to any reasonably conscious toddler. The "obscenity" charge really had nothing to do with sex or immorality. It had EVERYTHING to do with the impermissible, authority-threatening act of reporting critically about L.A.'s not-so-finest fuzz.

So what's my connection with all this? Simply that *Open City* and its "rad" lawyer, Mike Hannon, asked UCLA's deputy library director, a giant among the profession's intellectual freedom crowd, to testify for the defense. He refused. To this day I don't know precisely why. Possibly the scuzziness offended his sensibilities. Only a guess. Too bad he didn't do it, though, because his venerable age and august demeanor would surely have impressed the jury. Mine didn't. For, as a last resort, *I* was invited to go to court. And I did so willingly enough, bringing an armful of sample magazine copies from the periodicals reading room to demonstrate how nudity and other graphic sex were common enough in journals and newspapers published here and abroad—and freely available to the public in our library.

The first day, under direct, friendly examination, went great. Jurors even chuckled. But the next day's cross-examination, by a vicious, upwardly-mobile assistant D.A., who during the recess had audibly announced that he was going to "get that faggot" (me!), proved a disaster. I froze, became practically speechless and inaudible, and retired from the stand feeling like shit. *Open City* eventually lost the case. Later, I believe, they won on appeal, but the authorities achieved what they intended. They killed the rag. No shoestring operation could afford such enormous court costs and outlay of personal time and energy.

With hindsight, I realize that my lousy performance alone didn't wreck the paper, and no one associated with the case ever rebuked me for collapsing on the stand. But now, more than 20 years later, I want to say publicly that I'm sorry I didn't do better. I sure as hell *wanted* to.

The years 1968-71 my family and I spent in Zambia, where I worked at the university library. During that time I suspect we were the sole subscribers to the *L.A. Free Press* and *I.F. Stone's Weekly* in all of Sub-Saharan Africa. Who knows, possibly in the whole continent! In any event, those subs kept the underground press and sixties near and alive for us, even though we lived thousands of miles away from "the action." And maybe this is what I want to say about the undergrounds: their "gospel" was that the "action" is really where *you* are. So even in the middle of Africa they functioned as a context, as a moral and political inspiration, for my own thoughts and acts. And the same holds for the subsequent "alternative press." While not as psychedelic, frenzied, and flamboyant as their sixties' precursors, today's independent press and media do essentially the same job. They "keep the faith." They build community. They supply visions of a better life and world. They remind us about what issues and events and policies are truly important. And they provide facts and analyses that "somehow" the *New York Times* and NBC and even PBS miss altogether. Often they accomplish these deeds in memorable and moving prose and graphics reminiscent of the *Great Speckled Bird* and *Berkeley Barb*, but what's overridingly significant is that THEY DO IT.

Why should anyone buy, read, or browse *Voices from the Underground: A Directory of Resources and Sources on the Vietnam Era Underground Press*? By now you can certainly guess. Because it furnishes the tools for students, librarians, historians, sixties' veterans, and latter-day activists and journalists to variously identify, access, use, understand, appreciate, and perhaps be energized by that still vibrant, icon-toppling, uninhibited and hopeful corpus of newsprint called the "underground press." It distinctly helped to mould my views and invigorate my life. And I'm deeply thankful for it.

— SANFORD BERMAN —

EDITOR'S INTRODUCTION

Ken Wachsberger

The underground press in the United States during the Vietnam era was the major vehicle through which a major segment of this country's population conspired to defeat the policies of a government they believed had gone insane. In the pages of the underground press, readers from this "anti-establishment" community of the political and cultural left learned the phrases that we would chant together at antiwar rallies to spread our message and to defend ourselves against what we perceived to be the establishment enemy. At the same time, those phrases gave us collective strength and a way to communicate with each other in other forms of hostile territory—at school, on the job, in the company of our parents. We embraced those phrases as "revolutionary war cries," although we never used that descriptive term.

In the pages of *Joint Issue*, East Lansing, Michigan's Vietnam-era underground newspaper, where I spent my politically formative years, readers found sayings to live by—morals to help them relate to each other: Tip the dishwasher, Pick up hitchhikers, Sisters pick up sisters, Don't talk to the FBI, Chop down cars, Make love not war, Impeach Nixon, Boycott grapes, Boycott lettuce, Boycott Gallo and all wines from Modesto, California, Boycott Farah...

We honored such a long list of boycotts that even staff members couldn't keep track of them all so we devised a "JI Boycott Box" and updated it for every issue.

The establishment press tried to delegitimize these phrases by calling them rhetoric. We legitimized them

Wachsberger is editor of *Voices from the Underground: Insider Histories of the Vietnam Era Underground Press* and *Voices from the Underground: A Directory of Resources and Sources on the Vietnam Era Underground Press*. His article on the underground newspapers from East Lansing, Michigan appears in this collection.

by learning the meanings behind them and acting accordingly.

In *Voices from the Underground: Insider Histories of the Vietnam Era Underground Press*, the story of *Joint Issue* is told along with the stories of some two dozen other underground newspapers through the eyes of the people who were on the respective staffs at the time. These are not the first insider histories ever written. In fact, the subject of the underground press is already folklore, as veterans and fascinated onlookers have continued to embrace its memory, even while critically evaluating it. Raymond Mungo was cofounder of Liberation News Service, the underground press' counterpart to the establishment media's Associated Press and United Press International. In 1970, Beacon Press in Boston published Mungo's *Famous Long Ago: My Life and Hard Times with Liberation News Service*. Abe Peck was a staffer and editor of *Chicago Seed*, the vehicle of communication that helped mobilize anti-riot defense forces against Chicago police and members of the Democratic Party during the summer of 1968. Pantheon Books published Peck's *Uncovering the Sixties: The Life and Times of the Underground Press* in 1985. Citadel Underground Press is to be commended for recently republishing both books. David Armstrong is a former editor of *Berkeley Barb*, one of the best known and most important of the many underground newspapers that published on the two coasts. Armstrong's *A Trumpet to Arms: Alternative Media in America* was published by South End Press in 1981. In 1967, Andy Stapp founded *The Bond*, generally considered to be the first underground newspaper published by and for military personnel. His account of that period, *Up Against the Brass*, was published by Simon and Schuster in 1970 and is long overdue to be reprinted.

These memoirs and analyses from the left were, of course, generally positive in their regard for the influence of the underground press as a whole. One example of an attack from the right was Francis Watson's *The Alternative Media: Dismantling Two Centuries of Progress*, which was published by Rockford (Illinois) College Institute in 1979. According to Watson, the permissive culture in which the alternative press thrived "provides a force for self-indulgence in art and lifestyle that runs counter to the values of self-discipline and economic self-reliance associated with capitalism and liberty."

Other articles, books, master's theses, and doctoral dissertations have compared and contrasted the underground press to the mainstream press, spotlighted individuals from the underground press, and documented government harassment of the underground press. Numerous anthologies have brought together its best writings. These accounts and reprinted articles can be found today in many public libraries. But what are the titles of these works and how can they be found in libraries?

Answers to those questions can be found in the lead article to *Voices from the Underground: A Directory of Resources and Sources on the Vietnam Era Underground Press*, which supplements the volume of *Insider Histories*. "The Underground Press of the Vietnam Era: An Annotated Bibliography," by Anne Zald, reference librarian at University of Washington, and Cathy Whitaker, social work librarian at University of Pittsburgh, is the most extensive and substantively annotated bibliography available on this fascinating and important subject. Anne and Cathy are both members of the American Library Association's Alternatives in Print Task Force. Anne is a past chair. Cathy is editor of *Alternative Publications: A Guide to Directories, Indexes, Bibliographies and Other Sources*.

* * *

Librarians are the original packrats, and the Vietnam era was a packrat librarian's dream period. Collectible materials that originated then, in the form not only of books and underground newspapers but also bumperstickers, buttons, flyers, posters, films, and other vehicles of communication, as well as boxes and files of unpublished notes, were as colorful, inspiring, and intellectually stimulating as any our country's brief history has created. Always there to gather it up for posterity as it was being created and discarded were librarians, both vocational and avocational. Today, libraries with these special collections are scattered throughout the world. There is a good chance one is located not far from your own home.

Michigan State University's "American Radicalism Collection," for instance, provided me with yellowed but nevertheless original copies of every underground newspaper to appear in the Lansing area from 1965 to 1976, when I wrote and edited an eight-part series on the history of the underground press in East Lansing for the *Lansing Star*, *Joint Issue*'s successor paper. Years later, when I expanded that article for *Serials Review*, and again when I began my research that would lead to *Voices from the Underground: Insider Histories of the Vietnam Era Underground Press*, I returned there. I would like to thank at this time MSU special collections librarians past and present—Jannette Fiore, Peter Berg, and Anne Tracy—for their suggestions and their direction.

In "Directories of Special Collections on Social Movements Evolving from the Vietnam Era," Ellen Embardo brings us inside MSU's American Radicalism Collection, as well as approximately fifty other public and private special collections libraries in the United

States and Canada that have major holdings of primary and secondary materials from the Vietnam era. Ellen is curator of the Alternative Press Collection at Homer Babbidge Library at the University of Connecticut. Her research continues the work done by Patricia Case, James Danky, and Elliott Shore in 1982.

* * *

Finally, who would have guessed, while laying out the final pages of any issue of *Joint Issue* at 3 a.m. the day the galleys were due at the printer's, standing in front of a wobbly light table next to the kitty litter box under a basement window, that my beloved source of revolutionary information and outlet for revolutionary satire would one day be a commodity in the hi tech commercial market? Indeed, as Dan Tsang shows in "Preserving the U.S. Underground and Alternative Press of the 1960s and '70s: History, Prospects, and Microform Sources," a number of public and commercial organizations have gathered together complete or nearly complete collections of hundreds of underground papers for easy access and long-term preservation on microfilm. Dan's compilation of microform masters, which appears as appendix H of his article, is the first time these disparate sources have been gathered together in one place. Dan himself has been active in the underground and alternative press for many years. Besides being social sciences bibliographer at the University of California, Irvine, he is a volunteer indexer for the *Alternative Press Index* and head of the Lesbian and Gay Declassified Documentation Project.

* * *

If we as citizens of the nineties are to understand what the political, corporate, and banking leaders of the United States did during the Vietnam era to so anger so massive and so diverse a segment of the population that it could unite to bring down presidents of both major parties and end an insane war, and if we are to learn how they did it, we must read and understand the independent alternative media through which members of this dissident community communicated.

If we are to seek similar insights as to what our "leaders" did to us during the Reagan/Bush years in the name of "nationalism," "national security," "patriotism," "deregulation," "free trade," and other establishment rhetoric, and if we are to prevent such devastation from ever happening again, we must again look beyond the corporate media to the poets and visionaries of the independent alternative media.

As a journalist who has worked intimately with the librarian profession for the past four years, not only on this two-volume set of *Voices from the Underground* but as managing editor of Pierian Press' *Library Hi Tech*, *Library Hi Tech News*, *Serials Review*, and *Reference Services Review*, I've gained tremendous respect and appreciation for the efforts of its members, who are guided by the watchword "access" and whose career mission is to guide others to the materials that will answer their research questions. I am sincerely amazed at the efforts of the librarians with whom I collaborated on this second volume of *Voices from the Underground*. Anne Zald, Cathy Whitaker, Ellen Embardo, and Dan Tsang were always enthusiastic in their thirst for any leads, any ideas, any thoughts that I passed along to them even as we chased closing deadlines.

Voices from the Underground: A Directory of Resources and Sources on the Vietnam Era Underground Press is a unique and important addition to the collection of public and private libraries and social change organizations that hope to offer an understanding of the Vietnam era and its legacy.

MICA PRESS

In Memoriam

Michael "Mica" Kindman

May 8, 1945 - November 22, 1991

THE UNDERGROUND PRESS OF THE VIETNAM ERA:

An Annotated Bibliography

Anne E. Zald and **Cathy Seitz Whitaker**
with sidebars by Peggy D'Amato, Liz O'Lexa, and Sanford Berman

I.   **General Treatment of Underground Press**
  A.   History, Analysis
  B.   Comparison to/Critique of Mainstream Press
  C.   Anthologies
  D.   Government Harassment

II. **Individual Treatments**
  A.   Title or Organization
    1.   History, Analysis
    2.   Comparison to/Critique of Mainstream Press
    3.   Anthologies
    4.   Government Harassment
  B.   Geographic Area
  C.   Publisher
  D.   Personality

III. **Press Syndicates**

Zald is reference librarian, University of Washington Libraries, Seattle. She is past chair of the Alternatives in Print Task Force, Social Responsibilities Round Table, American Library Association. *Whitaker* is Buhl social work librarian, Hillman Library, University of Pittsburgh. She is the editor of *Alternative Publications: A Guide to Directories, Indexes, Bibliographies and Other Sources*.

Despite the title of this bibliography, there was not a truly underground press in the United States during the 1960s and 1970s. The phrase is a misnomer, reputedly coined on the spur of the moment in 1966 by Thomas Forcade when asked to describe the newly established news service, Underground Press Syndicate, of which he was an active member. The papers mentioned in this bibliography, except for the publications of the Weather Underground, were not published by secretive, covert organizations. Freedom of the press and of expression is protected by the First Amendment to the Constitution, although often only symbolically as the experience of the undergrounds will show. Most of the publications that fall into the "underground" described herein maintained public offices, contracted with commercial printers, and often used the U.S. Postal Service to distribute their publications.

The term "underground," then, has come to have another meaning. It has been used to describe publications, in particular those founded during the years of the Vietnam War, that presented a new, personalized approach to journalism. More people had access to the means of production, the printing press, due to advances in the offset printing process. The technical skills required to produce a newspaper were reduced to the ability to type, cut, and paste. Costs became affordable.

Concurrent with these technological developments was a growing dissatisfaction with the established media and its consistent failure to cover issues with any hint of critical inquiry. The voices unleashed in this enthusiasm for print were brash, opinionated, creative, and revolutionary. The underground press was born on the West Coast, but soon spread to every major city, and many smaller ones, in the United States. Laurence Leamer, in his book *The Paper Revolutionaries*, estimated in 1972 that the total underground press circulation may have been as high as 3,000,000 with an estimated readership of 18,000,000.[1]

Reviewing the literature about the underground press quickly reveals that "underground" was more a state of mind than a precise category. The concerns of the underground papers were highly individualistic and covered both political and cultural issues on the national and local scene. The appearance of the papers was as unique as their editorial opinions, with each paper developing a unique, often non-columnar, multi-colored graphic presentation.

This bibliography uses the term to describe those newspapers that shared the following characteristics:

1. They rejected the conventional journalistic notions of objectivity. Underground newspapers contended that mainstream newspapers published their biases but did not acknowledge them. Underground journalists and editors were blatantly subjective in their reporting, often participating in or even instigating the events covered in their papers.

2. They were almost uniformly non-commercial and unprofitable. A few notorious exceptions did exist but the majority of the papers founded during the period studied ceased to publish within twelve months of their first issue, due to financial difficulties. Those that survived did so with extreme tenacity.

3. They published strong anti-Vietnam War and anti-military draft articles and opinions. This was the one consistent theme among the various political and cultural emphases of the papers.

4. They served the opinions of a growing youth culture, interested in social change, self-expression, freedom from parental interference, and/or personal growth. Editorial staff and readership included students of high school and college age, young adults both civilian and military, and long-time radicals eternally young at heart.

5. They covered topics that were omitted by the mainstream press. These topics included the antiwar organizations and demonstrations, rock music, liberated mores regarding sexuality, drug use, communal living, environmental concerns, the women's movement, the gay liberation movement, and the movements of racial minorities for full social, legal, and economic rights.

6. Many of them experienced some form of harassment from federal or local law enforcement officials. Harassment ranged from the nuisance arrests of street peddlers who often sold the newspapers, to the intimidation of landlords and printers, and went to the extremes of disinformation, infiltration, and the destruction of offices and equipment.

The period studied for this bibliography is 1964-1975. While a few of the publications discussed precede or antedate this period in part, a publication was included if a substantial portion of its lifespan fell within these dates and it met with the definition provided above. The beginning date, 1964, marks the publication and distribution of Art Kunkin's *Faire Free Press* at the Los Angeles Renaissance Faire on May 1, 1964. The *Faire Free Press* later expanded to become the *Los Angeles Free Press*. The closing date for the bibliography, 1975, corresponds with the withdrawal of U.S. military forces from Vietnam. Without the unifying ideology of opposition to U.S. military terrorism in Southeast Asia, competing interests within The Movement began to tear it apart. The Movement became several movements, splintering into its constituent factions. The underground papers increasingly addressed smaller audiences, unified by their location or specialized interests (e.g., women's rights, gay rights, the environment, mystic and New Age religions). By this time, even the name of the underground press had changed. In 1973, the Underground Press Syndicate, which had originally christened the countercultural press, became the Alternative Press Syndicate, an acknowledgment of the changing times. "Alternative" has become the accepted term to describe the publications that today follow in the dissenting tradition and advocate social change. Not included here, although a worthy subject of study, is the rich and varied literature about the alternative press from the later seventies and into the eighties.

Although there is literature available about the underground press in Great Britain, Canada, and other regions of the world, we have included only those materials that are primarily about the underground press in the United States. Excluded also are materials written in languages other than English and non-print media.

Online databases searched in the process of compiling this bibliography include the following: America: History and Life, Arts and Humanities Citation Index, Dissertation Abstracts, ERIC, Humanities Index, Knowledge Index, LC MARC-BOOKS, Magazine Index, MLA International Bibliography, Public Affairs Information Service Bulletin, Social Sciences Citation Index, Social Sciences Index (also searched paper edition of *Social Sciences and Humanities Index* back to 1960), Sociological Abstracts, and

OCLC's EPIC database. In addition, Peggy D'Adamo and Liz O'Lexa, from the Alternative Press Collective (see sidebar 1), contributed annotations for articles listed in the *Alternative Press Index* from 1985 to 1989. Many of the references concerning the military underground newspapers were contributed by Harry W. Haines, whose own story, "Soldiers Against the War in Vietnam: The Story of *Aboveground*," appears in *Voices from the Underground: Insider Histories of the Vietnam Era Underground Press*, which complements this volume. In sidebar 2, Sanford Berman, head cataloger at Minnesota's Hennepin County Library, shows librarians how to add alternative substance to their collections.

To the best of our ability this bibliography is complete through 1989, with the exception of the *Alternative Press Index* from the years 1969 to 1984.

This bibliography originally appeared in an abbreviated form in *Reference Services Review* 18, no. 4 (Winter 1990). Although weaknesses then in the bibliography have been addressed in part, the authors continue to lament the shortage of studies about the gay/lesbian/feminist press and minority papers. For example, Clare Potter's *Lesbian Periodicals Index* (1986, Naiad Press) provides access to 42 publications of the 1960s and 1970s, but critical or descriptive works about these or other lesbian or gay papers have

yet to be identified. Some materials that looked promising have been omitted after examination due to their peripheral treatment of the underground press. One example of this is Huey Newton's doctoral dissertation, "War Against the Panthers: A Study of Repression in America" (University of California, Santa Cruz, 1980). This detailed account of the Black Panther Party only briefly discusses government harassment of the *Black Panther* newspaper. Certainly the *Alternative Press Index* for the years 1969-1984 is a valuable source for further research on these papers. Additional resources for the study of publications from this era include *From Radical Left to Extreme Right: A Bibliography of Current Periodicals of Protest, Controversy, Advocacy, or Dissent, with Dispassionate Content-Summaries to Guide Librarians and Other Educators* (3d edition, Scarecrow Press, 1987) and *The American Left, 1955-1970: A National Union Catalog of Pamphlets Published in the United States and Canada*, edited by Ned Kehde (Greenwood Press, 1976).

NOTES

1.   Laurence Leamer, *The Paper Revolutionaries: The Rise of the Underground Press*. (New York: Simon and Schuster, 1972), 14-15.

"Access to Alternatives," in *The Joy of Cataloging* (Phoenix, AZ: Oryx Press, 1981), 124-48.

This article offers guidelines and examples for improving catalog access to alternative and small press materials. Among the guidelines: "Make added entries for sponsoring, producing, or otherwise closely associated presses, groups, and agencies; and, for informational purposes, provide *public notes* in the catalog that briefly identify such producers and organizations. Make added entries for subtitles and catch-titles that catalog users may remember and seek. Impose no upper limit on subject tracings, applying as many as necessary to substantially and accurately reflect the content of each work. Assign subject tracings to novels, short stories, poetry, and other literary genres on the same basis as to nonfiction. Establish new descriptors to represent subjects not currently "legitimized" nor recognized in the LC [Library of Congress] thesaurus. Compose notes to clarify contents, indicate special features, and show relationships to other works, persons, or groups."

"Compare and Contrast, or, The Unexamined Cataloging Record Isn't Worth Inputting," *Alternative Library Literature, 1988/1989* (Jefferson, NC: McFarland, 1990), 173-81.

Comparisons are made between "Library of Congress and Hennepin County Library records for recent small and alternative press titles." Three examples follow:

+LC

Downing, John.
Radical media: the political experience of alternative communication. South End Press, 1984.

1. Mass media—Political aspects. 2. Mass media—Management. I. Title.

+HCL

Downing, John.
Radical media: the political experience of alternative communication. South End Press, 1984.
PARTIAL CONTENTS: United States. National Guardian/Guardian. KPFA, Berkeley. Union Wage. Akwesasne Notes and ERIN Bulletin. NACLA: Report on the Americas. Third World Newsreel. California Newsreel. Independent film-making in Puerto Rico. - Portugal and Italy. Radio Renascenca. Lutta Continua. - Eastern Europe.
1. Alternative mass media. 2. Akwesasne Notes—History and criticism. 3. The Guardian, New York City—History and criticism. 4. KPFA (Radio station). 5. Union Wage—History and criticism. 6. ERIN Bulletin—History and criticism. 7. NACLA Report on the Americas—History and criticism. 8.

Third World Newsreel. 9. California Newsreel. 10. Independent filmmakers—Puerto Rico. 11. Alternative mass media—Portugal. 12. Alternative mass media—Italy. 13. Alternative mass media—Eastern Europe. 14. Censorship—Eastern Europe. I. South End Press. II. Title. III. Title: The political experience of alternative communication.

+LC

Rule, Jane.
Memory board. Naiad Press, 1987.

I. Title.

+HCL

Rule, Jane.
Memory board. Naiad Press, 1987.

1. Twins—Fiction. 2. Lesbian seniors—Fiction. 3. Lesbians—Family relationships—Fiction. 4. Brothers and sisters—Fiction. I. Title. II. Naiad Press.

+LC

Seider, Maynard, 1943 -
A year in the life of a factory. Singlejack Books, 1984.

1. Electronic industry workers—California. 2. Collective bargaining—California. 3. Strikes and lockouts—California. 4. Seider, Maynard, 1943- . I. Title.

+HCL

Seider, Maynard, 1943-
A year in the life of a factory. Singlejack Books, 1984.

"Account of a run-of-the-mill year and run-of-the-mill strike" at a California electrical equipment firm, by a college teacher who became a factory worker for a year.
1. Electrical equipment industry workers—California—Personal narratives. 2. Collective bargaining—California—Personal narratives. 3. Strikes—Electrical equipment industry workers—California—Personal narratives. 4. Blue collar workers—California—Personal narratives. 5. College teachers—California—Personal narratives. 6. Working class literature (Non-fiction). I. Singlejack Books. II. Title. III. Title: The life of a factory. IV. Title: Factory life. V. Title: A factory year.

"Dissident Magazines," in Bill Katz, *Magazines for Libraries* (New York: Bowker, 1969), 104-14.

About those twenty-four annotated magazines, Berman writes this introduction (in part):

"None of these variously enraged, visionary, discontented, and rebellious magazines represents the American mainstream. None would win a national popularity contest. Few, if any, appear in doctors' waiting rooms. Depending on the reader's viewpoint, some might be derisively termed Fascist, racist, Red, unpatriotic, godless, utopian, Neanderthal, jingoist, reactionary, creeping Socialist, revolutionary, flag-waving, or crackpot. None, however—and this, paradoxically, may be all they have in common—is really happy with the way things are. Moreover…few have ever been stocked by public libraries. And the percentage in most colleges is probably low. Well, then, why bother with them at all? Simply because America is not all mainstream. It is not only Democrats and Republicans, capitalists and trade unionists, Catholics and Presbyterians, *but also* Wobblies and populists, socialists and tycoons, fundamentalists and atheists, white supremacists and egalitarians. In sum, America is diversity and ferment. It is a running battle between tradition and change. It is two unresolved questions: What is the 'good society'? and What are we all about?

"Bluntly put, the library that fails adequately to reflect the widespread and long-standing dissidence in American life is a lie. Worse, it is profoundly un-American, for it denies that very vitality, conflict, and color that help to make this country unique.

…[O]pen-minded[readers, even if they] can't agree fully with the dissidents, will nonetheless discover in their newspapers and journals much incisive criticism, many creative proposals, a host of genuine grievances that otherwise go unventilated, and often some inspired, engrossing prose."

"Libraries to the People!" in Celeste West and Elizabeth Katz, editors, *Revolting Librarians* (San Francisco: Booklegger Press, 1972), 51-57.

This updated reprint of a March 1971 *Los Angeles Free Press* article maintains that "the pressure for change—if it's to be effective—needs to come from *two* directions: not only from inside the traditionally straight-laced, stuffed-shirted, status-quo-hugging profession, but also from outside, from the liberationists and undergrounders themselves, from angry feminists and alienated students, warring Indians and unshackled Blacks, from proud Chicanos and no-longer-docile Asian-Americans, from boss-burdened workers and impatient peaceniks. It's not merely our right to enjoy easy access to the books, pamphlets, films, tapes, discs, and mags we want, but equally a necessity that the mass of uncommitted and largely uninformed citizens have access to sources that authentically explain what we're all about, that genuinely convey our vision of the 'alternative society.' If what Middle Amerika knows about the Black Panthers, as an example, derives solely from *Time* and tv, they'll never understand the BPs, nor all the fuss about 'persecution' and 'genocide.' The Movement, in short, if it's ever to shuck its insularity and really get its message to the Amerikan public, must be made more accessible. Libraries are one route."

"Where It's At: How to develop a meaningful, living, library periodical collection," *Library Journal* 93, no. 22 (15 December 1968), 4615-618.

This article features entries for over 50 magazines, from *Ally* and *Black Dialogue* to *El Papel* and *Vocations for Social Change*. It also offers selection tips (like buying Dustbooks' annual little-mag directory and visiting "offbeat bookshops…to discover new publications and trends") and begins with this declaration: "No amount of talk at library conferences and round tables about 'relevancy' and 'social responsibility' is itself going to enliven, enrich, un-barnacle, and, yes, *controversialize* library collections. Only librarians *themselves* can actually make their wares relevant to the *whole* community they serve: not just the respectable…middle class (who in any event, ought to know what's going on elsewhere from more trustworthy sources than *Time/Life*), but also the dissidents, the increasingly self-aware minorities, the forces in motion."

Reprinted, with corrections and revisions, in Eric Moon, editor, *Book Selection and Censorship in the Sixties* (New York: Bowker, 1969), 145-51.

"Why Should Librarians Give a Damn?" *Alternative Library Literature*, 1988/1989 (Jefferson, NC: McFarland, 1990), 171-72.

This report on harassment of alternative bookstores in the Twin Cities includes these remarks on the "library connections": "Given the *de facto* mainstream media exclusion of 'radical' opinions and of such vital issues as North-South relations, U.S. interventionism, multinational power, economic democracy, nuclearism, and comprehensive health care, it may be *only* librarians—explicitly committed to public access to a wide variety of ideas and topics—who *can* do something to remedy the imbalance. One step, of course, is to generously represent alternative materials—print and AV alike—in library collections. Another is to raise the otherwise *un*raised issues and spotlight nonmainstream resources by means of displays, bibliographies, bookmarks, and programs. And a third is to actively support beleaguered bookshops and other information-providers, both nationally and locally…If we truly give a damn and start to behave *pro*-actively, it just *could* make a difference. If we don't, the trend toward stifling conformity and regimentation will only worsen."

Yin-Yang, nos. 1-2 (1966). Coleman and Taukkunen Barracks Special Services Libraries, Worms/Mannheim-Sandhofen, West Germany.

Yin-Yang was "an independent journal of art, ideas, and imagination, published from time to time by Coleman Barracks Library" in Mannheim-Sandhofen, West Germany. GIs composed three-fourths of the editorial board. Copies are archived at Department of Special Collections, UCLA Research Library.

GENERAL TREATMENT OF UNDERGROUND PRESS

HISTORY, ANALYSIS

"Admen Groove on Underground." *Business Week* (12 April 1969): 84-86.

This explanation of the music industry's use of underground newspapers includes reviews of promotion budgets and techniques, along with the difficulties of working with underground papers. The undergrounds are described as "a highly logical medium for us. The people who read the papers are the ones who include music as essential to their way of life" (p. 84).

Agee, Philip. "CAIB - Eleven Years in Retrospect." *Covert Action Information Bulletin* 32 (Summer 1989): 4-6.

Covert Action Information Bulletin succeeded *Counterspy* as a publication "dedicated to exposing U.S. covert interventions around the world." Philip Agee, author of *Dirty Work* and *Dirty Work 2* (biographies of 600 CIA officers and employees), a former CIA employee himself, is the only American ever to have his passport revoked without being charged with a crime. This article is invaluable as both a history of *CAIB* and a testament to the lengths the U.S. government will go in order to suppress information. This issue of *CAIB* also contains a short article on present *CAIB* staff, "Who We Are" (p. 3), and a reprint of Agee's article "Where Myths Lead to Murder" (p. 7-9) from issue number 1. The issue reprints many of the best articles previously published in *CAIB*.

Allen, Gary. "Underground for Adults Only." *American Opinion* 10, no. 10 (December 1967): 1-16.

The author, described as "active in anti-Communist and other humanitarian causes," presents the underground press as one of many revolutionary tactics employed by the Left to conquer America. In this scenario the underground press is "now merchandising a new revolutionary Line to millions of teens and post adolescents. That Line seeks to promote the image of an exploited youthful minority—romantic and noble—in revolt to make America into a Flower Commune resisting the forces of war, wickedness, and Wall Street" (p. 2). This divisive "age consciousness," akin to class consciousness of Marxist theory, plays upon natural adolescent-parental tensions and should not be ignored. Several undergrounds are described.

Armstrong, David. *A Trumpet to Arms: Alternative Media in America.* Boston: South End Press, 1981.

This book traces the beginnings of underground comics, magazines, radio, and newspapers through the late 1960s and early 1970s, when many of the papers folded or changed their tone. It discusses obscure underground publications as well as popular dissident periodicals like *Rolling Stone* and *Mother Earth News*, and New Age media. One chapter focuses on the "new muckrakers," who cover stories one never sees on the evening news but that appear on the annual Project Censored list of the ten top stories ignored by mainstream media. The book's concluding analysis of the current (for 1981) state of alternative publishing suggests that "the assertion, frequently repeated in the mass media, that the really juicy stuff happened in those fabulous faded sixties, is rooted more in nostalgia than political reality" (p. 332). A major thesis of Armstrong's book (ignored by many of the other books that focus more on journalistic style than political context) is that alternative publishing has changed in response to the times, and that, as the times change again, alternative publishing will continue to play a vital role in American culture.

Askin, Richard Henry. "Comparative Characteristics of the Alternative Press." Master's thesis, University of Texas at Austin, 1970.

This is a "descriptive analysis of the major characteristics of the alternate press," with a focus on its content (p. 3). The author examined 45 underground papers and corresponded with their editors during the first four months of 1970. Four specific areas of these papers are examined at length: style, social content, political content, and cultural content (primarily music). A final chapter addresses advertising in the undergrounds. The author's major conclusions are unimpressive: namely that underground papers are characterized by highly personalized reporting of a variety of subjects including the individual as he relates to others and methods of political change.

Ben-Horin, D. "Alternative Press: Journalism as a Way of Life." *The Nation* 216 (19 February 1973): 238-45.

Ben-Horin asserts that there was a cross-fertilization between the underground and establishment press, both of staff and journalistic methods, that has been mutually beneficial. He examines the contradiction between the collectivist motivations that began many undergrounds and the longevity and success experienced by a few papers. With the decline in radical politics Ben-Horin identifies the following trend: undergrounds in large cities tend to accept financial success and work toward large circulation, higher staff wages, and bigger advertising budgets; whereas the undergrounds in medium- to smaller-sized cities tend to retain their smaller organization and community orientation.

Boles, Alan. "Upstarts in the Ivy." *The Nation* 208 (7 April 1969): 429-32.

Boles describes changes in college journalism on several campuses including Harvard, Yale, Stanford, University of Colorado at Boulder, Boston University, and Wesleyan. Changing political opinions gave rise to several new campus newspapers and changed editorial opinions at several extant papers. The author considered the changes temporary and indicative only of increased interest in journalism and the world of ideas.

____. "Books on the Underground/Alternative Press." *New Pages* 13 (Spring 1988): 14.

Annotated bibliography of ten books (two out of print) on the underground and alternative press in the United States, including: *Trumpet to Arms: Alternative Media in America; The Underground Press in America; The Dissident Press; Alternative Journalism in American History; The Paper Revolutionaries; The Rise of the Underground Press; Outlaws of America: The Underground Press and Its Context; Uncovering the Sixties: The Life & Times of the Underground Press*; and *From Radical Left to Extreme Right*.

Brackman, Jacob. "The Underground Press." *Playboy* (August 1967): 83, 96, 151-57.

Many undergrounds are described in this assessment of the underground press as a "vision of the world...loving...wildly messianic...passionate and venemous...against what it claims to be the repressive, monolithic vision of 'establishment blats'" (p. 96). It develops an historical overview by describing the *Village Voice*, several Beat papers of the 1950s, and other little magazines.

Brann, James W. "The Changing Student Press: Underground Papers Vie with Regulars." *Chronicle of Higher Education* (12 August 1968): 4-5.

Campus journalism underwent dramatic changes in the late 1960s, in part due to the influence of the underground press. Several leftist campus newspapers are described, as are networking organizations such as the College Press Service, U.S. Student Press Association, and Liberation News Service.

Bryan, Gene. "Underground Press Panel Holds Stormy Session." *Quill* (December 1969): 30.

Bryan reports on a panel discussion about the underground press held at the 60th anniversary session of Sigma Delta Chi in San Diego. Speakers included Thomas Forcade (Underground Press Syndicate), Art Kunkin (*Los Angeles Free Press*), Lowell Bergman (*San Diego Free Press, Long Beach Free Press*), Art

Seidenbaum (*Los Angeles Times*), and Dr. Robert Glessing (UCLA Department of Journalism).

Burke, John Gordon, ed. *Print, Image and Sound: Essays on Media*. Chicago: American Library Association, 1972.

This collection of five essays attempts to bring "conceptual and bibliographical perspective" to five areas of media in the 1960s (p. 1). Two such chapters touch upon the alternative press. The first, by James Ridgeway, editor of *Ramparts*, is a short history of the underground press of the sixties, focusing on details of specific titles and personal recollections. The other chapter, "Arima Rising," by small press guru Len Fulton, is both informative and insightful. Fulton describes the factors he sees behind the spread of small magazines in the period from 1963 to 1969. These are the "action ethic of youth"; offset printing; concrete poetry; and mimeography, among others. The essay includes an extensive annotated bibliography on small presses.

Burks, John. "The Underground Press." *Rolling Stone* (4 October 1969): 11-32.

Burks covered a lot of territory in compiling this subtly critical survey of the underground press. He spoke with editorial staff at Detroit's *Fifth Estate*, New York's *Rat*, the *Los Angeles Free Press*, Ann Arbor *Argus*, Washington, DC *Free Press*, Liberation News Service, Underground Press Syndicate, *Chicago Seed*, and many others while gathering information about editorial control, advertising, distribution, politics, and world views. Burks portrays a subculture at a point of transition. The material originally unique to the undergrounds (sex, drugs, and rock & roll) was increasingly appearing in the mainstream press resulting in introspection regarding objectives, a tilt to the left, and a move toward "revolutionary" rhetoric.

Commission of Inquiry into High School Journalism. *Captive Voices: The Report*. New York: Schocken Books, 1974.

The Commission of Inquiry into High School Journalism was established in the early 1970s by the Robert F. Kennedy Memorial. Its mission was to examine four areas of high school journalism: censorship, minority participation, journalism education, and its relationship with the established media. Data were gathered through public hearings, consultations with experts, surveys, a content analysis of 293 high school papers, and other research. The report is arranged around the four issue areas and concludes with recommendations. Its conclusions are predictable: censorship is rampant; racism, however subtle, precludes minority students from full participation; and professional journalists outside the schools have seldom done much to encourage high school journalism. Appendix A gives legal and other advice for school papers, Appendix B provides the results of surveys and other research, and Appendix C contains excerpts from student papers.

Danky, James. "Still Alive and Well: The Alternative Press in 1977, Part I." [See "Individual Treatments: Geographic Area"]

DeMaio, Don. "The Fate of the Underground Newspaper." *Distant Drummer* no. 69 (22-29 January 1970): 1, 11.

Factionalism of the New Left, staff burnout, declining advertising revenues, and formulaic writing styles are cited as contributing factors in the declining interest in and readership of the underground press. DeMaio's speculations regarding the introspection of the late 1960s and the challenge that would pose for undergrounds in the 1970s are remarkably prescient.

D'Emilio, John. *Sexual Politics, Sexual Communities: The Making of a Homosexual Minority in the United States, 1940-1970*. Chicago: The University of Chicago Press, 1983.

Begun as a doctoral dissertation while the author was a student at Columbia University, this book is seen now as one of the most important books on the history of the homophile movement in the United States during its formative years. Although World War II was a major catalyst to the awareness of a gay community in the United States, that consciousness grew slowly in the pre-Stonewall Riot years because gays had to overcome major social obstacles, especially in the religious, medical, and legal establishments. Thus, they had to affirm first within themselves individually and only then to the larger society the legitimacy, and even the existence, of their community. Despite the tendency of present-day activists to downplay the significance of their forebears and the organizations they represented, such as Mattachine Society and Daughters of Bilitis, D'Emilio concludes by saying, "The homophile movement deserves kinder treatment than it has received." One area that needs redefinition, he notes, is the press, where early activists "initiated what became a tradition of openly gay publishing and, through [the first independent gay magazine] *ONE*'s challenge of postal censorship, saw their constitutional right to freedom of speech upheld by the Supreme Court." Other gay publications that are discussed in some detail include *Advocate*, *Ladder*, *LCE* [League for Civil Education] *News*, *Mattachine Review*, *Vector*, and *Vice Versa*.

Dennis, Everette E., and William L. Rivers. *Other Voices: The New Journalism in America*. San Francisco: Canfield Press, 1974.

The authors have divided new journalism into seven categories that are systematically dealt with in a chapter devoted to each. The seven classes are: 1) new nonfiction, 2) alternative journalism, 3) journalism reviews, 4) advocacy journalism, 5) counterculture journalism, 6) alternative broadcasting, and 7) precision journalism. This book's emphasis is more on journalistic style than the socio-political context in which writers operate. The book closes with an analysis of what the future holds for each brand of new journalism, predicting that some (counterculture journalism) will face much trouble, while others (alternative broadcasting) will prosper. An annotated bibliography is included.

"Dissenting Servicemen and the First Amendment." *Georgetown Law Journal* 58 (1970): 534-68.

This article reviews existing statute and case law regarding the protection of constitutional rights of servicemen. The conflict between the need for military discipline and the right of free speech had not been explicitly remedied in the law to date, resulting in difficulties in protecting servicemen from retaliatory administrative action.

Divoky, Diane. "Revolt in the High Schools: The Way It's Going to Be." *Saturday Review* 52 (15 February 1969): 83-84, 89, 101-2.

The phenomenon of underground newspapers in the high school is described as a result of the conflict between student idealism and the narrow, or even repressive, response those ideals received from school administrators. Several high school papers are discussed, as is the High School Independent Press Syndicate (HIPS) and their relationships with SDS. A boxed supplement regarding black high school militants accompanies this story.

Divoky, Diane. "The 'Scoop' on the High School Underground Press." *Scholastic Teacher, Secondary Teachers' Supplement* (6 October 1969): 6-8.

This brief description of the high school underground press estimated its numbers to be at some 500 papers nationwide. Generally independent of outside organizations such as SDS, these papers dealt with issues of immediate importance to high school students (e.g., poor cafeteria conditions, meaningless student councils, and administrative restrictions). The writing may advocate revolution or reform, be "dreamy" or "angrily obscene," but Divoky notes that "the creativity displayed in the underground is the one resource teachers can't seem to tap" (p. 7).

Downie, Leonard, Jr. *The New Muckrakers*. [See "Individual Treatments: Title or Organization: History, Analysis"]

Echols, Alice. *Daring to Be Bad: Radical Feminism in America, 1967-1975*. Minneapolis: University of Minnesota Press, 1989.

This book-length scholarly study of the radical feminist movement, the author notes in her introduction, was written to fill the void that exists in that literature between publication of Sara Evans' *Personal Politics*—which ends in 1968, "as the first women's liberation groups were beginning to form"—and the present. In particular, the book "analyzes the trajectory of the radical feminist movement from its beleaguered beginnings in 1967, through its ascendance as the dominant tendency within the movement, to its decline and supplanting by cultural feminism in the mid-'70s." Tensions within American feminism today include feminism's relationship to other social change movements, women's differences from one another, whether sexuality should be seen mainly as a site of pleasure or of danger, and whether feminism entails the transcendence of gender or the celebration of female difference. Feminist publications that are discussed include *Come Out, Everywoman, The Furies, It Ain't Me Babe, Jane, off our backs, Ms.*, and *Quest*.

Ellis, Donna Lloyd. "The Underground Press in America: 1955-1970." *Journal of Popular Culture* 5, no. 1 (1971): 102-24.

This general discussion of underground newspapers in the United States examines its influence on popular culture, especially advertising and rock festivals, and includes their purposes, reasons for success, and history. Reasons cited for the success of the undergrounds include the emergence of an affluent young population, the failure of the establishment press to cover antiwar and minority issues, and the permissiveness in print that emerged following the 1966 Supreme Court ruling defining pornography. Histories of some of the major publications, such as *Village Voice* and *Los Angeles Free Press*, are described. The article also describes the alternative news services, Liberation News Service and Underground Press Syndicate. Finally the article addresses what the author sees as the "present stagnation" of the undergrounds, which she attributes to the decline of "freak society."

Farrell, Barry. "For the Only Freak in Ohio." *Life* 67 (21 November 1969): 32B.

This short opinion piece focuses on the influence of the underground papers, especially the sex papers. Farrell makes a distinction between underground papers that attempt to break the taboos regarding sex by

exalting the beauty of the body and those that cater to and depend upon the maintenance of those taboos.

Feigelson, Naomi. *The Underground Revolution: Hippies, Yippies, and Others*. New York: Funk & Wagnalls, 1970.

Feigelson examines the underground culture that flourished in the 1960s and early 1970s. A chapter on the underground press discusses many individual papers including *Village Voice, East Village Other, Rat, Oracle* (San Francisco), *Avatar* (Boston), *Los Angeles Free Press, Logos* (Montreal), and Liberation News Service. Feigelson emphasizes the origin and role of the underground press as a reaction against the establishment press presentation of the underground movement. In the other chapters of the book, which discuss the hippies, yippies, drug use, communes and new social forms, religious explorations, antiwar activism, and race conflict within the movement, Feigelson continually portrays a movement moving from individual exploration toward political activism. This expression is continually related to America's heritage of conflict between established orthodoxies and dissenting individualism, with references to Ann Hutchinson, Henry David Thoreau, Ralph Waldo Emerson, and quotations on the American character from Alexis de Tocqueville.

Feldman, Sam. "Going Underground." *Journalism Education Today* (Fall 1970): 10-12.

Feldman, a former high school teacher, advocates the value of student expression by means of underground newspapers. Legal issues pertaining to adolescent civil rights are examined, particularly in regard to the suspension of two students at Warren High School in Downey, California.

Feldman, Samuel Nathan. "The High School Underground Press: Content Analysis, Member Attitudes, and Beliefs." Ed.D. diss., University of California, Los Angeles, 1973.

The goal of this study was to determine why high school underground papers flourished from 1965 to 1973. It combines three separate methodological approaches: 1) a scale used to measure the attitudes of principals, underground editors, and student editors; 2) a content analysis of thirteen high school undergrounds; and 3) a content analysis of five major court decisions concerning issues of freedom, school, violence, and authority. The author concludes that underground papers were a "strategy to publish without punishment, gaining access to a student public that was denied them through the regular high school press" (p. 123).

Fire!: Reports from the Underground Press. Comp. by Paul, Jon and Charlotte. New York: E.P. Dutton & Co., 1970.

Photographs, drawings, and poetry (presumably from various underground publications, although uncredited) lace this rambling work. Peoples Park, the strike of high school students in Ocean Hill, New Jersey, the occupation of Columbia University and other universities, military papers, women's liberation, black power, and many other movements and events are worked into this collective account.

Frye, Patrick Keith. "The *Great Speckled Bird*: An Investigation of the Birth, Life, and Death of an Underground Newspaper." [See "Individual Treatments: Title or Organization: History, Analysis"]

Fudge, William, and John W. English. "Emergence of the Fifth Estate: The Underground Press." In *Mass News: Practices, Controversies, and Alternatives*, ed. by David J. Leroy and Christopher H. Sterling, 274-80. Englewood Cliffs, NJ: Prentice-Hall, Inc., 1973.

This brief, generally positive introduction to the underground press is included in a journalism textbook. The authors present a descriptive introduction to the strengths and weaknesses of the underground press and its value as a vehicle for dissent and minority opinions. Although Liberation News Syndicate (1968) and Underground Press Service (1966) are mentioned, the authors posit the underground phenomenon as beginning in 1968.

Fulbright, Newton H. "Underground Press Strives to Fuse Sex with Politics." *Editor and Publisher* 102 (27 December 1969): 34.

Fulbright reports the conclusions of a study of the underground press conducted by John R. Everett, president of the New School for Social Research. Quoting that study heavily, Fulbright illustrates that undergrounds use the philosophy and language of classical Marxism to blame all social ills on capitalism. Fulbright is particularly interested in the sex undergrounds and their social analysis. *Screw* and six other New York sex papers are discussed.

Garvey, Ellen. "From Outrage to Barometer: The Underground Press." *Library Journal* 99 (1 September 1974): 2,050.

Garvey, a member of the Liberation News Service collective, describes the current state of affairs among the alternative press. The changing focus of LNS is described, as is the staff composition and product.

"GI Press." *WIN* 5, no. 21 (1 December 1969): 22-23.

Written by "A Marine Lance Corporal," this guide for the GI underground newspaperman describes what works and what doesn't when producing a paper for military personnel. Constructive advice is provided on how to organize, how to communicate your ideas, and how to distribute your paper without getting caught. A list of 48 GI papers is included.

Glasser, Theodore L. "Semantics of an Alternative: The Language of the Underground Press." *ETC: A Review of General Semantics* 31 (1974): 201-14.

This article is a short examination of the language used in underground newspapers. The author puzzles over why so many underground papers use language that most people do not understand. Various scholars have proposed reasons for this and seem to agree that it is to limit readership to a small population. He suggests that the "primary symbols of the underground press suggest two probable categories" (p. 202). These are "new words," invented to express a feeling for which there is no word (such as "bummer"), and conventional words given new meaning (such as "trip"). Even more restricting is the use of "snarl-utterances" and "purr-utterances," words that "by themselves are used as direct expressions of approval or disapproval" (p. 202). A study using Fishbein's Attitude-Belief Scales found that the word "freak" was used often as a purr-utterance and "establishment" was often used as a snarl-utterance. Use of these devices makes underground papers rigid in their opinions and limits their contribution to serious writing and thinking. Consequently, the undergrounds have "remained largely a nonextensional medium, primarily a forum for the exchange of judgments" (p. 203).

Glenn, Charles Craig. "Citizenship Education and the First Amendment in Public Schools." Ph.D. diss., University of Illinois at Urbana-Champaign, 1982.

Glenn reviews court cases and decisions bearing upon First Amendment issues in the public schools affecting both teachers and students. The author hopes to provide guidance through the complexities of various decisions, and between conflicting decisions, and analyze them in light of three models of citizenship education: the indoctrination method, the marketplace of ideas method, and the Socratic method. Of particular interest to this bibliography are the cases reviewed involving underground newspapers, school-sponsored newspapers, and library and text books. Other issues studied include teacher freedom to select books, freedom to conduct unlimited classroom discussions, and freedom of political speech. With regard to the issues pertinent to the underground press, Glenn found that student self-expression was most strongly supported in the early 1970s, following the Supreme Court decision in *Tinker* v. *Des Moines*, which made the test for restriction of student expression the material or substantial disruption of school activities. Subsequent decisions at the circuit court level tinkered with this ruling, imposing limits based upon possible psychological harm or danger to student health and safety. Prior restraint of publication was an issue upheld in theory by later decisions, but never in an actual case. Glenn concludes with suggested policies for teachers and administrators in light of these protections and restraints on student and teacher rights.

Glessing, Robert J. *The Underground Press in America*. Westport, CT: Greenwood Press, 1970.

This book is an excellent introduction to the underground press of the 1960s. Three distinct sections deal with "The Past," "The Present," and "The Future." The first section covers the roots of the underground press, including the New Left and student movements, and a relatively unique chapter on graphic innovation in the undergrounds. The second part provides an in-depth description of the underground's financial picture, editorial content, and "hip" language. The last part is written by two editors of underground papers, who make no notable predictions as to the future of the media. The general theme (if there is one—the book is mostly descriptive) is that, although the underground press is a reaction to, rather than a cause of, social change, its "message is getting through."

Gruen, John. "The Earsplitting Underground Press." *Vogue* 151 (15 February 1968): 44.

In this short assessment of the underground press, undergrounds are deemed to be effective due to the candor of their published interviews. However, "its literary style is negligible. Ennui is the all-pervasive commodity."

Harper, Paul Dean. "Rhetorical Analysis of Motive Attribution in the Alternative Press." Ph.D. diss., University of Kansas, 1974.

This study of print media issued by several extremist groups uses symbolic interaction theory as a means of motive analysis. Arguing that other analyses of the underground press have limited their definition to include only those papers on the left end of the political and social spectrum, Harper has broadened the definition of underground to include the publications, issued between 1964 and 1974, of four extremist social groups. The groups studied, and their publications, are as follows: black supremacists, using *Black Panther* and *Muhammad Speaks* (Nation of Islam); white supremacists, using *White Power* (American Nazi

Party), *Thunderbolt* (National States Rights Party), and *American Opinion* (John Birch Society); the radical political Right, using *The Cross and the Flag* (an anti-Semitic fundamentalist paper); and the radical political Left, using *Weekly People, Workers World, The Militant, The Liberator, Berkeley Tribe*, and *East Village Other*. Despite the widely differing views expressed, Harper found strong similarities in the rhetoric used in each of the papers examined and the motivations revealed therein. He states, "[T]he purpose of this rhetoric is not to persuade, but to sustain believers in their beliefs..." (p. 24). In addition, Harper applies analyses of paranoid social psychology to the shared theme of conspiracy found in the papers. "[T]he eight extremist groups posit a world in which people plot genocide, the destruction of nations, exercise political control of other people, engage in national power struggles, destroy morals, reap vast profits without concern for human values, and brainwash those whom they can use and whom they wish to control. The agents of these conspiracies are willing to go to great lengths to cover their activities. These lengths include the control of mass media, the corruption of governments, and the destruction of anyone who would oppose them" (p. 164).

Heussenstamm, F. K. "Activism in Adolescence: An Analysis of the High School Underground Press." *Adolescence* 6, no. 23 (Fall 1971): 317-36.

This article discusses the high school underground press of the 1960s as an illustration of Robert Merton's theories regarding innovative reactions to alienation and anomie. It reviews studies of the high school press and provides a profile of the press. A content analysis performed on *The Loudmouth*, published by students at a southern California high school, illustrated a radical, critical attitude toward school policies. The adolescents involved were committed to a more democratic, creative society and were involved with political and social movements. The author advocated using the press as an insight into student convictions in order to enhance dialogue between adults and adolescents.

Johnson, Michael L. *The New Journalism*. Lawrence: University of Kansas, 1971.

Opening with a short history of new journalism from the 1950s, this book focuses on the publications and writers of new journalism, rather than its political and social context. The histories of such notable titles as *Berkeley Barb* and *Los Angeles Free Press* are discussed at length. A chapter is devoted to Truman Capote, Tom Wolfe, and Norman Mailer, leaders of the new journalism movement. A few chapters discuss a more obscure but "illustrative cross section" of new journalists (p. 87) and their work. These chapters tend to focus on the writing style of the author in question, but do address "the race and war scene" and the "youth and radical scene" of the 1960s. The final chapter concludes with the somewhat bland assertion that new journalism has produced a greater selection of writing for the public to choose from.

Kessler, Lauren. *The Dissident Press: Alternative Journalism in American History*. The SAGE CommText Series, vol. 13, ed. by F. Gerald Kline. Beverly Hills, CA: Sage Publications, 1984.

Kessler puts the underground, anti-Vietnam War press in its context in the tradition of American dissident journalism. Kessler uses a proactive definition of the constitutional protection of the freedom of speech and of the press to include not only freedom of expression and the toleration of diverse ideas, but also the encouragement of diversity by granting access to the "marketplace of ideas" to a wide variety of ideas that may be controversial or even unpopular. Examined in this context, journalistic media throughout U.S. history has not been upholding its constitutional imperative. Therefore, various populations and organizations have sought the freedom of the press that A.J. Leibling identified, that which exists "for the guy who owns one." African Americans, utopian reformers and new age visionaries, feminist activists, immigrant non-English speaking communities, agrarian and industrial labor organizations, and war resisters have all responded to the limited access to media by publishing papers that communicated ideas not addressed elsewhere. This book offers a good introductory overview of important dissenting organizations and their publications.

Kessler, Lauren. "Up the Creek without a Paddle." *The Quill* 72 (November 1984): 40-42 + .

This article offers an explanation of why Americans throughout our history have launched alternative publications (primarily newspapers). The author cites such factors as commitment to their cause and the failure of the mainstream press to publicize unpopular issues. Publishers of alternative materials have faced harassment and financial troubles. Their papers often preached to the converted, but they occasionally helped to legitimize now-acceptable causes. Regardless of the views expressed in the alternative press, the author concludes that the First Amendment guarantees their right to express those views.

Kornbluth, Jesse. "This Place of Entertainment Has No Fire Exit: The Underground Press and How It Went." *Antioch Review* 29 (1969): 91-99.

This short essay laments the "death" of the underground press, which, the author says, only really

lived for a brief time in the mid-1960s. The press' demise is blamed on the mass production of underground papers which caused the local underground to "become as institutionalized as the head shop" (p. 95). This is an impressionistic overview of the 1960s and its culture. Kornbluth's opinions are steeped in a classic sixties aura (his prose is filled with "groovy"s and "hip"s) and provide as much insight into the period's thought as to its press.

Kronenberger, John. "What's Black and White and Pink and Green and Dirty and Read All Over." *Look* 32, no. 20 (1 October 1968): 21-22.

The underground press is described as the true voice of the sixties. Sample story topics are presented.

Leamer, Laurence. *The Paper Revolutionaries: The Rise of the Underground Press*. New York: Simon and Schuster, 1972.

In this strongly sympathetic, heavily illustrated account of the underground press from its roots in the early twentieth-century publication, *The Masses*, through 1971, the underground papers of the 1960s and 1970s are described as the direct descendants of the middle-class, intellectual, cultural radicals of the 1910s and 1920s. Leamer describes two "generations" of underground papers in the 1960s. The first generation consisted of the cultural revolutionaries, *Village Voice, The Realist*, and *Berkeley Barb*. Each of these papers was founded, written, edited, and produced by one or two primary individuals. These papers reflected the idiosyncracies of their makers, and were generally outside of the radical movement as well as the mainstream. The second generation of newspapers was characterized by their effort to speak to and for a specific community. That community may have been defined by geographic or intellectual territory. In the pages of *Rat, Chicago Seed, Great Speckled Bird, Space City!*, and others, the political and cultural issues of the day were debated. Despite the political extremism of the left-wing papers and the right-wing governmental agencies, which at the time of this book were damping circulation figures, Leamer was tremendously positive about the influence and revolutionary prospects for the underground press.

Lewis, Rap. "Shop Papers—Catalysts for Action." *Political Affairs* 64, no. 4 (April 1985): 35-36, 40.

Lewis provides an overview of some of the shop newspapers started by the American Communist Party and includes information on how to start and maintain such newspapers.

Lewis, Roger. *Outlaws of America: The Underground Press and Its Context*. Harmondsworth, Middlesex, England: Penguin, 1972.

Lewis' descriptive account of the underground press and the surrounding cultural, political, and economic conditions provides a great deal of information, as well as a comparison to British underground or alternative publishing of the day. He takes a topical approach, examining the widely varied nature of the response to America's "national neurosis." Movements for free speech, against the war and the draft, for the liberation of oppressed minorities such as blacks, Hispanics, Native Americans, and women, political activism, increased concern over the state of the environment, communal living, mystical religious concerns, and, of course, drugs and rock and roll music are touched upon in Lewis' account. Lewis clearly believed in the revolutionary nature of the social changes underway. Despite his recognition of the commercialization of rock music, he was still able to assert that it was "one of the most dynamic radicalizing forces within the counterculture" (p. 100). The underground papers were developing from the politically unconscious to the politically radical and, when this book was published, were the harbinger of the revolutionary struggle to come.

Lydon, Michael, "The Word Gets Out." *Esquire* 68, no. 3 (September 1967): 106-7, 156, 158, 165-68.

Several conflicts that occurred in 1967 between university student newspaper staff and university administrations are reviewed. When student editors were unable to publish without censorship they turned to the underground format and forum. Interactions between campus press and the Underground Press Syndicate are described. This is one of several articles in the issue describing changes on campuses across the country, including such topics as drug use, men and women co-habitating without marital contracts, and establishment reactions.

MacDonald, Ingrid. "Pushing the Press." *Rites* 5, no. 5 (October 1988): 14.

This discussion of lesbian/gay press history is often newsy and chatty but does not engage in political vision. In the seventies the gay press mixed sexual openness with analysis of political issues (*The Body Politic*). In the eighties the gay press became more commercial and more directed exclusively at the male market. Currently the lesbian press is typified by small circulation publications that cater to specific audiences.

"Making It—Underground." *Newsweek* 71, no. 10 (4 March 1968): 58-59.

Several individual papers are described to illustrate the growing underground press phenomenon.

Marks, Jane. "Paper Tiger with Teeth." *Mademoiselle* 71 (August 1970): 226-27, 326-27.

Administrative reactions to the changing editorial content of campus newspapers varied from withholding funds to firing of editorial staff. Specific instances of such censorship are described, as are the resulting underground campus papers. Some campus papers continued to work within the system for independence (e.g., establishing an advertising co-op, the U.S. Student Press Association, and legal actions).

Marshall, Joan. "Indexing the Underground." *Library Journal* 97, no. 2 (February 1972): 734-35.

The activities and difficulties of the American Library Association Social Responsibilities Round Table Task Force on Subject Indexing the Bell & Howell/Underground Press Syndicate Underground Newspaper Microfilm Collection 1965-1969 are described.

Merlis, George. "The Underground Press." *Signature* (April 1970): 49, 74, 78, 82, 83.

Underground papers are dismissed as graffiti since they are not truly underground, nor revolutionary, nor a new journalistic trend.

Miller, Timothy A. "Ethics and the Counter-Culture." Ph.D. diss., University of Kansas, 1973.

This study uses the Bell & Howell underground press collection on microfilm to analyze papers published from 1965 to 1970 in order to delineate the ethical value structure of the counterculture. Miller focused on the cultural rather than the political elements of the countercultural movement. He found that, despite new rhetoric and some unique contributions, the counterculture of the 1960s drew heavily upon traditional American ethical values of individualism, iconoclasm, action as opposed to philosophical speculation, and the effort to change human hearts. The primary ethical concerns revolved around drugs (among which distinctions were made between "good" and "bad" drugs), sexuality as a vehicle of interpersonal communication and freedom, rock music as a communication vehicle for the movement, and communal living.

Murphy, Sharon. *Other Voices: Black, Chicano, and American Indian Press*. Dayton, OH: Pflaum/Standard, 1974.

Intended as a textbook, this book provides information about the history, motivations, and organizations of the minority press in the United States.

Nelson, Jack A. *The Underground Press.* Freedom of Information Center Report No. 226. Columbia: School of Journalism, University of Missouri, August 1969.

In this brief, informative overview of the underground press phenomenon, Nelson describes, not necessarily for a sympathetic audience, the scope of the underground papers in cities, colleges, high schools, and military bases, as well as news services networking these papers. He also provides some statistical data regarding circulation and number of papers. Two factors are described as stimuli to the development of the underground papers: the technological development of offset printing, which provided an inexpensive means of communication; and the prevailing climate of dissent focusing on the youth culture, drugs, sexual liberation, and the antiwar movement, accentuating a growing dissatisfaction with the establishment print media as a source of news and information. Nelson cites some establishment press sources as well as further reading then available about the underground press.

"Notes from Underground." *Newsweek* 72, no. 2 (8 July 1968): 76.

The invasion and disruption of a televised interview with Jeff Shero (*Rat*), Marvin Fishman (Newsreel), and Allan Katzman (*East Village Other*) is described. Although the invaders were happy with the action, the interviewer, Steve Roberts (*New York Times*), suggested that the method obscured the message.

"Opposition Press on Campus." *Time* 94, no. 24 (12 December 1969): 48.

Several campus newspapers have taken an editorial turn to the left. In response, moderates and conservatives have started publications to air their own views.

"The Peace GI's." *Newsweek* 73, no. 16 (21 April 1969): 36-37.

Antiwar GI actions, organizations, coffeehouses, and newspapers are described.

Peck, Abe. "Faded Flowers, the Legacy of the Underground Press." *The Quill* 73 (June 1985): 34-37.

An impressionistic recounting of the major underground papers and their fate, this article includes an account of the 1973 conference sponsored by the Underground Press Syndicate where its name was changed to the Alternative Press Syndicate. Successes and failures are reviewed in a nostalgic, yet hopeful, tone, asserting that "polarization is in the air. Whether defending gains, or pushing the pendulum back in the other direction, counter-media will have their role" (p. 37).

Peck, Abe. *Uncovering the Sixties: The Life and Times of the Underground Press.* New York: Pantheon Books, 1985.

The author was on staff at the *Chicago Seed* from 1967, soon after it was founded, to 1971, and later worked at *Rat* in New York, *Rolling Stone*, Chicago *Daily News* and *Sun-Times*, and the Northwestern University Medill School of Journalism. His history of the underground press of the 1960s and early 1970s provides a broad detailed account while focusing upon the events in Chicago and at the *Seed* itself. Benefiting from historical perspective and documents released in response to Freedom of Information Act requests (see work of Geoffrey Rips included in this bibliography), Peck portrays a movement increasingly factionalized after the high point of unity experienced during the Summer of Love in 1967. Ideological, racial, and sexual politics served to divide the movement from within, aided and abetted by agents of the FBI, CIA, IRS, and other governmental agencies. The underground press was instrumental in mainstreaming the culture and politics of the New Left while increasingly isolated, attacked, and financially distressed. A reprint edition of this work was released by Citadel Underground Press in May 1991.

Pelz, William A. "The Decline and Fall of the Underground Press." In *Proceedings of the Sixth National Convention of the Popular Culture Association*, 22-24 April 1976, Chicago, Illinois, comp. by Michael T. Marsden, 35-51. Bowling Green, OH: Bowling Green State University Popular Press, 1976.

Pelz illustrates the decline of the underground periodical press by noting that only seven publications listed in the 1969 issues of *Alternative Press Index* continued to be listed in the 1971 issues. However, the growth of the "alternative" press between 1969 and 1975 is also demonstrated. Several factors are advanced as explanations for the "decline and fall," including: the inherent contradictions between the political and cultural segments of the underground movement; the dismantling of Students for a Democratic Society in 1969 and the loss of that focal organizing body; the splintering of "movement" forces into narrower issue-oriented organizations (e.g., gay liberation and women's liberation, which issued their own publications); friction between traditional male attitudes toward sexuality expressed in the undergrounds' advocacy of sexual liberation and the growing women's movement; and external harassment and pressure from police and government agencies.

Pelz, William A. "The Decline and Fall of the Underground Press, 1969-1974." *Indian Journal of American Studies* 10, no. 2 (1980): 58-66.

This is one of the few articles to spend some time defining radical and underground papers ("radical" papers are distributed nationally, have a consistent editorial policy and a Marxist-oriented ideology; "underground" papers are distributed locally, have an erratic editorial policy and a "cultural-radicalism/anarchism" ideology). After telling us what he means by underground, Pelz gives a thorough review of the scale and causes of the undergrounds' decline. Some factors in this decline include the waning of radical left political groups, staff members with opposing goals, and the sexist attitudes of the men in the underground press movement. The decline began in 1969 and "grew progressively sicker until 1974, by which time it was clear that the Empire was dead" (p. 64). The author ends on a positive note, saying that the underground press' death means that its rebirth will be free of earlier defects.

Pepper, Thomas. "Underground Press: Growing Rich on the Hippie." *Nation* 206 (29 April 1968): 569-72.

This critique of the underground press asserts that the underground press has not contributed anything of value to journalism in terms of editorial value or advancements in content or style. Nor is it a harbinger of revolution, since it is largely the product of children of wealth or the middle class. Its primary value has been to identify new markets for journalistic endeavors by speaking to sub-cultures not addressed by the mainstream press. In this way, it is compared to the development of suburban newspapers which provide similar feature items such as artistic and social commentary, calendars of events, and advertisements. "The underground papers are not a quality press because they pander to their readers with a dexterity befitting the establishment papers they criticize so bitterly. In their own pages, instead of stimulating political and social discussion worthy of the society they seek, the underground papers offer nothing more than a stylized theory of protest" (p. 572).

Piloti, Joe. "The Underground GI Press: Pens Against the Pentagon." *Commonweal* 90, no. 21 (19 September 1969): 559-61.

The Bond, The Ally, Vietnam GI, Shakedown, and F.T.A. (*Fun Travel and Adventure* or the more expressive *Fuck the Army*) are the GI underground papers mentioned in this account of the growing phenomenon that linked the civilian antiwar movement with the soldiers on active duty in the United States and overseas. The origin and distribution of the papers are described. A boxed story written by Murray Polner about the charges filed by the navy against Roger Priest and his publication *OM: The Liberation Newsletter*,

entitled "An Enemy of the People," accompanies this article.

Plowman, Edward. "Jesus Presses Are Rolling." *Christianity Today* (April 1971): 38.

Several Christian street publications are described, in particular the *Oracle*, which originally advocated the glories of sex, drugs, and rock and roll. Editor-publisher David Abraham and Chris D'Alessandro ("a former junkie and heroin dealer who led Abraham to Christ") revived *Oracle*, which "has always been dedicated to a search for truth."

Polner, Murray, "The Underground GI Press." *Columbia Journalism Review* (Fall 1970): 54-56.

This is a brief review of underground papers at military bases, the varying brass reactions, and the legal issues surrounding these activities. Excerpts from several papers are included.

Preble, Lee A. "The GI Antiwar Press: What It Says and Why." Master's thesis, University of Wisconsin, 1971.

This thesis combines the methods of content analysis, survey research, and historical review to provide an in-depth study of the GI antiwar press. The author studied 33 papers published between January and June 1970. Examples of both military post and nationally oriented papers were included in the sample, from a wide geographical distribution. These papers are placed in the context of antiwar dissent throughout American history. Preble examines the who, what, when, where, and why of these papers. He finds that the educational level of those printing papers is higher than that of the military at large and that priority in the papers is given to stories that advocate GI rights and cover protest activities. Preble argues that the press is not a centrally organized phenomenon and that the military administration should not ignore the concerns published here. The GI underground papers raise genuine concerns that repression only lends a stronger focus.

Romm, Ethel G. "Campus Protest Movement: You Go Underground for 'Inside' Report." *Editor and Publisher* 101 (11 May 1968): 12, 82.

The occupation of buildings at Columbia University and the exclusive coverage of that story by the Liberation News Service are described.

Romm, Ethel Grodzins. *The Open Conspiracy: What America's Angry Generation Is Saying*. Harrisburg, PA: Stackpole Books, 1970.

Of all the books examined, this might well qualify as the coffee table book on the underground press. The book is off-sized and the author's topical essays alternate pages with black-and-white illustrations from a wide selection of underground papers. Romm addresses issues such as obscenity, drug use, and religious and political movements covered in the pages of undergrounds in an interpretive, not analytical, style.

Romm, Ethel G. "Psychedelics by Offset: Protest Tabloids Turn On to Color Printing." *Editor and Publisher* 101 (11 May 1968): 15, 68, 70.

This critique of the underground press emphasizes their physical appearance and production process. Romm interviewed printer Howard Quinn and distributor Morris Moskowitz in this review of the underground press production process.

Sanford, David. "The Seedier Media." *The New Republic* 157, no. 23 (2 December 1967): 7-8.

This short piece dismisses the underground press as a badly written exercise in yellow journalism, both biased and predictable.

Sherman, Edward F. "Dissenters and Deserters." *New Republic* 158, no. 1 (6 January 1968): 23-26.

Sherman presents a brief history to date (January 1968) of the state of internal military resistance to the war in Vietnam. Several cases are reviewed, including the court martials of Henry Howe, Howard Levy, the "Fort Hood Three," Richard Perrin, and Andrew Stapp. Sherman highlights the influence of civilian courts on military discipline in these cases. Sherman also illustrates the development of RITA (Resistance Inside the Army) and how non-military antiwar organizations became interested in organizing and propagandizing military personnel. Newspapers and coffeehouses are mentioned as instrumental to these organizing efforts.

Smith, John C. "What's Up Underground." *National Review* 8 (October 1971): 1,130.

This is a short, non-complimentary assessment of the underground press.

Spencer, Michael J. "Why Is Youth So Revolting Nowadays?" *Wilson Library Bulletin* 43, no. 7 (March 1969): 640-47.

Idealism vs. reality is the explanation provided for the burgeoning youth rebellion expressed in underground newspapers, guerrilla theater, New Left politics, and drug use. Several underground papers are described, and an annotated list of the underground and New Left press follows this article on pages 648-52.

Stapp, Andrew. "Dissent in Uniform." *Time* 93 (25 April 1969): 20-21.

Dissent within the military, evidenced by underground newspapers, desertions, and the organizing efforts of the American Serviceman's Union, is described as a phenomenon affecting only a small percentage of the armed forces.

Star, Jack. "Uproar Hits the Campus Press." *Look* 33, no. 4 (18 February 1969): 36, 38, 40.

Star gives an account of the administrative reaction to use of four-letter words in campus newspapers at Purdue and Wayne State universities. The explicit and implicit exercise of editorial control over campus papers is described.

Tebbel, John. "What's Happening to the Underground Press." *Saturday Review* 54 (13 November 1971): 89-90.

The underground press is described as having passed its peak and facing the challenges of surviving through economic hard times.

Tischler, Barbara L. "Breaking Ranks: GI Antiwar Newspapers and the Culture of Protest." *Vietnam Generation* 2, no. 1 (1990): 20-50.

This is one of several articles in a special issue devoted to "GI Resistance: Soldiers and Veterans Against the War" guest edited by Harry Haines. The other articles examine topics such as GI resistance within the military, black GI resistance, and the Presidio mutiny. Also included is a selective bibliography of the literature on this topic. Tischler's article emphasizes the role that GI underground newspapers played in providing a forum and organizing tool for dissent against military involvement in Vietnam as well as the growing demand for civil and human rights for military personnel. The impact of and linkage to civilian social change movements can be seen in the pages of GI underground papers which published articles and letters from the GIs themselves, raising issues of civil rights, racism, and sex discrimination in military life.

Tischler, Barbara L. "Voices of Protest: Women and the GI Antiwar Press." In *Sights on the Sixties*, ed. by Barbara L. Tischler. New Brunswick, NJ: Rutgers University Press, 1992.

This one chapter in Tischler's forthcoming book discusses the role of women in the military protest movement during the Vietnam War. She spotlights the particular problems women faced and the issues that either prevented them from being more vocal—such as their fears of being charged with being lesbians—or that became the focus of their dissent when they finally began speaking out—such as the difficulties women had being promoted without having to lie horizontal for their male superiors or the fact that they were being recruited to serve as morale boosters, or "adjuncts," of the male soldiers, whose work was considered more important. The military underground press was the vehicle, Tischler shows, through which women GIs expressed their grievances.

Todd, Richard. "Life and Letters: Alternatives." *The Atlantic* 226 (November 1970): 112-20.

This description of the Alternative Media Project Conference concludes with a critique of the underground, now alternative, press for its lack of substantive political analysis.

Trager, Robert, and Donna L. Dickerson. "Prior Restraint in High School: Law, Attitudes, and Practice." *Journalism Quarterly* 57 (Spring 1980): 135-38.

The authors conducted a survey of high school administrator responses to the non-definitive U.S. Court of Appeals rulings that 1) allow prior restraint if precise guidelines for review are established, 2) insist upon explicit guidelines for acceptable content, and 3) are in disagreement with a single court ruling that rejects both of these as justifications for prior restraint. The authors determined that these rulings appear to have little influence on the existence of student papers, and in fact that school administrators are generally ignorant of these decisions.

"Underground Trips." *Newsweek* 69, no. 18 (1 May 1967): 65.

This is a brief, early description of the underground newspaper phenomenon.

Waterhouse, Larry G., and Mariann G. Wizard. *Turning the Guns Around: Notes on the GI Movement.* New York: Praeger, 1971.

Using many excerpts from the GI underground papers, this book describes the GI movement, protests, and various organizations that support dissent within the ranks. Military reforms enacted to counter this dissent are also analyzed.

Watson, Francis M. *The Alternative Media: Dismantling Two Centuries of Progress.* Rockford, IL: Rockford College Institute, 1979.

In his effort to unmask and discredit the alternative press, which is merely a semantic relabeling for the radical and subversive underground press of the 1960s, Watson succeeds in providing extensive information regarding active underground and alternative publications, including addresses, Alternative Press Syndicate membership, political orientation and activism, subjects of editorial interest, and sources for further research. This analysis is an effort to illustrate the pervasive,

influential, and subversive goals of the alternative media. While sounding the warning cry against the permissive culture that "provides a force for self-indulgence in art and lifestyle that runs counter to the values of self-discipline and economic self-reliance associated with capitalism and liberty" (p. 19), Watson also implicitly denounces the causes common to these deceptive radicals, such as child care, health care, transferring money from defense spending to "human needs," "collectivist economic ideas," and the elimination of racism.

White, Mary Ann. "Social and Political Upheaval as Reflected in the Underground Press of the 1960s." Master's thesis, University of Texas at El Paso, 1986.

This rather lightweight thesis opens with an analysis of the roots and concerns of the 1960s underground press. According to this author, the press—called underground because it "mirrored the illegal drug culture" (p. 10)—was most concerned with domestic opposition to the Vietnam War, rather than the war itself. Most of the thesis consists of brief histories of individual papers while continually returning to the saga of the *Berkeley Barb.* How the author chose which papers to cover is left unstated. A section of political papers focuses on *New Left Notes*, published by Students for a Democratic Society. White differs from most authors in this bibliography in that she was not active in the underground press or sympathetic to it. Her critical comments, while grating to some, do present an alternative and outside view of the press.

Wickboldt, Mae McCarter. "Police and Courts: Themes of Individualism and Authority in the Underground Press." Ph.D diss., University of Texas at Austin, 1975.

This study reports the results of a content analysis of seven geographically diverse underground papers to determine their views of the police and courts from 1965 to 1971. The study showed that individual rights were valued more highly than the rejection of institutional authority by the undergrounds.

COMPARISON TO/CRITIQUE OF MAINSTREAM PRESS

Aronson, James. *Deadline for the Media.* New York: Bobbs-Merrill Company, 1972.

Most of this book is a critique of the mainstream press. Part One focuses on network television, the *New York Times,* and *Washington Post*, and how they covered specific events such as the Cuban Missile Crisis. Part Two discusses publications whose mission is to criticize the popular press from the left, devoting a chapter to Cleveland's *Point of View*. The treatment of blacks and women in journalism wraps up this second part. Part Three devotes a chapter to underground papers for servicemen in Vietnam, a topic rarely written about, but crucial to the study of Vietnam-era undergrounds. Socialist newspapers get their turn next, followed by a brief general history of the underground press. As with most books under review here, the author concludes with an "attitude of realistic optimism" (p. 296) concerning the alternative press, based of his judgment that by its very existence it has a positive effect by keeping the mainstream press (more) honest.

Didion, Joan. "Alicia and the Underground Press." *Saturday Evening Post* 241 (13 January 1968): 14.

In this short opinion piece, Didion defends the underground press while openly acknowledging their faults and weaknesses, stating, "I have never read anything I needed to know in an underground paper. But to think that these papers are read for 'facts' is to misapprehend their appeal. It is the genius of these papers that they talk directly to their readers." Integral to her argument is a critique of the establishment media that claims objectivity and yet is institutionally dependent upon biases that are unclear to the reader.

Holt, Patricia. "Len Fulton." [See "Individual Treatments: Personality"]

Kazan, Nick. "Underground Press." *Earth* (July 1971): 82.

The transforming influence of the underground press on establishment journalistic style is described in this introduction to the underground press phenomenon. Prominent undergrounds are listed.

Pepper, Thomas. "Underground Press: Growing Rich on the Hippie." [See "General Treatment: History, Analysis"]

Spates, James L. "Counterculture and Dominant Culture Values: A Cross-National Analysis of the Underground Press and Dominant Culture Magazines." *American Sociological Review* 41 (October 1976): 868-83.

This article reports the results of a study done to determine if the counterculture of the 1960s changed the American preoccupation with instrumental values to a concern with more expressive values. Content analysis was done on alternative and "dominant culture" magazines for the time periods 1957-59, 1967-69, and 1970-72. No change was found in the values expressed in the dominant culture magazines. Moreover, the study found that the counterculture magazines became less

expressive, but more political, as time progressed, suggesting a "major change in the underground press between 1967-69 and 1970-72" (p. 877).

Spates, James L., and Jack Levin. "Beats, Hippies, the Hip Generation and the American Middle Class: An Analysis of Values." *International Social Science Journal* 24, no. 4 (1972): 326-53.

The authors sample Beat publications (1957-1959) and Hippie publications (1967-1969) and compare them with middle-class publications to test hypotheses regarding the expressive values of the underground press and their influence upon the larger society. Middle-class publications of the 1950s and 1960s were examined, and little change in values was noted. The authors conclude that either values may take longer to change or the underground press has had little influence.

Stanfield, Douglas W. "Alternative Newspapers and Mobilizing Information." *Journalism Quarterly* 64 (Summer/Autumn 1987): 604-7.

Mobilizing information (MI) is information "that helps people act on the attitudes they already have" (p. 604). MI is usually left out of stories for mainstream newspapers in order to avoid charges of bias. This article reports the results of a study to measure the difference in MI provided by alternative, "active" alternative, and mainstream newspapers. As expected, the active alternative provided more MI than the alternative paper. The alternative paper actually gave less MI than the mainstream newspaper.

ANTHOLOGIES

Birmingham, John. *Our Time Is Now: Notes from the High School Underground.* New York: Praeger, 1970.

Using the anthology format, the editor, himself a recent high school graduate at the time this volume was published and an underground editor during his high school career, presents the issues, methods, organization, and most importantly the many voices of his subject. By broadly defining "underground" to include any paper that takes the high school as its subject but is produced outside the authority or premises of the school, Birmingham includes selections from individual papers across the spectrum of political ideologies, as well as black, Latino, and Puerto Rican papers, and the High School Independent Press Service (HIPS). Birmingham attempts to illustrate the independence of the high school movement from outside organizers such as Students for a Democratic Society (SDS), focusing on the issues of concern to the high school student (i.e., censorship, dress codes, unrepresentative student government, authoritarian school administrations, unresponsive curricula, racism, sexism, and the youth culture). Using the Spring Offensive of 1969, Birmingham describes the difficulties of organizing students and forming coalitions between groups, particularly black, Latino, and white groups.

Divoky, Diane. *How Old Will You Be in 1984?: Expressions of Outrage from the High School-Free Press*. New York: Avon, 1969.

This book is an anthology of writings by 14- to 18-year olds as printed in the pages of high school underground newspapers. The high school underground press was largely independent of outside organizations, and was printed in all areas of the country by students from across a broad economic and racial spectrum. The anthology represents this diversity in its selections. The articles, cartoons, illustrations, poetry, and editorials are arranged topically to focus on schools, students, and society. The volume concludes with a study report on the Montgomery County Public School System issued by the Montgomery County Student Alliance, which outlines the problems students perceive with the educational system and recommendations for correcting those problems. Divoky identifies two unifying trends among the various papers, the first being advocating the use of emotion to counter depersonalization in a technocratic society, and the second being the students' puritanical zeal for absolute honesty. "Here the students are themselves: original, sarcastic, vulnerable, earnest. They are speaking for themselves, talking to each other...Although they are often thought of as the radicals of their generation, they are the writers of tomorrow" (p. 12).

Forcade, Thomas King, ed. *Underground Press Anthology*. New York: Ace Books, 1972.

Edited by the head of the Underground Press Syndicate, this pithy anthology contains classic pieces from the underground press by Tim Leary, John Sinclair, Huey Newton, Bernadine Dohrn, and others. Unfortunately each piece lacks an introduction to place it in context. The book is illustrated with photographs and cartoons.

Howard, Mel, and Thomas King Forcade, eds. *The Underground Reader*. New York: New American Library, 1972.

The 47 articles from underground papers in this anthology were chosen to "allow the initiated and uninitiated underground-press reader to follow the Movement and Counter-Culture Movement through the great adventure of these last five years" (p. v). They are arranged chronologically, beginning in 1966. Included are such well-known authors as Tom Hayden,

Tim Leary, and Eldridge Cleaver, and classic pieces such as "Student as Nigger." A short history essay on the underground press and some underground comics round out this excellent sampling of the underground press.

Kornbluth, Jesse, ed. *Notes from the New Underground: An Anthology*. New York: Viking Press, 1968.

This book is an anthology of writings from the underground press published during 1966-1967 by writers as varied as William Burroughs, Tom Robbins, Allen Ginsberg, Allen Katzman, Richard Goldstein, and others. The essays are grouped into topical chapters commenting on American society, culture, alternative politics, alternative lifestyles, and the rise and radicalization of the children of love. Kornbluth keeps his own voice muted and lets the authors speak for themselves, presenting the "underground newspaper...preoccupations with the truth; at least what we are predisposed to hear" (p. xi). Kornbluth is clear about the strengths and weaknesses of the undergrounds, and concludes that they are "an attempt to legitimize dissenting reporting, to develop a constituency for radical politics, and, of course, to titillate an audience too well versed in political and cultural affairs to enjoy the mindlessness of mass journalism" (p. vx).

Shelton, Gilbert. *The Fabulous Furry Freak Brothers in the Idiots Abroad*. Auburn, CA: Rip Off Press, 1987.

Cartoons in this anthology originally appeared in the underground press across the country celebrating the adventures of the Fabulous Furry Freak Brothers. This is just one volume of the twelve volumes in the *Underground Classics* series reprinted by Rip Off Press. Other cartoonists and their strips featured in the series include Dave Sheridan (Dealer McDope), Greg Irons and Gilbert Shelton (Wonder Wart-Hog), Jack Jackson (God Nose), Ted Richards (Forty year old Hippie), and Foolbert Sturgeon (New Adventures of Jesus).

GOVERNMENT HARASSMENT

Agee, Philip. "CAIB - Eleven Years in Retrospect." [See "General Treatment: History, Analysis"]

Barnes, Peter. "The Army and the First Amendment." *The New Republic* 160, no. 21 (24 May 1969): 13-14.

Barnes describes the case of two soldiers at Fort Ord in California who were court-martialed for distributing a leaflet expressing their views about the Vietnam War. Although the pamphlet was an independent action, devoid of revolutionary language, these soldiers were sentenced under the Uniform Code of Military Justice to four years hard labor.

Berlet, Chip. "COINTELPRO: The FBI's Zany and Disruptive War on the Alternative Press." *Alternative Media* 10, no. 2 (1978): 10-14.

Various efforts by the FBI to disrupt the activities of the underground press, and particularly the underground news services, are described. Disinformation and infiltration were just two of the methods employed. The conclusion lists organizations that can assist individuals when requesting FBI files using the Freedom of Information Act.

Berlet, Chip. "Media OP." *The Public Eye* 1, no. 2 (1978): 28-38.

One of a series of articles in this issue about COINTELPRO, Berlet's piece describes FBI activities to interfere with and disrupt the alternative media. Based upon documents released through Freedom of Information Act requests, Berlet emphasizes the methods of cooperation between mainstream journalists and the FBI, including lists of media organizations that cooperated with COINTELPRO activities.

Blackstock, Nelson. *COINTELPRO: The FBI's Secret War on Political Freedom*. [See "Individual Treatments: Title or Organization: Government Harassment"]

Churchill, Ward, and Jim Vander Hall. *The COINTELPRO Papers: Documents from the FBI's Secret Wars Against Domestic Dissent*. Boston: South End Press, 1990.

FBI documents released in response to Freedom of Information Act requests are reproduced. The COINTELPRO campaigns against the Communist Party USA, Socialist Workers Party, Puerto Rican independence movement, black liberation movement, New Left, and American Indian Movement are illustrated here. The documents are presented within the context of an extensive history and analysis of COINTELPRO activities that, despite the dropping of the COINTELPRO label, the authors assert continue to the present day. An extensive bibliography and listing of organizational contacts complete the book.

"Dissenting Servicemen and the First Amendment." [See "General Treatment: History, Analysis"]

Eshenaur, Ruth Marie. "Censorship of the Alternative Press: A Descriptive Study of the Social and Political Control of Radical Periodicals (1964-1973)." Ph.D. diss., Southern Illinois University at Carbondale, 1975.

The core of this lengthy dissertation is the results of a study to determine the extent and nature of censorship of radical periodicals in the United States during the period 1964 through 1973. It was based on a survey of 297 (responding) alternative newspapers from 40 states. The author found that most of the papers had faced formal legal action against them, and that half had been subject to informal persecution by private parties. Detailed statistical analyses are included, and periodicals for servicemen and school and college papers are treated separately. Eshenaur's bibliography is extensive and focuses on legal issues.

Mackenzie, Angus. "Sabotaging the Dissident Press." *Columbia Journalism Review* 19 (March/April 1981): 57-63.

This article reviews the findings of the Church Committee Report (Senate Select Committee to Study Governmental Operations with Respect to Intelligence Activities chaired by Senator Frank Church, see entry below) with particular attention to harassment of underground publications and New Left organizations. The CIA, FBI, and Internal Revenue Service were the primary agents in the harassment of domestic dissidents. CHAOS and Project Resistance, two CIA programs, are described by Mackenzie.

O'Neill, Frank. "Censorship: In the South the Means of Resisting Are Weak." [See "Individual Treatments: Geographic Area"]

Peck, Abe. *Uncovering the Sixties: The Life and Times of the Underground Press*. [See "General Treatment: History, Analysis"]

Rips, Geoffrey. *The Campaign Against the Underground Press: PEN American Center Report*. San Francisco: City Lights Books, 1981.

Essays by Aryeh Neier, Todd Gitlin, Angus Mackenzie, and Allen Ginsberg frame Rips' detailed account of local, state, and federal harassment of the underground press. Rips has researched his topic using documents released through various Freedom of Information Act requests, many of which illustrate the volume. Harassment was carried out by several government agencies, most notably the FBI-coordinated COINTELPRO (Counterintelligence Program), established in 1956 to "expose, discredit, and otherwise neutralize the United States Communist Party and related organizations." CIA domestic activities, under the aptly named CHAOS program, were justified as efforts to identify foreign funding for "subversive" organizations. Also documented are the violations of the civil rights of servicemen by military intelligence efforts to eliminate the underground papers produced during off-duty time. Rips is able to demonstrate that a vast secret campaign was directed against New Left, antiwar, women's liberation, black liberation, and civil rights organizations, often with the cooperation of local police. Techniques included, but were not limited to, the annoying harassment and arrest of street vendors, illegal search of editorial offices, seizure of publications, equipment, and records, destruction of equipment, intimidation of landlords, publishers, and advertisers, active disinformation programs, and infiltration of newspaper and left organizations. Legal action against underground papers and their staff created financial difficulties that forced several papers to fail. The larger, more devastating effects of the disinformation and infiltration activities are only hinted at in this report. What is perhaps more distressing than the widespread violation of constitutional rights, which is illustrated in lavish detail, was the lack of any protest from mainstream journalists.

Rips, Geoffrey. "Dirty Tricks on the Underground Press." *Index on Censorship* 10, no. 2 (April 1981): 47-50.

Rips recounts many of the methods of legal and illegal harassment inflicted by local citizens and police against the *San Diego Free Press and Street Journal*. Many of the techniques used against this paper, which eventually forced it to cease publication, were used in other cities against underground papers. These are described in greater detail in Rips' book, *The Campaign Against the Underground Press*, from which this article is an excerpt.

Sherman, Edward F. "The Military Courts and the Serviceman's First Amendment Rights." *Hastings Law Journal* 22 (January 1971): 325-73.

This article is a legal analysis of the principal military First Amendment cases decided by the Court of Military Appeals during the Korean and Vietnam Wars. Sherman asserts that the military courts are isolated from academic discussion of these issues and also from civilian court review. Therefore, this developing area of the law has limits peculiar to the military context. Cases studied include *United States* v. *Voorhees, United States* v. *Howe, United States* v. *Daniels, United States* v. *Harvey*, and *United States* v. *Gray*.

Sherrill, Robert. "Must the Citizen Give Up His Civil Liberties When He Joins the Army?" *New York Times Magazine* (18 May 1969): 25-27 +.

Dissent within the military is viewed as a threat to military discipline and mission and results in sometimes arbitrary disciplinary action. Specific instances of disciplinary action, reassignment, and harassment are described. The GI movement and organizations that attempt to promote GI civil rights are discussed.

Underground publications are discussed in the context of these efforts.

"Soldiers on the War." *The New Republic* 161, no. 23 (6 December 1969): 5-6.

This editorial contrasts the rights of free speech accorded to military personnel who support the war and those of military personnel who do not support the war effort.

U.S. Congress. House of Representatives. Committee on Internal Security. *Investigation of Attempts to Subvert the United States Armed Forces*. Washington, DC: U.S. Government Printing Office, 1972.

In three parts, these hearings present testimony, press releases, articles, meeting minutes, correspondence, Department of Defense directives and correspondence, and answers to submitted committee questions regarding the threat of subversion among U.S. military personnel. The hearings begin with the text of a speech by committee chair Richard Ichord about factors contributing to the crisis of morale in the armed forces. The hearings were conducted in response to a congressional resolution passed April 28, 1971, and were intended, "to better determine the true nature and extent of the GI movement and its ties with revolutionary groups of the new and old left" (p. 6384). Each volume includes an index to individuals, organizations, and publications.

U.S. Congress. Senate. Committee on the Judiciary. *Organized Subversion in the U.S. Armed Forces*, hearings before the Subcommittee to Investigate the Administration of Internal Security Act and other Internal Security Laws. 1975. Washington, DC: Government Printing Office. (Y4.J 89/2:Ar 5/4/pt.1 + appendixes 1 & 2).

Presided over by Senator Strom Thurmond, part one of these hearings, with its two appendixes, explores communist and leftist subversion of the Navy in particular. Witnesses testifying before the committee are Navy spokesmen bringing evidence (letters, project reports, news releases, cartoons, movement music) of specific instances of sabotage and subversion. Organizations specifically discussed include the National Lawyer's Guild, Pacific Counseling Service, and the Lawyers Military Defense Committee, which was active both in the United States and abroad. Particular attention is paid to publications and underground newspapers published for military personnel. The work is indexed with supplemental indexes for personalities and groups and organizations. It also includes lists of GI coffeehouses and publications in the Far East.

U.S. Congress. Senate. Select Committee to Study Governmental Operations with Respect to Intelligence Activities. *Final Report of the Select Committee to Study Governmental Operations with Respect to Intelligence Activities, United States Senate: Together with Additional, Supplemental, and Separate Views.* Washington, DC: U.S. Government Printing Office, 1976. (Report, 94th Congress, 2d session, Senate; no. 94-755).

Popularly known as the Church Report, for committee chair Frank Church, this six-volume report is the result of a fifteen-month long inquiry into the practices and abuses of the various agencies involved in intelligence activities. Books 2 and 3 examine "Intelligence Activities and the Rights of Americans," including descriptions of the domestic surveillance activities (COINTELPRO, CHAOS, military surveillance of civilians) against organizations of the New Left, the Black Panthers, and Martin Luther King, Jr., among others. The other volumes of this report examine "Foreign and Military Intelligence" (books 1 & 4), "Investigation of the Assassination of President John F. Kennedy and Performance of Intelligence Agencies" (book 5), and "Supplementary Reports on Intelligence Activities" (book 6).

Wickboldt, Mae McCarter. "Police and Courts: Themes of Individualism and Authority in the Underground Press." [See "General Treatment: History, Analysis"]

INDIVIDUAL TREATMENTS

TITLE OR ORGANIZATION

History, Analysis

Allen, Douglas. "Antiwar Asian Scholars and the Vietnam/Indochina War." *Bulletin of Concerned Asian Scholars* 21, nos. 2-4 (April-December 1989): 122-34.

This is an in-depth history of the CCAS (Committee of Concerned Asian Scholars), an antiwar group that was instrumental in supporting the Bulletin of Concerned Asian Scholars. It includes a series of interesting short interviews that touch on topics such as scholarship vs. activism, the invisibility of the Asian community, and personal activism within the Vietnam antiwar movement. Those interviewed include Ngo Vinh Long, *BCAS* co-editor Christine White, Nina Adams, Noam Chomsky, and Sandy Sturdevant.

Aronson, James. *Deadline for the Media.* [See "General Treatment: Comparison to/Critique of Mainstream Press"]

Belfrage, Cedric, and James Aronson. *Something to Guard: The Stormy Life of the National Guardian 1948-1967.* New York: Columbia University Press, 1978.

The *National Guardian* (now the *Guardian*) was first published on October 18, 1948. This is the story of that paper, told by two of its three founders. The paper originally began as a vehicle for supporting the "progressive tradition" of FDR and preventing a resurgence of fascism. Detailed here is a tale of financial crisis, shifting ideological priorities, McCarthyism, and the personalities in radical publishing during that era. The final chapters describe the authors' decision to resign after internal division in 1967, and address such weighty issues as why the *Guardian* was not more critical of the Soviet Union.

Brody, Michal, ed. *Are We There Yet? A Continuing History of Lavender Woman, a Chicago Lesbian Newspaper, 1971-1976.* Iowa City: Aunt Lute Book Company, 1985. (Now published by The Institute of Lesbian Studies, PO Box 60242, Palo Alto, CA 94306.)

Lavender Woman appeared 26 times between 1971 and 1976. This book reprints 50 articles and many of the lively graphics from this Chicago lesbian newspaper. In addition, interviews with seven collective members are presented. An introductory chapter provides the historical background as well as the story of how the paper got started.

Cliff, Eleanor. "Read It First in the *Bird.*" *McCalls* (June 1971): 45.

Although the reasons are unclear why this account of the editorial content and staff lifestyles of Atlanta's *Great Speckled Bird* appeared in *McCalls* magazine, Cliff praises the *Bird* for its involvement with important national and local issues.

Doggett, David. "Underground in Mississippi." *Southern Exposure* 2, no. 4 (1975): 86-95.

Doggett gives an account of the four-year life of *Kudzu,* an underground paper he published in Jackson, Mississippi. Doggett became founder, writer, and editor when he sought a means of communicating information regarding national movements and local events to people who might otherwise have had no access to that information. Doggett was active in the civil rights movement through the Southern Student Organizing Committee and had published two short-lived papers before starting *Kudzu.* A small group of people worked collectively and intensively to produce *Kudzu* with him. Financial difficulties, long hours, and police harassment are described. With the disintegration of national organizations and the New Left movement, *Kudzu* became increasingly isolated, resulting in a slow decline in readership and staff and the paper's demise in 1972.

Doggett, Martha Lynn. "Worse Than Infamy." *NACLA* 22, no. 1 (January 1988): 3.

In this article on testifying before a House subcommittee as one of the 96 leftist organizations burglarized by the right wing, the author turns these attacks around and credits them with having made *NACLA* "the country's most widely read periodical covering Latin America and the Caribbean. In 1970 we had 1,400 subscribers. Today we print 11,500 copies of the magazine." Doggett goes on to state that, despite financial support from subscribers, they are still $98,000 in debt and goes on to appeal for funds.

Downie, Leonard, Jr. *The New Muckrakers*. Washington, DC: New Republic Book Company, Inc., 1976.

This book is divided into chapters on various "muckrakers," or investigative reporters. Most of them hardly fall into the category of "underground" (Seymour Hersh, Bob Woodward), but three of the book's chapters are within the scope of this bibliography. The first profiles the weekly *San Francisco Guardian* and other "hell-raising" advocacy journalism efforts. The next chapter examines *The Nation* and "free lance" muckrakers such as Tad Szulc. The final chapter, "The Future of Muckraking," looks at muckraking's shortcomings, such as occasionally damaging, inaccurate stories and the tendency of muckrakers to avoid investigating the corporate world. The author stresses muckraking's accomplishments, however, and urges more papers and television networks to pursue investigative stories.

Downing, John. *Radical Media: The Political Experience of Alternative Communication*. Boston: South End Press, 1984.

Downing examines the political context and structural characteristics of media (print and broadcast) in industrialized nations. Section One focuses on the United States, with chapters on the *National Guardian*, KPFA, Berkeley, *Union Wage, Akwesasne Notes, ERIN Bulletin, NACLA Report on the Americas*, Third World Newsreel, and California Newsreel. Section Two looks at Portugal and Italy, while Section Three examines media in Eastern Europe.

"Easygoing Advocate of the Outrageous." *Life* 65 (4 October 1968): 41-43.

In this brief profile, with photographs and quotations, *Life* introduces its readers to Paul Krassner's satirical point of view. *The Realist*, of which Krassner was the editor and chief writer, had a circulation of over 100,000 at the time.

"Editorial." *Cineaste* 16, nos. 1-2 (1978): 6.

This editorial gives a fairly brief history of the magazine's 20 years, from its first 30-page, 50-cent issue with a 500-copy print run, to its political commitment. It includes an "honor roll" of *Cineaste* staff members from 1967 to 1987. The article states that "apart from our frugalities, *Cineaste*'s secret weapon, the ultimate key to our survival, has been the volunteer labor of our editors and other staff members."

Ehrenreich, Barbara. "Poppa of the PAC: An Interview with Health/PAC Founder Robb Burlage." *Health/PAC Bulletin* 18, no. 4 (Winter 1988): 23-27.

Ehrenreich interviews the founder of Health Policy Advisory Center. This entire special issue celebrates the 20th anniversary of *Health/Pac Bulletin*. It also includes a reproduction of the first issue dated June 1968.

Ellis, Donna Lloyd. "The Underground Press in America: 1955-1970." [See "General Treatment: History, Analysis"]

Evans, Larry. "Steel Voices—The *Mill Hunk Herald* Saga." *Changing Work* 10 (Summer 1989): 3-7.

Evans tells the story of the *Mill Hunk Herald*, a Pittsburgh working class literary journal. *Mill Hunk*'s vision was to empower workers by encouraging them to write and by raising their political consciousness. *Mill Hunk* grew from the unorthodox though short-lived Committee of Concerned Union lists. This is an article on a unique publication written by a self-proclaimed anarchist-hedonist.

Frye, Patrick Keith. "The *Great Speckled Bird*: An Investigation of the Birth, Life, and Death of an Underground Newspaper." Master's thesis, University of Georgia, 1981.

Frye gives a detailed history of *Great Speckled Bird*, Atlanta's major underground newspaper. Begun by a small collective of graduate students at Emory University in 1967, the *Bird* grew to be the largest paid weekly publication in Georgia at its peak circulation of 23,000 in July of 1970. Fluctuations in circulation, advertising, editorial and management organization, and editorial content are given detailed attention. The influence of the women's movement on the editorial structure and content of the paper is indicative of the time, as is the decline of "The Strip," a hippie section of Atlanta, which co-existed and supported the *Bird*, and whose decline only shortly anticipated that of the paper. Throughout its life, the *Bird* was sustained by its identification with the antiwar, left wing politicos and avant-garde artists of Atlanta. Although the *Bird* survived intense political and legal harassment, it could not survive the decline in its base readership and its drift into the leftist, Maoist, political extreme. An attempt to cling to life as a free drop monthly failed and the paper ceased publication in 1976.

Frye's thesis, in its "effort to fill the void in research of the underground press" (p. 8), sheds much light on underground papers in general during the *Bird*'s era. While much of the thesis is based on personal interviews, it does cite many short articles from the popular press on alternative newspapers. The conclusion is a thoughtful analysis of the social factors that produced an enthusiastic readership for the *Bird*.

Fudge, William G., Jr. "A Descriptive Readership Study of the Atlanta Underground Newspaper: The *Great Speckled Bird*." Ph.D. diss., Florida State University, 1975.

This thesis is based upon a readership study of the Atlanta underground newspaper, *Great Speckled Bird*, conducted in February of 1972. The only other readership study for an underground paper that has been conducted was a small sampling of *East Village Other* readership in 1968. Fudge worked with the collective that produced the paper to devise an acceptable survey, which was then printed in the paper. The goal was to determine the demographic and behavioral characteristics of the *Bird* audience. Fudge asked questions regarding age, education, employment, income, living arrangements, geographic location, and other media use including print and broadcast media "consumption." Fudge explains the biases in his results due to the lack of any follow-up or control procedures as well as omissions in the data. For example, the editorial collective found questions about gender of respondent to be offensive, yet questions about race were left in. In brief summary, the readership was young with the median age being 24.5 years, predominantly poor (85 percent earned less than $10,000 per year), highly educated (85 percent had graduated high school, 40 percent had college degrees), and heavy media consumers reading books, attending concerts, listening to the radio, and more, 96 percent of the respondents were white, and 60 percent lived outside of Georgia. These last two statistics highlight the difficulty of viewing Fudge's work as a representative sampling of the readership.

Fulbright, Newton H. "Underground Press Strives to Fuse Sex with Politics." [See "General Treatment: History, Analysis"]

Gordon, Douglas E. "The *Great Speckled Bird*: Harassment of an Underground Newspaper." [See Individual Treatments: Title or Organization: Government Harassment"]

Haines, Harry William. "The GI Underground Press: Two Case Studies of Alternative Military Newspapers." Master's thesis, University of Utah, 1976.

In this in-depth study of two military underground newspapers, *The Ally* and *Aboveground*, based upon interviews with their founding editors, Haines examines the motivations for founding the papers, objectives of the papers, editorial control, methods of distribution, financial support, and political affiliations. After surveying several GI undergrounds, Haines selected the two studied as representative of several trends. *The Ally* was published by civilians in Berkeley from 1968-1974 and was distributed nationally. The editors made an effort to focus on GI civil rights and assess and address the needs of their GI readership. *Aboveground* was printed and read by military personnel at Fort Carson, Colorado, from 1969-1971. More strongly influenced by outside political organizations through contacts at the local Homefront cafe, this paper presented a Marxist analysis of military organization in its effort to radicalize GIs. Haines concludes that the Left failed to propagandize the disaffected among military personnel due to their reliance upon Marxist analysis and their inability to capitalize upon the experiences and needs of GIs and veterans. He concludes with a listing of 120 military undergrounds and major ephemera collections containing GI underground newspapers. Updated versions of this thesis and the listing of military undergrounds appear in *Voices from the Underground: Insider Histories of the Vietnam Era Underground Press* (Ann Arbor, MI: Pierian Press, 1991).

Hairston, Julie B. "The *Great Speckled Bird* Flies into the '80s." *Southern Exposure* 16, no. 2 (Summer 1988): 59-62.

One of the late great underground newspapers of the sixties and seventies, the *Great Speckled Bird*, held a 20-year reunion in Atlanta in 1988. This article offers a choice description of the *Bird*'s life, with the accuracy only hindsight can give. The article has a few choice photos and graphics from the *Bird* as well as a rundown of where former staffers are today. It should not be annotated, it should be read.

Hale, Dennis. "Boston's New Journalism: Prospects for the Alternative Press." *The Nation* 216 (23 April 1973): 529-33.

Hale offers a detailed account of the ownership, editorial content, and mutual influence of Boston's alternative papers, the *Boston Phoenix, Boston After Dark*, and *The Real Paper*, which was started by former *Phoenix* staff members after a labor dispute with the management.

Heussenstamm, F.K. "Activism in Adolescence: An Analysis of the High School Underground Press." [See "General Treatment: History, Analysis"]

Hoffman, Amy. "My Interview." *Gay Community News* 17, no. 2 (9-15 July 1989): 8-9.

    The former *Gay Community News* editor offers a chapter of her novel-in-progress about a Boston gay and lesbian newspaper, the *Gay Weekly*. "Any resemblance to any real person, place, or thing, is, of course, purely coincidental." An amusing way to publish everything-you've-always-wanted-to-say-about-the-collective-but-were-afraid-to.

"How Free Should the High School Press Be?" *Today's Education* (September 1969): 52-54, 85.

    This article examines the role of the faculty advisor for *Silver Chips*, the student paper at the Montgomery Blair High School in Silver Springs, Maryland. By respecting the students and avoiding external censorship, the paper had a successful career and the students have wrestled with the ethical dilemmas inherent in publishing. There has also been no underground paper at this school.

Johnson, Michael L. *The New Journalism*. [See "General Treatment: History, Analysis"]

Kaiser, Ernest. "25 Years of *Freedomways*." *Freedomways* 25, no. 3 (Fall 1985): 204-16.

    This in-depth history of *Freedomways*, a major black journal which began publishing in 1961, includes an issue-by-issue review, states the editorial policy, and credits Shirley Graham and Esther Jackson with being the founding editors.

Keller, Nancy J. "Case Study of an Alternative Newspaper: The *Sonoma County Stump*, 1972-1982." Master's thesis, Sonoma State University, 1986.

    This thesis was a labor of love by Keller, who worked for the *Sonoma County Stump* for two years. A paper started as a means of communication for the urban refugees from the political and cultural movements of the day, the story of the *Stump* is that of the growth of the alternative press from the rubble of the underground press. The movements of the 1960s splintered into a variety of racial, sexual, political, and cultural organizations, publications, and activities that led to the decline of many underground papers. Those people who joined the "back to the land" wave and moved from San Francisco to the Russia River Valley of northern California had the *Stump* to look to for news, calendars of events, police blotter reports, and other information. Keller examines the editorial content, graphic design, production methods, advertising,

economic crises, editorial and ownership changes, community and readership, circulation, and distribution, as well as the paper's demise after ten years of travail and triumph.

Kessler, Lauren. "Sixties Survivors: The Persistence of Counter-Cultural Values in the Lives of Underground Journalists." *Journalism History* 16, nos. 1-2 (Spring/Summer 1989): 2-11.

    Kessler conducted interviews with fourteen former staff/commune members of the *San Diego Street Journal* in order to determine the degree to which their values relating to family, lifestyle, politics and activism, and career continue to be influenced by the experiences of their youth. The interviews were conducted twenty years after involvement with the commune and newspaper, a much longer time span than in previous studies. Most of those interviewed have maintained strong values of social responsibility that are demonstrated in their nontraditional family structures, continued urban (rather than suburban) residence, career choices and trajectories, leftist politics, and non-conspicuously consumerist lifestyles.

Kleiner, Art. "A Short History of the First 50 Issues of *CoEvolution Quarterly* and *Whole Earth Review*." *Whole Earth Review* 51 (Summer 1986): 128-38.

    This issue-by-issue listing of contents also reveals in a chatty style editor's and writers' visions of the magazine.

Knoll, Erwin. "*Ramparts*' Red Glare." *Progressive* 49, no. 5 (May 1985): 4.

    Knoll offers a brief history of the glory and demise of *Ramparts*, a major antiwar publication of the sixties. Knoll then criticizes a *Washington Post Magazine* article by two former *Ramparts* editors, Peter Collier and David Horowitz.

Leamer, Laurence. *The Paper Revolutionaries: The Rise of the Underground Press*. [See "General Treatment: History, Analysis"]

Livingston, John, and Bryant Avery. "The *Bulletin of Concerned Asian Scholars* from the Perspective of Past and Present Managing Editors." *Bulletin of Concerned Asian Scholars* 21, nos. 2-4 (April-December 1989): 180-83.

    A look back on the 20-year publishing history of the *Bulletin of Concerned Asian Scholars* by two of its editors. Each gives a state and vision of the journal as it was during his tenure (Livingston 1971-1976 and Avery 1976-1981). Both talk about the role the Committee of Concerned Asian Scholars played in the *Bulletin*'s history.

Lydon, Michael. "The Word Gets Out." [See "General Treatment: History, Analysis"]

McAuliffe, Kevin. *The Great American Newspaper: The Rise and Fall of the Village Voice*. New York: Scribner, 1978.

A detailed account of the founding, growth, and various ownership changes of the *Village Voice*, a precursor to and model for many underground papers of the 1960s and 1970s. McAuliffe has laced this history with many personal accounts of the writers and editors, as well as information on their subsequent contributions to American letters.

McQuistion, Iris. "School Paper Learns from Underground." *Communication: Journalism Education Today* (Spring 1971): 11.

The author reports on a section meeting held on "School Paper and the Underground: Friendly Rivals" at the 47th Annual Conference of the Columbia Scholastic Press Conference. Two Pelham Memorial High School papers were represented, the official *Pel Mel* and the underground *The Paper*. The underground, having more editorial freedom, pushed the official paper to be timely in their news coverage. Life expectancy of the underground paper was reported shaky, due to staff graduations.

Mills, Howard A. "The Seattle *Helix*: An Underground Looks at the Times." Master's thesis, University of Montana, 1970.

This history of the Seattle *Helix* reviews staff composition as well as production and distribution patterns and provides an extensive content analysis. Topics covered in the paper reflect the times and include drug use, spirituality and moral issues, minority population concerns, and local issues. Mills glosses over issues of harassment in his analysis, which presents the paper evolving from its original drug orientation to a focus for political activism and local organizing.

Peck, Abe. "The Death of a Founding Father." [See "Individual Treatments: Personality"]

Peck, Abe. *Uncovering the Sixties: The Life and Times of the Underground Press*. [See "General Treatment: History, Analysis"]

Picciotto, Sol. "Ten Years of *Capital and Class*." *Capital and Class* 30 (Winter 1986): 7.

This personal view of the journal's complete history speaks mainly to the vision and scope of the journal, though it is not hesitant to criticize its own shortcomings.

Piloti, Joe. "The Underground GI Press: Pens Against the Pentagon." [See "General Treatment: History, Analysis]

Plowman, Edward. "Jesus Presses Are Rolling." [See "General Treatment: History, Analysis"]

Roth, Moira. "The Tangled Skein: On Re-Reading *Heresies*." *Heresies* 24 (1989): 84-88.

Written by a faithful reader of *Heresies*, this article offers a critique of the magazine and of the collective process while providing a revealing look at both the development of *Heresies* itself and the women's movement since 1977.

Sale, J. Kirk. "The *Village Voice* (You've Come a Long Way Baby, but You Got Stuck There)." *Evergreen Review* (December 1969): 25-27, 61-67.

Sale's history and assessment of the *Village Voice* focuses on personnel and personalities of Dan Wolf and Ed Fancher, founding editors. While the *Voice* is credited with initiating a new literary journalistic style, offering a new bo-lib political viewpoint (bohemian-liberalism), and having a wide cultural influence, Sale petulantly concludes that the *Voice* "is not as good as it should be."

Seeger, Arthur August, Jr. "Pig Paper: A Case Study of Social Control in the Newsroom of a Controversial Underground Newspaper." Ph.D. diss., University of California, 1976.

The author, a self-described "conventional" journalist, spent time as a participant-observer at the *Berkeley Barb* as both reporter and editor beginning in 1970, after the staff strike against publisher Max Scherr and the founding of the rival *Berkeley Tribe*. The image of the *Berkeley Barb* as the voice of the hippie/"head" element of the counterculture is disputed. Seeger's original framework for the thesis, that the influential *Barb* had a role as "molder" of and socialization mechanism for hippie values and culture, had to be radically restructured. He found that the *Barb* more often mirrored values of a small portion of the community, that which was vocal, militant, and strategically placed. After the strike, the *Barb* was particularly vulnerable to criticism as a "pig paper" and many editorial decisions were made to counter that loss of "face." Game theory is a major analytical framework for this thesis. Descriptive information regarding how the paper was put together each week, Scherr's role as publisher and editor, what stories were covered (or not covered), and the infamous sex advertisements provide a glimpse into what life at the *Barb* was like.

Smith, Gar. "Sour Notes from the Underground." [See Individual Treatments: Personality"]

Stapp, Andy. *Up Against the Brass*. [See "Individual Treatments: Personality"]

"The Tribe Is Restless." *Time* 94, no. 3 (18 July 1969): 46.

This account of the *Berkeley Barb* staff conflict with owner/publisher Max Scherr came prior to the staff strike and split that produced the *Berkeley Tribe* newspaper.

"The Way We Were: An *East West* Journal Retrospective." *East West* 16, no. 3 (March 1986): 55-75.

This retrospective for their 15th anniversary issue includes statements of the magazine's goals and beliefs and two interesting staff photos from 1977 and 1983. Also included are many brief reprints of *East West*'s most significant articles.

Williams, R.M. "San Francisco *Bay Guardian* Blues." *Columbia Journalism Review* 15 (November 1976): 42-44.

The long, bitter strike at the *Bay Guardian* is described. Despite the views printed in the paper, the management (owner/publisher Bruce Brugmann) is described as a benevolent despot who would not automatically knuckle under to union demands. The strike was in process at the time of this account, so the resolution is not included.

Winter, Michael, and Ellen Robert. "A Swift Backward Glance: Thirty Years of the *BJS*." *Berkeley Journal of Sociology* 31 (1986): 201-12.

This in-depth history of the *Berkeley Journal of Sociology* traces its development of a Marxist-inspired critical sociology perspective. Two prominent themes are the women's movement and colonialism and the Third World.

Comparison to/Critique of Mainstream Press

Cobb, Ron. *Mah Fellow Americans: Editorial Cartoons from the Underground Press Syndicate*. Los Angeles: Sawyer Press, 1970.

This collection of Cobb's cartoons contains little text, presumably a tribute to the axiom that a picture is worth a thousand words.

Kimball, Bruce A. "A Case Study in Alternative Journalism: The Santa Barbara Bribery Exposé." *Journalism Quarterly* 51, no. 2 (1974): 303-6.

The author analyzes coverage of the same story by two different newspapers, the establishment *Santa Barbara News-Press* and the alternative *Santa Barbara News & Review*. Kimball argues that investigative journalism and opinionated presentation of the news can be as responsible as the objective journalism of the establishment press.

Levin, Jack, and James L. Spates. "Hippie Values: An Analysis of the Underground Press." *Youth and Society* 2, no. 1 (September 1970): 59-73.

Expressive values are those favoring self-expression, affiliation, and concern for others. Instrumental values stress achievement, cognitive growth, and economic status. The authors argue that the hippie movement was a rejection of the middle-class pursuit of instrumental values in favor of expressive values. This article describes a study to test the hypothesis that "contrary to the middle class pattern, hippie values stress expressive concerns and de-emphasize instrumental concerns" (p. 64). A content analysis was done of the *Reader's Digest* to test for middle-class values and of various underground newspapers to test for hippie values. The results supported the thesis, showing that the underground newspapers showed more expressive concerns while the *Reader's Digest* conveyed instrumental concerns. The authors suggest that hippies may make a higher level of expressivism more acceptable in American culture.

Schoenfeld, Eugene. *Dear Doctor Hip Pocrates: Advice Your Family Doctor Never Gave You*. New York: Grove Press, 1968. 2d edition, 1973.

Schoenfeld wrote a medical advice column that appeared in several underground newspapers. This anthology demonstrates that his column emphasized practical, straightforward advice, laced with a strong sense of humor.

Smith, Gaye Sandler. "The Underground Press in Los Angeles." [See "Individual Treatments: Geographic Area"]

Anthologies

Carson, Clayborne, senior ed. *The Student Voice, 1960-1965: Periodical of the Student Nonviolent Coordinating Committee*. Westport, CT: Meckler, 1990.

This reprint was compiled by the staff of the Martin Luther King, Jr. Papers Project. A one-page introduction by Carson gives a brief overview of the paper's history. *Student Voice* was begun in June 1960 as a vehicle to spread news about black student lunch counter sit-ins, mass mobilizations, and other protests. In addition, the paper published reports on the activities of SNCC field secretaries, especially in the Black Belt areas of Georgia, Alabama, and Mississippi. One purpose of the paper was to provide Northern supporters with news that the mainstream press was not covering.

Grier, Barbara. *Lesbiana: Book Reviews from The Ladder, 1966-1972*. Reno: Naiad Press, 1976.

The Ladder first appeared in October 1956 as a "twelve-page poorly mimeographed magazine with a paid subscription list of seventeen and a mailing list of two hundred professionals" (p. 15). It was intended as a national magazine and was published by the San Francisco group Daughters of Bilitis, a social group for lesbians founded a year earlier. By 1968 *The Ladder* was a glossy bimonthly with a paid subscription list of about 1,000. In 1970, the magazine became independent and shifted its focus from lesbian and gay liberation to lesbian and feminist issues. These changes coincided with the growth of the women's movement and saw the magazine's circulation more than triple. *The Ladder* folded at the height of success in 1972, from lack of funds and apathy according to Grier in *Lesbiana*, and is still revered as the first (and for a long time only) national publication for lesbians.

In 1966, *The Ladder* began a book review column written by Gene Damon (Barbara Grier's pseudonym) called "Lesbiana." The columns are reprinted in their entirety here, arranged chronologically. The chatty review essays covering several books each issue are supplemented by an author and title index, making this a useful reference book.

Grier, Barbara, and Coletta Reid, eds. *The Lavender Herring: Lesbian Essays from The Ladder*. Baltimore: Diana Press, 1976.

The 37 essays appearing in *Lavender Herring* cover a range of topics, including lifestyle, sexuality, feminism, and culture.

Grier, Barbara, and Coletta Reid, eds. *The Lesbians Home Journal: Stories from The Ladder*. Baltimore: Diana Press, 1976.

Short stories, especially romances, were a favorite with readers of *The Ladder*. Twenty-two of them are reproduced here. Rather than lighthearted fluff, they address the difficulties our society imposes on lesbians.

Grier, Barbara, and Coletta Reid, eds. *Lesbians Lives: Biographies of Women from The Ladder*. Baltimore: Diana Press, 1976.

From 1957 to 1972, *The Ladder* published numerous articles about lesbians from different eras and backgrounds. These popular biographies and biographical essays helped to fill the great void of information

on famous lesbians. All of them are included in this anthology. Most of them are accompanied by references to other sources and a photograph. This collection doubles as a readable account of fascinating women ("I didn't know she was a lesbian!") and reference books of hard-to-find facts.

Katzman, Allen, comp. and ed. *Our Time: An Anthology of Interviews from the East Village Other*. New York: Dial Press, 1972.

The *East Village Other* was established in 1966 as an underground paper for the growing East Greenwich Village community and as an alternative to the *Village Voice*. In this anthology are reproduced 45 interviews with a wide range of the leading writers, thinkers, and activists—both cultural and political—that were published between 1966 to 1971. Bobby Seale, Timothy Leary, Andy Stapp, Grace Slick, Kate Millett, Alan Watts, an anonymous GI, and a Buddhist monk are a sample of the people whose conversations are reproduced here. "Our format was simple. We were involved. We participated. We talked to the people who were doing it. This is the result; a series of interviews which, when woven together, give a clear pattern of what is happening in the world today." (From the introduction.)

Krassner, Paul, ed. *The Best of the Realist*. Philadelphia: Running Press, 1984.

In this book are a selection of articles, essays, cartoons, and "interviews" from the pages of *The Realist*, a satirical magazine published by Krassner from 1958 to 1974. Authors included in this anthology include Krassner, Timothy Leary, Lenny Bruce, Abbie Hoffman, Jerry Rubin, Richard Pryor, Joe E. Brown Jr., and Kurt Vonnegut, to mention only a few. *The Realist* was a precursor to, and one of the best examples of, the underground press and served as a means to "liberate communication, even if as a byproduct bad taste has now become an industry" (p. 8).

Krassner, Paul. *How a Satirical Editor Became a Yippie Conspirator in Ten Easy Years*. New York: Putnam, 1971.

This memoir, in the form of excerpts from *The Realist*, reflects Krassner's view of the world and particularly the events of the day. *The Realist* was a satirical review originally founded by Krassner in 1958. It was revived in 1984 to express some of the same outrage at the public manipulations of reality. Krassner titles his introduction "The Truth Is Silly Putty," and proceeds to illustrate the legitimating power of the printed word. Stories issued by "legitimate" sources can be as outrageously funny, or horrifyingly absurd, as some of Krassner's stories printed as satire and mistaken for reality. The issues covered range from stag parties to abortion, the "swami scene" to the founding of the Yippies, and present a lively portrait of an era.

The Ladder. New York: Arno Press, 1975.

This is a reprint, in 16 volumes, of *The Ladder*, the longest running monthly lesbian periodical. Originally affiliated with the Daughters of Bilitis, it was published in San Francisco from October 1956 to August 1968, when it moved its base of operation to Reno, Nevada. In August 1970, *The Ladder* became an independent publication, with Barbara Grier as editor and publisher. *The Ladder* ceased publication in October 1972.

Outlaws of Amerika: Communiques from the Weather Underground. New York: Liberated Guardian, 1971.

The Weathermen were the only true underground organization of the era in question, in the sense of using illegal, violent tactics. The nine numbered communiques and six additional messages included in this pamphlet were originally published in the *Liberated Guardian, Berkeley Tribe*, and other underground newspapers. In this pamphlet, they are arranged with a chronology of events beginning with the May 1, 1970, Mayday demonstrations and the killings at Kent State and then Jackson State. The first communique is a Declaration of War issued on May 21. Subsequent messages celebrate or commemorate such events as the escape of Timothy Leary from prison, various bombings carried out by the Weathermen, prison uprisings, and the flights of Black Panther leader Huey Newton, Rap Brown, and Angela Davis. The rhetoric of revolution is fierce, reflecting the sense that extreme measures were required to change "Amerika" and end its racist, imperialist, capitalist war against humanity. This rhetoric is modified dramatically beginning with the message entitled "New Morning—Changing Weather," and communique number 7, issued December 6, 1970, after three Weathermen were killed in the accidental explosion of a bomb. The change in language and tone in message 7 revealed internal conflicts regarding the use of violence. In later communiques, feminist ideology becomes more evident as a motivation and strategy. The Underground as an active organization did not last long after that event. The last message is dated Mayday 1971, one year after its inception.

The San Francisco Oracle: The Psychedelic Newspaper of the Haight-Ashbury 1966-1968. Facsimile edition by Allen Cohen. Berkeley, CA: Regent Press, 1991.

This limited edition facsimile reprint edition was named Book of the Year by Noel Peattie (*Sipapu* 21, no. 1, 1991, pages 3-4). Issues 1-12 of the *Oracle*, the most daring graphic innovator among the underground newspapers, are included in this full-color reproduction. Essays by Allen Cohen and John Montgomery are included.

Government Harassment

Blackstock, Nelson. *COINTELPRO: The FBI's Secret War on Political Freedom*. New York: Vintage Books, 1976.

In 1973, the Socialist Worker's Party (SWP) and the Young Socialist Alliance (YSA) filed a lawsuit against the FBI for spying, harassment, and disruption. FBI files were released during the trial and form the basis for this book. Originally published in 1976, it has been updated following the completion of the lawsuit (the SWP and YSA won their case; a U.S. district judge ruled that the FBI violated the groups' constitutional rights). With numerous reproductions of declassified documents, the book details the FBI's program in the 1960s to impede the SWP, which had spill-over effects on other movement groups. While most of their efforts did not focus on stopping the alternative press, the book exposes the techniques used by the FBI to crush the American socialist movement, which included the disruption of its publications.

Cook, Fred J. "On Being an Enemy of the FBI." *The Nation* 242, no. 11 (22 March 1986): 426-29.

This is the afterword to the article by Penn Kimball (see below) on the FBI surveillance of *The Nation* over a period of 68 years.

Flannery, Gregory. "Hot on the Press: Did Police Torch a Cincinnati Paper?" *In These Times* 13, no. 33 (6-12 September 1989): 7.

Flannery, author of the two-part series of articles "Reach Out and Torch Someone," was investigating a Cincinnati Bell telephone installer's admission of placing 1,000 illegal wiretaps between 1972 and 1984 at the request of local police and the FBI. Through this investigation, Flannery uncovered charges that in 1970 the Cincinnati police torched an underground paper, *Independent Eye*. After the fire—which did not destroy the office—50 people witnessed undercover officers carrying out armloads of files. A classic story of police harassment of a radical underground newspaper.

Gordon, Douglas E. "The *Great Speckled Bird*: Harassment of an Underground Newspaper." *Journalism Quarterly* 56, no. 2 (1979): 289-95.

The *Great Speckled Bird* was an underground newspaper published in Atlanta, Georgia. This article describes its evolution from a community paper for

Atlanta's street, hippie population to a radical intellectual paper engaging in investigative reporting on urban development projects. Police harassment accompanied this shift, in odd correlation to investigations into the mayor's involvement with developers. Legal and extra-legal tangles with Atlanta authorities are described regarding issues of obscenity, street peddling of papers, and sales in high schools and neighboring communities. Arrests, firebombing of the editorial offices, and legal actions were some of the harassment techniques employed.

Kimball, Penn. "The History of *The Nation* According to the FBI." *The Nation* 242, no. 11 (22 March 1986): 399-426.

Kimball provides an exhaustive presentation of materials gleaned from the twelve bound volumes obtained under the Freedom of Information Act. The request took five years to process and includes more than 2,000 pages.

Knoll, Erwin. "Filed but Not Forgotten: The FBI and *The Progressive*." *The Progressive* 50, no. 10 (October 1986): 24-25.

In this story of the FBI files on *The Progressive*, editor Knoll notes that most of what drew the FBI's attention were articles critical of them. He offers an interesting view of Hoover's anti-communism.

"Not So Free Press." *Time* 95, no. 12 (23 March 1970): 38.

Harassment of the *San Diego Street Journal and Free Press* within the conservative political and journalistic environment of San Diego is described.

Rechy, John. "GI's for Peace: The Army Fights an Idea." [See "Individual Treatments: Geographic Area"]

Rips, Geoffrey. *The Campaign Against the Underground Press: PEN American Center Report*. [See "General Treatment: Government Harassment"]

Rips, Geoffrey. "Dirty Tricks on the Underground Press." [See "General Treatment: Government Harassment"]

Widmer, Kingsley. "Censorship by Harassment." *The Nation* 210 (30 March 1970): 336-69.

Harassment of the *San Diego Street Journal* and the GI paper *Duck Power* is reviewed. Widmer connects the harassment to the publication by the *Street Journal* of investigative stories regarding the San Diego Copley newspapers.

Withum, Ronald E. "GI Communication." *The New Republic* 161, no. 23 (6 December 1969): 29-30.

This letter to the magazine from Private Ronald E. Withum at Fort Bliss, Texas, describes two recent events on base where military authorities reassigned personnel due to political activities, one of many forms of harassment short of court martial employed to discourage dissent within the military.

GEOGRAPHIC AREA

Danky, James. "Still Alive and Well: The Alternative Press in 1977, Part I." *Harvest Quarterly* no. 5 (Spring 1977): 5-11.

Looks at the founding and content of the *Los Angeles Free Press* and the *Berkeley Barb*, two of the early underground papers of the Vietnam era.

Danky, James. "Still Alive and Well: The Alternative Press in 1977, Part II. *Harvest Quarterly* no. 6 (Summer 1977): 17-22.

Danky describes several alternative newspapers that appeared in Madison, Wisconsin, between 1967 and 1977. Content, format, and lifespan of each paper are discussed. The papers are described in chronological order of appearance.

Feldman, Sam. "Going Underground." [See "General Treatment: History, Analysis"]

Feldman, Sam, "To Publish Underground Newspapers." *Journalism Education Today* (Fall 1968): 7, 18.

Feldman reports the results of a survey sent to 400 California high schools. A 40 percent response rate indicated that 18 schools had underground papers, 52 "indicated rumblings" of a potential underground paper, and 21 had previously had underground papers on campus. Also surveyed were advisor reactions to undergrounds, which ranged from the opinion that undergrounds represent a form of Communist subversion to strong encouragement. He concludes that rigid administrative response to expression will encourage formation of underground papers. The converse is also true on occasion, that the threat of an underground will encourage principals to grant more editorial freedom and motivate staff advisors to do a better job. Feldman encourages school administrators to use these papers for educational purposes.

Hale, Dennis. "Boston's New Journalism: Prospects for the Alternative Press." *Nation* 216 (23 April 1973): 529-33.

When purchased in 1970 by Richard Missner, the *Boston Phoenix* had 800 readers. By 1972, it had almost 6,000. Its leading competitor, *Boston After Dark*, changed its style in order to compete with it. This article relates the history of Boston's two best-known undergrounds. It focuses on the papers' evolution, their editors, and, in the case of the *Phoenix*, the conflict between the editorial staff's aims and Missner's business interests. A drawn-out battle between Missner and his staff described here is a nightmare of organizational disarray producing a strike, firings, and reorganization. The end result of this mess was Missner's decision to sell the *Phoenix* to its competitor, *Boston After Dark*, and the birth of a new underground by former *Phoenix* staffers. The article concludes with a cogent discussion of how Boston makes possible two alternative papers (heavy on advertising and entertainment listings), as well as the author's doubts about how "alternative" the papers really are.

Letwin, Leon. "Regulation of Underground Newspapers on Public School Campuses in California." *UCLA Law Review* 22 (1974): 141-218.

Letwin provides an extensive legal review of statutory and constitutional bases for prior restraint of public high school publications. He critiques school administrative policies that are based upon the theory that the rights of children are not co-extensive with those of adults.

O'Neill, Frank. "Censorship: In the South the Means of Resisting Are Weak." *South Today* (January/February 1971): 4-6.

O'Neill cites several instances of censorship in publications, the performing arts, and elsewhere and indicates that the tendencies toward censorship are strong in the South, although not exclusive to the South. The best means of resisting censorship is a demanding public, while the average educational attainment level among the southern population is the eighth grade. Power is also concentrated in fewer hands in the South. Often the press abdicates its critical role because of close relationships to the power structure. Liberal and underground publications are available in the South, but they are not widely influential. A box story recounts harassment of the underground press and the lack of support from establishment journalists.

Rechy, John. "GI's for Peace: The Army Fights an Idea." *The Nation* 210 (12 January 1970): 8-12.

GI's for Peace is an organization founded at Biggs Field and Fort Bliss in El Paso, Texas. Their founding and underground publication, *Gigline*, is described. Harassment from military administration took the form of reassignment, informal harassment, and punishment without trial, in disregard of army protections for free expression. Events at the Defense Language Institute are described in detail.

Shore, Elliott. "Decade of Dissent: The Alternative Press in Philadelphia, 1966-1976." *Drexel Library Quarterly* 12 (1976): 58-74.

In this clear, detailed description of Philadelphia's underground papers from 1966 to 1976, Shore admits that Philadelphia followed trends set in more radical areas such as San Francisco or New York. The papers were "outstanding however, in the official opposition that they provoked, and in the high quality of the writing and production of some of the work" (p. 59). The article traces the history and describes each of the city's undergrounds—from *Graffiti* in 1967 through 1973 with *Recon*. Throughout the article, Philadelphia's experience is chronicled within the context of alternative papers and sixties culture in general.

Slater, Paul. "The Fifth Estate: Underground Newspapers as an Alternative Press in California." Master's thesis, University of California, Berkeley, 1969.

Slater discusses the role of underground newspapers in California in the mid- to late-1960s. He traces the origin of the underground press and focuses on its influence on the establishment media in terms of news coverage and graphics. Newspapers examined range from the *Los Angeles Free Press* and *Berkeley Barb* to many smaller papers that did not survive more than a few issues. It includes a comprehensive listing of underground newspapers published in California in 1969.

Smith, Gaye Sandler. "The Underground Press in Los Angeles." Master's thesis, University of California, Los Angeles, 1968.

This analysis of eight consecutive issues of four underground Los Angeles newspapers compares content, format, emphasis, and style, as well as relationships with the other underground and establishment papers in the city. All issues compared were printed prior to October 5, 1967. Therefore, this thesis provides a look at the early undergrounds, generally acknowledged to have been started by Art Kunkin's *Los Angeles Free Press* in 1964. The papers studied include the *Free Press* along with *Open City*, started in May 1967 as a sensationalizing tabloid focusing on racial and sexual minorities; the *Oracle*, a short-lived paper dedicated to the religious experience of drug use; and the *Los Angeles Underground,* which grew from a series of protest pamphlets in 1966 to a paper that was antiwar, anti-drug, anti-obscenity, anti-establishment, and occasionally anti-underground press. The thesis provides a detailed breakdown of paper content, review of stories covered, editorial content, illustrative matter, classified and display advertisements, events calendars, layout, and more, and extrapolates regarding the typical readership of each paper. A comparative analysis of underground and establishment press coverage of the same story, the antiwar demonstrations at the Century Plaza Hotel on June 23, 1967, leads Sandler to conclude that the undergrounds were less thorough and professional, and served as a sort of "house organ," serving a networking function, for the counterculture and racial and sexual minorities.

Wakefield, Dan. "Up from Underground: Boston's Weekly Alternative Papers." *New York Times Magazine* (15 February 1967): 14-17.

An account of the format, content, history, staff, readership, and relationship of Boston's two underground papers, *The Phoenix* and *The Real Paper*. Short descriptions of five additional undergrounds follow the article.

PUBLISHER

Bongartz, Roy. "South End Press: The Long March Continues." *Publishers' Weekly* 232 (7 July 1987): 17-22.

South End Press began in 1985 as a group of graduates from the University of Massachusetts who coalesced to start a publishing house that would publish the texts they felt their own education had lacked. The house was formed as a collective operation that searched for a "new political outlook that considered class, race and sex as equally important" (p. 17). This article describes South End's shaky start and growing success. It addresses such issues as the difficulty of getting mainstream review sources to review left wing books and self-censorship in writing and publishing. It also has a one-page insert on three other left wing presses, comparing them to South End.

Romm, Ethel G. "Psychedelics by Offset: Protest Tabloids Turn On to Color Printing." [See "General Greatment: History, Analysis"]

Sargent, Lydia. "Beyond the Small Press as a Dinner Roll in the Main Course of Life." *New Pages* 13 (Spring 1988): 9-11.

This article is adapted from a speech at the 1987 Small Press Conference. Sargent, co-founder of *Z Magazine* and South End Press, discusses the founding of South End Press, a radical book publisher, by a group of sixties activists to publish perspectives on feminism, racism, the Vietnam War, social movements, and other issues that are ignored by the mainstream press.

PERSONALITY

Alterman, Eric. "The Ironies of Izzymania." *Mother Jones* 8, no. 5 (June 1988): 34-37.

Alterman profiles I.F. Stone, publisher of *I.F. Stone's Weekly*, a newsletter he published for 19 years. Stone had recently published *The Trial of Socrates*, an analysis of the Athenian side of the debate. Alterman discusses Stone's popularity, his contribution to journalism, and his uncovering in 1958 of the U.S. Atomic Energy Commission's first underground nuclear tests.

"Ask Dr. Hip." *Newsweek* 73, no. 20 (19 May 1969): 118-19.

The medical column that appeared in many undergrounds, authored by Eugene Schoenfeld of the UC Berkeley Student Health Service, is described.

Berlet, Chip. "The Tom Forcade Story: The Death of an Activist." *Alternative Media* 11, no. 1 (1979): 26+.

This obituary following Forcade's suicide celebrates his ceaseless productivity as founder of the Underground Press Syndicate and publisher of *High Times* and *Orpheus*, two unrelated undergrounds, and his outrageous behavior in defense of free speech. The article is followed by an interview with Forcade by Gabrielle Schang-Forcade, accounts from his friends, and his own statement regarding the "Repression of the Underground Press."

Downie, Leonard, Jr. *The New Muckrakers*. [See "Individual Treatments: Title or Organization: History, Analysis"]

Holt, Patricia. "Len Fulton." *Publisher's Weekly* 218 (5 December 1980): 6-7.

Dustbooks, Len Fulton's publishing company, has been called the "RR Bowker" of the small press. Beginning in 1963 with *International Directory of Little Magazines and Small Presses*, Fulton publishes *Small Press Review* and a variety of guides to the small press as well as individual books. This short report of an interview with Fulton and his partner, Ellen Ferber, covers their views on the role of the small press and how it differs from mainstream publishing.

Levitt Lanyi, Ronald. "Trina, Queen of the Underground Cartoonists: An Interview." *Journal of Popular Culture* 12, no. 4 (1979): 737-54.

In response to the Senate Subcommittee on Juvenile Delinquency investigation into the propriety of comic books in 1955, major comics publishers hastily created a "Comics Code." The burgeoning underground press in the 1960s created a forum for underground cartoonists who felt no need to be restrained by the major publishers' code. An influential underground cartoonist, the first woman in the field, was Trina Robbins. This interview, conducted in July of 1977, covers a variety of topics, including women in comics, popular subjects for underground cartoons, and the meaning of her own work.

Peck, Abe. "The Death of a Founding Father." *Rolling Stone* 17 (21 January 1982): 17-18.

Peck presents a sensitive chronicle of Max Scherr and the *Berkeley Barb*, which Scherr founded and edited. The *Barb*, begun in 1965, quickly became a "flagship" of sixties underground papers—reaching a circulation of over 90,000—and was an integral part of Berkeley's counterculture movement. Unfortunately, as so often happens with undergrounds, editor and writers were often at odds over wages and Scherr's acceptance of sexist advertisements. Staffers went on strike and began their own paper, the *Berkeley Tribe* in 1969. The paper and Max survived the seventies, but faced falling circulation, heart attacks, and a divorce. Scherr sold the *Barb* in 1980, shortly before he died of cancer. The article portrays both the man and his magazine, both philosophically locked in the sixties, unable to accept changing times.

Purnick, Joyce. "Editing the Mayor (Dan Wolf)." *New York* (12 February 1979): 10.

Purnick gives a succinct account of the role played by former *Village Voice* editor Dan Wolf in the office of Mayor Ed Koch as special advisor to the mayor. The author outlines Wolf's longtime friendship with Koch—beginning in the 1950s—and draws parallels between Wolf's style at the *Voice* and in city hall: "In first encouraging writers' individuality and in now doing the same with Koch, he is in fact orchestrating things, editing them. Whether what worked in a counterculture newspaper of the fifties and sixties will work in the decidedly unradical Koch administration of the seventies and eighties remains to be seen" (p. 11).

Sinclair, John. *Guitar Army: Street Writings/Prison Writings*. New York: Douglas Book Corp., 1972.

On December 22, 1966, John Sinclair, in the spirit of countercultural good feelings, gave two joints to a fellow freek. Surprise, the man turned out to be an undercover government informer. Sinclair—poet, activist, underground paper writer, manager of the rock group MC5, and a founder of the Ann Arbor-based White Panther Party/Rainbow People's Party, as well as bane of the Detroit-Ann Arbor repressive establishment—was given a prison sentence of 9 1/2 to 10 years. By the time he was freed, on December 13, 1971, some

29 months after his sentencing, and only after a massive nationwide publicity campaign led by his fellow party members, he had become a counterculture folk hero and symbol of the free marijuana movement. *Guitar Army*, Sinclair's call for a society based on love, rock & roll, and good pot, is a collection largely of prison writings and of newspaper articles he wrote for the *Warren-Forest Sun* (Detroit), Detroit's *Fifth Estate, Ann Arbor Argus, Ann Arbor Sun, Sun/Dance*, and *Creem*. It concludes with a "Rainbow Reading & Listening List." His listening list ("Jams") is subdivided according to Rock & Roll, Rhythm & Blues, Spoken, and New Black Music.

Smith, Gar. "Sour Notes from the Underground." *New West* 4 (1 January 1979): 52-60.

Smith describes the complex and suspicious financial dealings made during the sale of the *Berkeley Barb* by its founder and publisher, Max Scherr. As a result of the sale, the sex ads, which were both the fame and infamy of the *Barb*, were to be moved to a companion paper, *The Spectator*, described as "a poor man's Penthouse."

Stapp, Andy. *Up Against the Brass*. New York: Simon & Schuster, 1970.

This book is an account of Stapp's effort to radicalize the armed forces from within the ranks. Himself radicalized against the Vietnam War while a Pennsylvania State University student, Stapp was drafted in May 1966 (after burning his draft card). Between then and his undesirable discharge four weeks before the end of his tour of duty in April 1968, Stapp attempted to organize what became the American Servicemen's Union (ASU) to counter the inequitable treatment of enlisted men by the officer corp, institutionalized racism, and violation of the constitutional rights of servicemen. The eight-point program of the ASU included the demand for election of officers by enlisted men, the right to disobey illegal and immoral orders, and the right of servicemen to collective bargaining. Stapp's first court-martial, on the grounds of refusing an officer access to his personal library, elicited a great deal of publicity and enabled him to link up with external legal counsel and organizing staff from such organizations as National Emergency Civil Liberties Committee, Youth Against War and Fascism, and the American Civil Liberties Union. ASU experienced its real growth after Stapp was discharged, aided by the founding of *The Bond* in mid-1967, the first but not the only underground newspaper published by and for military personnel.

Press Syndicates

Berlet, Chip. "A Guide to Alternative News Services in the U.S." *Alternative Journalism Review* 9, no. 1 (1976): 13-14.

This descriptive listing of ten alternative news services includes address, frequency, format, number of pages and stories, camera ready copy, graphics pages, mail class, and rates.

Berlet, Chip. "Alternative News Services in the U.S.—Part II." *Alternative Journalism Review* 9, no. 2 (1976): 16-19.

Berlet provides the who, what, where, and so on for several alternative news services and important conferences convened for these services. Important stories seen first through the alternative services are reviewed (e.g., the My Lai massacre and the CIA role in the Southeast Asian heroin trade) as are some critiques of the services.

Berlet, Chip. "COINTELPRO: The FBI's Zany and Disruptive War on the Alternative Press." [See "General Treatment: Government Harassment"]

Collins, Deaver. "The Liberation News Service, [ca. May 1973]." Contemporary Culture Collection. Temple University Libraries, Philadelphia.

When you think about Liberation News Service, the images you probably get are of the Virtuous Caucus and the Vulgar Marxists, LNS co-founder Ray Mungo's respective terms for the post-split Massachusetts and New York contingents. This unpublished research paper is interesting, then, in that it provides a glimpse at the story of LNS from the perspective of the New York contingent. Written in first person, it is based on information and quotes the author obtained during a two-week stay with the collective.

His pro-New York contingent bias is so obvious that selective quotes are unnecessary. This fact is not objectionable—certainly Mungo's *Famous Long Ago* is no less objective. Irritating, however, is the author's habit of tossing out negative connotations and then moving on to new territory without elaborating. A few examples: Why was LNS co-founder Marshall Bloom "dismissed" from the presidency of the U.S. Student Press Association? Does the author side with the USSPA in the decision? Or, what is meant by "Marshall's gay irresponsibility"? What is meant by "Ray wrote his memoirs, of a sort..."? What is meant by the suggested racism behind the fact that "a *black* [reviewer's emphasis] printer had to be hired to make up for the reduced staff..."?

The writing itself sounds too carefully worded at times, to the point of appearing defensive. The fact that it appears on LNS letterhead suggests that it was commissioned as a public relations piece. A better discussion of why the research was done in the first place would have been helpful.

Nevertheless, the paper contains a few illuminating elements. One is the discussion of the difficulty LNS members had in resolving the issue of leadership vs. ego that paralyzed so many movement groups and did more than its share to burn out talented individuals who had to stifle their talents or die in order to behave as correct-acting collective members. In part, the author shows, this issue was behind the LNS split all along, and in fact served to turn away leaders even after Mungo and Bloom and Co. had moved north. Later on Allen Young, George Cavelletto, and Sheila Ryan appear to have been phased out also, because they had radical politics in their backgrounds. "Now in LNS there are substantially no heavies," says Beryl Epstein. "So people feel generally on a fairly equal footing." Yes, but at what cost to talent?

Ellis, Donna Lloyd. "The Underground Press in America: 1955-1970." [See "General Treatment: History, Analysis"]

Garvey, Ellen. "From Outrage to Barometer: The Underground Press." [See "General Treatment: History, Analysis"]

Mungo, Raymond. *Famous Long Ago: My Life and Hard Times with Liberation News Service*. Boston: Beacon Press, 1970.

In this intensely personal account, Mungo recalls his two-year involvement with the Liberation News Service (LNS), which he conceived with Marshall Bloom at a U.S. Student Press Association (USSPA) conference and established December 1968 in Washington, DC. After eighteen months as a communal collective, LNS merged with the added resources of the SDS in New York. The merger and move were traumatic, and a rift developed between the "vulgar Marxists" and the "virtuous caucus." When the latter group retreated to rural Massachusetts in 1969 with money, equipment, and mailing list stolen from LNS offices in the dead of night, the New York staff responded with violence and a lawsuit, the emotional traces of which are evident throughout Mungo's presentation. Personal philosophy, various drug scores, people, and events (the levitation of the Pentagon, attending services at LBJ's church, King's assassination, and the subsequent days of rage) twine into a powerful account of a search for a way of life. Despite Mungo's involvement and commitment to the Movement and revolutionary change, he ultimately abandoned organized efforts. As he states, "Here's a lesson

I honestly believe I learned in my lifetime: ideals cannot be institutionalized. You cannot put your ideals into practice, so to speak, in any way more 'ambitious' than through your own private life" (p. 69).

Mungo's three books were reprinted by Citadel Underground Press, an imprint of Carol Publishing, in 1990. The new title is *Famous Long Ago: My Life and Hard Times with Liberation News Service, at Total Loss Farm and on the Dharma Trail*, and includes a new foreword by Eric Utne and Jay Walljasper as well as two dozen photographs by Peter Simon.

Peck, Abe. "Faded Flowers, the Legacy of the Underground Press." [See "General Treatment: History, Analysis"]

Romm, Ethel G. "Campus Protest Movement: You Go Underground for 'Inside' Report." [See "General Treatment: History, Analysis"]

"Underground Alliance." *Time* 88, no. 5 (29 July 1966): 57.

This description of the five founding members of the Underground Press Syndicate, one of the earliest accounts, notes that "shoestring papers of the strident left are popping up like weeds across the United States."

AUTHOR INDEX

TITLE INDEX

DIRECTORIES OF SPECIAL COLLECTIONS ON SOCIAL MOVEMENTS EVOLVING FROM THE VIETNAM ERA

Ellen E. Embardo

In 1982, Scarecrow Press published *Alternative Materials in Libraries*. As one chapter, the book included a directory of collections of contemporary alternative materials in libraries. That directory, compiled by Patricia J. Case and edited by James P. Danky and Elliott Shore, proved immensely useful as a reference tool for identifying libraries throughout the United States and Canada that contain original source materials emanating from the social and political upheavals of that period which is known loosely as "the sixties."

These repositories contain a broad range of primary research materials that document social and political movements for radical change. Most function as sub-units of large research libraries, many in university settings. A large number were created during the heyday of the political activism, such as those at University of Connecticut, University of California (Berkeley), and Northwestern University. Some predate the Vietnam era by decades, such as the Tamiment Library in New York, the State Historical Society of Wisconsin, or the Labadie Collection at the University of Michigan. Many, on the other hand, were started far away from any academic setting, by individuals who had the sense that they were living, and making, history and who had the foresight to preserve primary materials from the period for the documentary record. Many of the gay and lesbian collections, for instance, still operate out of private homes.

Whether connected with a large research institution or cared for by a committed individual or group of people, the collections listed in this directory constitute an enormous resource for scholars or casual users,

Embardo is curator of the Alternative Press Collection, Special Collections Department, Homer Babbidge Library, University of Connecticut, Storrs, Connecticut.

veterans of the period, or students of today who seek the unadulterated words of activists from across the progressive political and social spectrum.

The usefulness of the original directory was such that I was excited when Jim Danky asked me to update and expand it for a new edition of the Scarecrow Press book. Since publication of the first edition, other institutions or individuals had amassed similar collections. Also, many of the collections listed in the first edition had stopped adding materials or had been sent elsewhere by their curators. The University of California, San Diego, for example, donated its collection to the University of Connecticut, after the collection's usefulness had dissipated on the California campus.

The new edition of *Alternative Materials in Libraries*, unfortunately, never materialized. Nevertheless, by the time the decision was made to retire the project, questionnaires that were to be used for updating the directory had already been sent to collections and returned by the majority of curators. Additionally, notices about the upcoming directory, which appeared in *American Libraries, College and Research Libraries News, Library Journal, Wilson Library Bulletin*, and other library journals in the United States and Canada, resulted in additional entries. It seemed a shame to have wasted all the efforts of so many people.

When Edward Wall, publisher of Pierian Press, expressed an interest in publishing a series of articles about the Vietnam-era alternative press in one of his quarterly publications, *Serials Review*, he asked me to update the information I had compiled, in order to publish it as a companion directory. For a number of reasons all relating to growing interest in this project, this material found its way over time first into *Reference Services Review* (vol. 18, no. 3, Fall 1990), another Pierian Press publication, and now into this anthology by Mica's Press.

Only a few minor changes distinguish the *RSR* version from this one. For example, we have added three collections: the unique collection at La Salle University entitled "Imaginative Representations of the Vietnam War"; The Henry Gerber-Pearl M. Hart Library of Chicago's Midwest Lesbian & Gay Resource Center; and the National Museum of Lesbian & Gay History from New York.

The directory in its present form actually appears as three directories. The first includes the general collections from Jim Danky's list, with a few additions and deletions. The second is of gay and lesbian collections, some from the general list and others found in Cal Gough's 1989 "Gay/Lesbian Archives and Libraries in North America," which itself is a revised version of a similar list compiled by Allen Miller in 1987. The third directory incorporates non-respondents from both of the first two directories.

Any directory of collections of alternative materials in libraries must of necessity include a definition of what is "alternative." The Social Responsibilities Round Table, Task Force on Alternatives in Print of the American Library Association recently ventured to define an "alternative publisher" in their new book, *Alternative Publications* (Chicago: ALA, 1989), as follows:

1. The publisher is noncommercial (i.e., more concerned with communicating ideas than making money).

2. The subject matter pertains to social responsibility, such as the attempt to: a) achieve rights for an oppressed group of people; b) see economic justice for all individuals; c) disperse political power among members of society. [I would add here a fourth category: achieve a sustainable, ecologically sound culture.]

3. The publisher would define itself as a publisher of alternative materials.

4. The work is published by a small press poetry or literary publisher.

Despite number four above, I did not actively solicit information about literary collections. Rather, throughout work on the directory, my focus remained on non-literary social and political movements. Nonetheless, many curators chose to include data on their literary as well as their non-literary materials. That material has been retained for this directory.

The questionnaires used for this directory were filled out with varying degrees of completeness. Most curators took a great deal of time and effort in answering yet one more questionnaire of the many they receive regularly regarding their specialized collections. One curator responded that his effort was a labor of love, given the tremendous amount of time he spends filling out questionnaires "for other people's research projects." To all who took time out of their very busy schedules, I am heartily grateful; I hope the directory proves useful enough to reward their considerable efforts. In addition, Mica's Press hopes to periodically update this directory. If you know of a collection that should be added, or if you know the whereabouts of those collections listed in directory 3, please pass along to the appropriate person a copy of the questionnaire, which is included in figure 1.

Respondents who wish to update and expand their responses that follow are strongly encouraged to do so also. Address all inquiries or suggestions to Ken Wachsberger, editor of *Voices from the Underground*, PO Box 15152, Ann Arbor, Michigan 48106.

Institution:

Address:

Phone number:

Collection name:

Curator or contact person:

Public service hours:

Restrictions on use (if any):

Inclusive years represented in collection:

Principal years represented in collection:

Primary subjects included in the collection:

Secondary subjects included in the collection:

Formats collected:

Imprints collected:

Number of volumes [break down by type, if necessary (e.g., number of monographs, reels of microfilm)]:

Number of journals or newspapers currently on subscription:

Housing considerations [Please describe how the collection is housed, including an indication of the shelf arrangement]:

Bibliographic control provided [Please describe the methods used for processing, cataloging, and accessing the collection bibliographically]:

Published guides to the collection [Are any of these publications available for purchase?]:

Other publications/services:

Date the collection was established:

History/Description of the collection:

Citation of descriptive articles about your collection (e.g., newspaper or journal articles):

Additional information:

Are you still adding materials to the collection?

DIRECTORY 1: SPECIAL COLLECTIONS LIBRARIES WITH MAJOR HOLDINGS ON VIETNAM ERA SOCIAL MOVEMENTS
(IN ORDER BY STATE, THEN COLLECTION)

ARIZONA

Institution: *Northern Arizona University Library*

Address: Box 6022
Flagstaff, AZ 86011-6022

Phone number: (602) 523-5551

Collection name: Allderdice Collection

Curator or contact person: Coordinator, Special Collections

Public service hours: 8 a.m. to 5 p.m., M-F only.

Restrictions on use: No lending. All materials used in high-security reading room. No ILL (this is an OCLC institution). Most books cataloged, OCLC.

Inclusive years represented in collection: 1910 (very roughly) to 1970s (also extremely rough).

Principal years represented in collection: Both world wars (I & II), labor movements, social movements Russia, China (respective years of these activities).

Primary subjects included in the collection: Leninism, John Birch, McCarthy, Chinese social movements.

Secondary subjects included in the collection: Eight four-drawer file cabinets of pamphlet, brochure materials covering proper names of people and organizations, fully indexed and analyzed in a catalog—really too numerous to mention.

Formats collected: Books (about 3,000 volumes), newspapers, periodicals (extensive runs of bound backfiles), clippings, pamphlets, brochures.

Imprints collected: Wide range, foreign and domestic, alternative press oriented, however, with extremist publications represented of common domestic publishers.

Number of volumes: 3,000 volumes, approximately 500 bound volumes.

Number of journals or newspapers currently on subscription: Fewer than two dozen, mainly those from Russia and China.

Housing considerations: Part of special collections' stack area (three ranges) is devoted to books and bound periodicals, eight four-drawer file cabinets contain clipping/pamphlet collection, flat metal shelves (approximately 50) hold flat larger-format [newspapers] materials.

Bibliographic control provided: Books in regular card catalog, with OCLC location indicating "Allderdice" above call number, with everyone here knowing "Allderdice" is located within special collections. Periodicals listed in main periodicals holdings list, partially cataloged.

Published guides to the collection: There is a brochure. Nothing is available for purchase.

History/Description of the collection: Norman Allderdice (Tucson) died in 1966, leaving his extremist literature collection to Northern Arizona University.

Additional information: This collection covers the years from the 1930s up through 1973, which was the "official" end of the Vietnam War. For this reason, it is primarily a historical collection rather than a current one.

Are you still adding materials to the collection? No, except occasional gifts.

Institution: *Hayden Library*

Address: Hayden Library
Arizona State University
Tempe, AZ 85287

Phone number: (602) 965-3145

Collection name: Chicano Research Collection

Curator or contact person: Christine Marin

Public service hours: 9 a.m. to 5 p.m., M-F; 1 p.m. to 5 p.m., Saturday.

Restrictions on use: All materials must be used in the Luhrs Reading Room of the Hayden Library, Department of Archives & Manuscripts. As we are a public institution, no one is denied access to materials.

Inclusive years represented in collection: 1848 to present.

Principal years represented in collection: 1848 to present.

Primary subjects included in the collection: Mexican Americans in the United States, from 1848 to present.

Formats collected: Books, newspapers, microforms, pamphlets, periodicals, ephemera, microfilm, manuscripts, photographs, videos, posters, buttons, and cassettes.

Number of volumes: Approximately 5,000.

Number of journals or newspapers currently on subscription: Approximately 50.

Housing considerations: Housed by format; then by LC.

Bibliographic control provided: CARL, MSS.-CARL, Colorado Alliance Research Libraries, the online catalog that includes books, manuscripts, and photographs, and is linked to both OCLC and RLIN.

Published guides to the collection: None.

Date the collection was established: 1969.

Citation of descriptive articles about your collection: Brochure is available.

Additional information: Manuscript collections include The Alberto Francisco Pradeau Collection; The Tiburcio Sotelo Family Papers; the Rose Marie and Joe Eddie López Papers; and The Armando Ruíz Papers, 1987-1988 (re: the pros and cons of the English Only Movement in Arizona).

Are you still adding materials to the collection? Yes.

CALIFORNIA

Institution: *DataCenter*

Address: 464 19th St.
Oakland, CA 94612

Phone number: (510) 835-4692

Collection name: DataCenter

Curator or contact person: Contact library department.

Public service hours: 1 p.m. to 5 p.m., T and Th, 5 p.m. to 9 p.m., W.

Restrictions on use: Use by members only (memberships available to the public for modest fee).

Inclusive years represented in collection: 1950s.

Principal years represented in collection: 1966 to present.

Primary subjects included in the collection: Alternative and underground press, political economic issues, United States and Third World from progressive perspective.

Secondary subjects included in the collection: Corporations, conservative and right-wing movements/organizations.

Formats collected: Serial publications, subject clippings files, and posters.

Number of volumes: Approximately 2,000 cubic feet.

Number of journals or newspapers currently on subscription: 250.

Housing considerations: Storage boxes, vertical files, library stacks; serials arranged alphabetically; vertical files by record groups.

Bibliographic control provided: Accessible through electronic and hard copy catalogs and inventories.

Other publications/services: Free-based custom research services, public-access library, Third World resource guide series including *Women in the Third World, Food, Hunger and Agribusiness*, and *Transnational Corporations and Labor*, and press-reprint publications.

Date the collection was established: 1977.

History/Description of the collection: The DataCenter collection began as an outgrowth of the research and publishing activities of the North American Congress on Latin America (NACLA) established in 1966. In 1977, the center was established as a non-profit educational organization dedicated to collecting and providing information services to progressive social change efforts. In addition to our historical material, the center continues to develop and maintain a collection of periodicals and subject files drawn from the alternative and mainstream press covering contemporary political economic and social issues.

Citation of descriptive articles about your collection: Horn, Zoia, and Karen O'Neill. "Data Center: A Very Special Library." *Collection Building* (Spring 1985). Setterberg, Fred. "A Library for Dissenters." *American Libraries* 20, no. 7 (July/August 1989): 702-4.

Are you still adding materials to the collection? Yes.

Institution: *University Library, California State University, Sacramento*

Address: 2000 Jed Smith Dr.
Sacramento, CA 95819

Phone number: (916) 278-7958

Collection name: Dissent and Social Change Collection

Curator or contact person: John Liberty

Public service hours: 8 a.m. to 9 p.m., M-Th; 8 a.m. to 4:30 p.m., F; 1 p.m. to 4:30 p.m., Saturdays and Sundays throughout the academic year; 8 a.m. to 4:30 p.m. during summer session and breaks.

Restrictions on use: The collection is open to the general public. Materials do not circulate to individuals. Most materials are available for limited loan to academic institutions.

Inclusive years represented in collection: 1880 to present.

Principal years represented in collection: 1965 to present.

Primary subjects included in the collection: Primary subjects included in the Dissent and Social Change Collection are materials on Afro-American history, alternative lifestyles, Asian-American history, civil rights, civil liberties, environmental movements, gay and lesbian movements, right-wing and left-wing activities, Mexican-American and Native American history, peace movement, and women's movement history and activities.

Secondary subjects included in the collection: The original archives of the Sacramento Peace Center (founded 1962) are housed in the University Library as a part of the Dissent and Social Change Collection. At present there are approximately 21 standard archive boxes of files and historical records of the Sacramento Peace Center.

Formats collected: Although thousands of monographs are included, the Dissent and Social Change Collection consists primarily of journals, with emphasis upon left-wing, right-wing, women's movement, and alternative lifestyle periodicals. A substantial portion of the material is now on microfilm.

Number of volumes: Journals, periodicals, newspapers: approximately 4,000; periodical titles, reels of microfilm: approximately 1,500; reels of film and monographs: estimate not available.

Number of journals or newspapers currently on subscription: 250.

Housing considerations: With the exception of rare or archival items, the books and journals of the Dissent and Social Change Collection are integrated into the University Library. Periodicals are shelved alphabetically, monographs by Library of Congress classification, and archival items by organization and topic.

Bibliographic control provided: Monographs are cataloged into Library of Congress classifications through OCLC; periodicals are recorded by a computerized serials control system. Periodicals are assigned a unique Dissent and Social Change Collection number and sub-number within the serials control system.

Published guides to the collection: The primary guide to the collection is John Liberty's *Journals of Dissent and Social Change*, 6th edition, 1986. This 500-page, subject-arranged bibliographic catalog is for sale through the University Bookstore, California State University, 6000 J St., Sacramento, California 95819. The price is $21.50, including shipping. (California residents should add 6 percent sales tax.)

Other publications/services: Microfilm and paper photocopying facilities are available.

Date the collection was established: 1965.

History/Description of the collection: The Dissent and Social Change Collection was begun by Social Science Librarian John Liberty in the mid-1960s. The collection is strongest in left-wing materials from 1890 to 1940 and from 1965 to the present. Right-wing periodicals run from the 1950s to the present. Women's movement and alternative lifestyle journals are strongest from 1965 to the present. Microfilmed newspaper clippings are available on the Berkeley Free Speech Movement, the San Francisco State College student strike, and California student protest demonstrations in the 1960s. Commercially produced indexes and guides are available, such as the *Alternative Press Index*, the *Left Index*, the *Catalog of the Tamiment Institute Library*, the *Students for a Democratic Society Papers Guide*, and the *Socialist Party of America Papers Guide*. Other guides include the *Herstory Microfilm Collection* table of contents, the *Right-Wing Collection of the University of Iowa Libraries Guide*, and the *Underground Newspaper Microfilm Collection* table of contents.

Are you still adding materials to the collection? New materials are continually being added to the Dissent and Social Change Collection to the extent that the University Library budget permits.

———

Institution: *California State University, Fullerton*

Address: University Archives and Special Collections Section
Library
California State University, Fullerton
PO Box 4150
Fullerton, CA 92634

Phone number: (714) 773-3444; 773-3445

Collection name: Freedom Center Collection (FC)

Curator or contact person: Sharon K. Perry

Public service hours: 1 p.m. to 4 p.m., M-Tu; 9 a.m. to 12 p.m., W-F; or by appointment; contact library reference desk: (714) 773-2633 (recess hours).

Restrictions on use: All materials must be used in the University Archives and Special Collections reading room. As we are a public institution, nobody is denied access to use of the materials. Xeroxing permitted—none on rare or fragile items. Some materials may circulate for a week to card holders.

Inclusive years represented in collection: Approximately early pre-World War I to present.

Principal years represented in collection: 1959 to present.

Primary subjects included in the collection: Political, social, and religious organizations and movements representing a variety of viewpoints—emphasis on right-wing and left-wing materials. Labor movement in the United States and elsewhere, principally Great Britain. Grassroots political literature—local campaign literature from all parties. (Local in terms of California and Orange County.)

Secondary subjects included in the collection: Sixties' arms control and disarmament, Holocaust, civil rights, Vietnam War, alternative newspapers ("underground" newspapers of the sixties and seventies), and women's movement.

Formats collected: Books, pamphlets (usually cataloged as monographs), periodicals, folders of ephemera, some posters, banners, and bumper stickers. Microfilm copies of some journals are purchased or owned in the library's general microform collection.

Imprints collected: Not limited to a particular kind; but most materials collected are published by "alternative" publishers or organizations.

Number of volumes: Periodical titles—4,079 journals, 272 newspapers (of this total library currently receives about 300 titles regularly); approximately 8,000 books and pamphlets (including uncataloged backlog); approximately 7,400 organizational folders.

Number of journals or newspapers currently on subscription: 376.

Housing considerations: Cataloged materials are shelved by LC call numbers. Periodicals are shelved alphabetically by name of periodical. Folders are shelved alphabetically by personal name or organization's name on tab. Housed in closed stacks.

Bibliographic control provided: All monographs are cataloged on OCLC. Some serials are cataloged on OCLC and listed in the library's periodicals computer print-out. Currently received serials are listed in a kardex; many of these serials are not yet cataloged or listed in the general periodicals print-out. A shelflist is used for non-LC cataloged pamphlets shelved by an in-house system. Eventually these will be cataloged LC on OCLC; name authority file for organizations filed in ephemera folders.

Published guides to the collection: None at this time.

Other publications/services: No publications; will help with any reference query as time and limited staff permit. ILL; yes.

Date the collection was established: 1965.

History/Description of the collection: Began under impetus of faculty in the political science and history departments as well as university librarian to build a collection of political pamphlets and materials, and the literature of grassroots political and social organizations in Orange County, Southern California, and the United States. Greatly augmented in the mid-1970s by the library's acquisition of the Benedict Collection from the University of Nevada, Reno.

Citation of descriptive articles about your collection: Coppel, Lynn M. "Fullerton: A Multitude of Sins." *Wilson Library Bulletin* (November 1973): 248-49.

Are you still adding materials to the collection? Yes; due to limited space and staff and a large backlog of unprocessed materials, new items are added at a slow rate. New items are processed immediately.

————

Institution: *Hoover Institution Archives*

Address: Hoover Institution
Stanford University
Stanford, CA 94305

Phone number: (415) 723-3563

Collection name: "New Left" collection

Curator or contact person: Elena S. Danielson

Public service hours: 8:15 a.m. to 4:45 p.m., M-F.

Restrictions on use: None.

Inclusive years represented in collection: 1962 to 1979.

Principal years represented in collection: 1964 to 1974.

Primary subjects included in the collection: The anti-Vietnam War movement, draft resistance, civil rights movement, various left-wing political groups, student activism, also includes some right-wing literature.

Formats collected: Booklets, leaflets, reports, newspaper clippings, and correspondence of various political groups.

Number of volumes: 67 manuscript boxes.

Housing considerations: Ephemera is housed in manuscript boxes in the Hoover Institution Archives. Serials are housed in the Hoover Institution Library.

Bibliographic control provided: There is a register to the ephemera in the archives. Unpublished register available in the Hoover Institution Archives Reading Room.

Published guides to the collection: Collection-level description available on RLIN AMC for ephemera. A published guide to the Bell and Howell microfilm, entitled *Underground Newspaper Microfilm Collection* (PN 4827 U 55 Index 1963/74).

Citation of descriptive articles about your collection: Bacciocco, Edward J., Jr. "Stanford: Hoover's New Left." *Wilson Library Bulletin* (November 1973): 241-42.

Institution: *Graduate Theological Union*

Address: Flora Lamson Hewlett Library
2400 Ridge Rd.
Berkeley, CA 94709

Phone number: (510) 649-2508 (Wait at least six rings; telephone will be answered.)

Collection name: New Religious Movements Research Collection

Curator or contact person: Gilles Poitras

Public service hours: 9 a.m. to 5 p.m., M-F; 1 p.m. to 5 p.m., Saturday (academic year); 9 a.m. to 5 p.m., M-F, summer and Christmas holidays through the end of January.

Restrictions on use: Ephemeral materials must be used in the library and identification, such as a driver's license, retained at the reference desk. Anyone may use the collection.

Inclusive years represented in collection: From about 1860 to the present.

Principal years represented in collection: From 1960 onwards.

Primary subjects included in the collection: Publications by and about Hindu, Buddhist, New Age, neo-pagan, Sufi, and Sikh religious groups new in the United States. Issues surrounding them such as psychological coercion, deprogramming, counter-culture organizations, responses of mainstream religious groups, and church/state concerns.

Secondary subjects included in the collection: Occultism, UFO contactee cults, and metaphysical movements of the late nineteenth and early twentieth centuries.

Formats collected: Books, serials, some audio and videocassettes, pamphlets, flyers, broadsides, posters, and unpublished papers.

Imprints collected: Any related to religious groups of interest to the collection. Primarily U.S. publishers.

Number of volumes: 3,000 books, 800 organizational files, 830 periodical titles, and 300 papers.

Number of journals or newspapers currently on subscription: Approximately 150.

Housing considerations: Books and audiocassettes are housed in the main stacks in Library of Congress call number order. Some periodicals are housed in the main stacks in alphabetical order by title. Other periodicals of an ephemeral nature are housed with ephemera by issuing organization in acid-free folders in approximately 34 linear feet of filing cabinets. The entire library building is temperature/humidity controlled.

Bibliographic control provided: All monographs, audiocassettes, videocassettes, and some periodical titles are cataloged on RLIN. Titles cataloged between 1978 and June 1988, also appear on OCLC. The library participates in ILL through RLIN, but not OCLC. A separate card catalog with its own subject authority provides access to the ephemera collection by organization names, alternative names and affiliates, founder or director, periodical title, and type of organization.

Published guides to the collection: Choquette, Diane, comp. *The Goddess Walks Among Us: Feminist Spirituality in Thought and Action.* Berkeley: Graduate Theological Union Library, 1981. ($2); *Audiocassettes and Phonodiscs: A Complete Bibliography of New Acquisitions, May 1978-February 1979.* Berkeley: Graduate Theological Union, Center for the Study of New Religious Movements, 1979. ($2); *New Religious Movements Newtitles.* Berkeley: Graduate Theological Union, Center for the Study of New Religious Movements, vol. 1-6; 1978-1983. ($6 per volume; 6-10 issues per volume).

Other publications/services: Listings of periodical holdings may be requested. Complete list available for $5. Subject lists available for $1 per page. Prepared on demand.

Date the collection was established: 1977.

History/Description of the collection: The New Religious Movements Research Collection of the Flora Lamson Hewlett Library, Graduate Theological Union was begun in 1977. The collection focuses on alternative religious and quasi-religious groups that are new to the United States or have grown significantly since 1960. Information concerning Hinduism, Buddhism, Sikhism, Sufism, Occult and metaphysical movements, neo-paganism, witchcraft, new age communes, and human potential movements is included. Related issues such as legal concerns and the response of mainstream religions are also covered. Approximately 3,000 books and audiocassettes are integrated into the main collection. A collection comprised of research papers and ephemera from and about 800 organizations is housed separately and is available during reference desk hours. Periodicals, 830 titles, are housed in either the main stacks or in the ephemera files.

Citation of descriptive articles about your collection: Choquette, Diane. "The New Religious Movements Research Collection: A History and Description of Alternative Subject Cataloging." In *Subject Cataloging: Critiques and Innovations*, ed. by Sanford Berman, 19-34. New York: Haworth Press, 1984; Choquette, Diane. "Alternative Publications in Theological Libraries." In *Summary of Proceedings, Forty-first Annual Conference of the American Theological Library Association*, 78-88. St. Meinrad, IN: American Theological Library Association, 1987.

Additional information: A bibliography of new acquisitions since 1984 is available for in-house use. It partially supplements: Choquette, Diane, comp. *New Religious Movements in the United States and Canada: A Critical Assessment and Annotated Bibliography*. Bibliographies and Indexes in Religious Studies, no. 5. Westport, CT: Greenwood Press, 1985.

Are you still adding materials to the collection? Yes, but staff support is minimal, so we are not very active.

———

Institution: *UCLA*

Address: Public Affairs Service
University Research Library
UCLA
Los Angeles, CA 90024-1575

Phone number: (310) 825-1088

Collection name: Non-Governmental Organization Collection (NGO)

Curator or contact person: Roberta Medford

Public service hours: 10 a.m. to 7 p.m., M-Th; 10 a.m. to 5 p.m., F; 1 p.m. to 5 p.m., Saturday and Sunday. (No weekend or evening hours during summer or intersessions.)

Restrictions on use: Some items are non-circulating, including all political campaign literature.

Inclusive years represented in collection: Emphasis is on very current materials (i.e., latest ten years approximately). Campaign literature covers 1930-present.

Principal years represented in collection: (See above.)

Primary subjects included in the collection: Current political and social movements, issues and viewpoints, with emphasis on U.S. English-language materials only.

Secondary subjects included in the collection: Some items are collected on industrial relations and social welfare issues, also emphasizing the United States.

Formats collected: Pamphlets of approximately 100 pages or less, newsletters, leaflets, brochures, and other ephemera.

Imprints collected: Generally publications of organizations or of "alternative" presses, occasionally commercially published pamphlets, no government publications.

Number of volumes: Approximate number of pamphlets is 23,560.

Number of journals or newspapers currently on subscription: Approximately 250.

Housing considerations: Pamphlets are in file cabinets, arranged by subject headings. Newsletters are arranged on shelf by main entry, in magafiles. Campaign literature is filed chronologically, then alphabetically by office.

Bibliographic control provided: Each item has a minimum-level record in ORION, UCLA's online information system. One LCSH subject heading is assigned per pamphlet. (PAIS subject headings were used until 1987; we are now converting to LCSH.) Campaign literature: Collection-level brief records in ORION. Newsletters: Each title has a full MARC bibliographic record in ORION. ORION records are searchable by any words in author, title, series, or subject.

Date the collection was established: 1970.

History/Description of the collection: The current NGO collection resulted from the merger of several previous UCLA library collections. Material that is no longer current is evaluated for its historic value and either discarded, given full cataloging for the UCLA Research Library stacks, or transferred to the library's Special Collections Department.

Citation of descriptive articles about your collection: Danks, Lora E. "The Public Affairs Service at UCLA: A Unique Concept in the Provision of Government Information?" *Government Publications Review* 14 (1987): 89-101; Eaton, Eugenia, James R. Cox, and Joyce Toscan. "Collection Highlights Sixty Years of Campaigns." *UCLA Librarian* 35, no. 9 (1982): 66.

Are you still adding materials to the collection? Yes.

———

Institution: *The Bancroft Library*

Address: University of California
Berkeley, CA 94720

Phone number: (510) 642-6481

Collection name: Social Protest Collection

Curator or contact person: Dr. Bonnie Hardwick

Public service hours: 9 a.m. to 5 p.m., M-F; 1 p.m. to 5 p.m., Saturday when classes are in session.

Restrictions on use: None.

Inclusive years represented in collection: 1960-1982.

Primary subjects included in the collection: Anti-Vietnam War, civil rights/civil liberties, community movements, counterculture, ecology, electoral politics, foreign movements, gay movement, intentional communities, international support organizations, labor, the Left, minorities, peace/anti-nuclear, professional/academic organizations, religion, the Right, student movement, women's movement.

Formats collected: Leaflets, handbills, posters, and short-lived serials.

Number of volumes: 25 boxes.

Number of journals or newspapers currently on subscription: None.

Housing considerations: Boxed and housed within the archives, within manuscript containers. The collection is organized into nineteen subject series reflecting the major movements of the 1960s and 1970s. Within each, the vast majority of folder titles are the names of organizations whose leaflets and literature have been preserved. For the most part, material is arranged chronologically within folders.

Published guides to the collection: Unpublished finding aid available in repository.

Date the collection was established: 1969.

History/Description of the collection: The Social Protest Collection was begun in 1969 as a special project to gather and archive the ephemera of the 1960s protest movements on the University of California, Berkeley campus and in the Berkeley community. Known as the Social Protest *Project* until its reorganization in 1986, the collection was originally developed in the undergraduate library, then transferred to the custody of the Collection Development office, and finally placed in the Bancroft Library in 1972. Placed with the Manuscripts Division, it joins the collection on the Berkeley campus Free Speech Movement of 1964.

Additional information: The accumulation of a sizeable backlog of unprocessed flyers and literature and the lack of sufficient staff to maintain the collection led to the decision to close it to new additions and reorganize it as a special collection primarily documenting social movements between 1960 and 1982.

Citation of descriptive articles about your collection: Maskaleris, Gerda, and Gerald Simerman. "Berkeley: Sproul Plaza Spillover." *Wilson Library Bulletin* (November 1973): 239-41.

Are you still adding materials to the collection? No.

Institution: *Southern California Library for Social Studies and Research*

Address: 6100 South Vermont Ave.
Los Angeles, CA 90044

Phone number: (213) 759-6063

Collection name: Southern California Library for Social Studies and Research

Curator or contact person: Sarah Cooper, director

Public service hours: 10 a.m. to 4 p.m., T-Saturday.

Restrictions on use: None on access. Friends of the Library ($26/year) may check out books. All other materials are non-circulating.

Inclusive years represented in collection: ca. 1910-present.

Principal years represented in collection: 1930s-1980s.

Primary subjects included in the collection: Radicalism, communism, labor, black studies, civil rights, civil liberties. The pamphlet and book collections cover most of these areas; the film collection is strongest on labor history.

Secondary subjects included in the collection: Women, international movements, proletarian literature.

Formats collected: Books, pamphlets, periodicals, tapes, films, manuscript collections, photographs.

Imprints collected: Books in subject areas described above from diverse publishers but especially alternative publishers or organizations.

Number of volumes: 16,000 books, 2,800 periodical titles, 21,000 pamphlets, 3,500 tape recordings, 100 documentary films, and 2,000 photographs and posters.

Number of journals or newspapers currently on subscription: 50.

Housing considerations: Books are shelved by author; periodicals are boxed and shelved alphabetically. Books and periodicals are in open stacks. All other material receives or will receive archival handling and is stored in closed stacks or other non-public storage areas.

Bibliographic control provided: The book and pamphlet collections have separate manual card catalogs; the periodicals have holdings records created for each title; tapes have a manual card catalog; and films are described in a holdings list. Manuscript collections have individual registers that include a history, scope and content note, and container list.

Published guides to the collection: There are currently no up-to-date published guides to any aspect of the collection.

Other publications/services: Bi-monthly newsletter HERITAGE.

Date the collection was established: 1963.

History/Description of the collection: The Southern California Library for Social Studies and Research was established in 1963 by Emil Freed, a longtime political activist in Los Angeles. The initial collection included the vast pamphlet holdings he had accumulated beginning in the 1930s when he participated in labor and Left movements as well as the book collections of the California Labor School (Southern branch) and the Progressive Bookstore. Until Freed's death in 1982 he continued to expand the collection. Work since 1982 has concentrated on consolidation and weeding of the basic collection, establishing systems of access for each format, and developing a modest collective program to continue to develop the library's holdings on Los Angeles labor and progressive movements.

Citation of descriptive articles about your collection: "Research Library Chronicles Career: Labor Chief Bridges to Be Feted." (feature on SCL and its collection on Harry Bridges) *Los Angeles Times* (6 February 1986); Cooper, Sarah. "The Southern California Library for Social Studies and Research." *Library Quarterly* (April 1989): 47-54.

Are you still adding materials to the collection? Yes.

Institution: *J. Paul Leonard Library, San Francisco State University*

Address: 1630 Holloway Ave.
San Francisco, CA 94132

Phone number: (415) 338-1856

Collection name: Strike Materials Collection

Curator or contact person: Helene Whitson, Special Collections/Archives

Public service hours: 8 a.m. to 5 p.m., M-F.

Restrictions on use: Anyone may use. Copying depends on nature and fragility of material. Material does not circulate. A large portion of the collection has been microfilmed.

Inclusive years represented in collection: 1967 to 1969.

Principal years represented in collection: 1967 to 1969.

Primary subjects included in the collection: Strike at San Francisco State College, 1968-1969; earlier activities beginning in 1967.

Formats collected: Broadsides, publications, posters, campus newspapers, other newspapers, reports, correspondence, and scrapbooks.

Imprints collected: Anything that would describe the events that took place.

Number of volumes: Approximately 20 books, publications that cover the subject.

Housing considerations: One four-drawer filing cabinet for most of the papers, which are arranged by subject/organization; posters in a map cabinet; scrapbooks on regular library shelves.

Bibliographic control provided: New material is received and added to the archives accession log; accessioned; placed in appropriate folder. The collection is not formally cataloged.

Published guides to the collection: Whitson, Helene. *Strike! A Chronology, Bibliography, and List of Archival Materials Concerning the 1968-1969 Strike at San Francisco State College.* ERIC, 1979. ED 158-735.

Other publications/services: *Strike!* lists many books and articles concerning the strike. There is nothing published by the archives.

Date the collection was established: 1970.

History/Description of the collection: I was at San Francisco State during the strike, and began collecting materials as actions developed. Many other people on campus collected, too, and later gave me their materials. People still are cleaning out offices and attics and finding strike materials, that they donate to the collection. It took me two years to organize the collection, and it was available for public use in 1971. The materials in the collection document the activities that happened during this specific confrontation.

Are you still adding materials to the collection? Yes.

CONNECTICUT

Institution: *University of Connecticut, Storrs*

Address: Special Collections Dept.
Homer Babbidge Library

University of Connecticut
U-5sc
Storrs, CT 06269-1005

Phone number: (203) 486-1149

Collection name: Alternative Press Collection [APC]

Curator or contact person: Ellen E. Embardo

Public service hours: 9 a.m. to 12 p.m., 1 p.m. to 5 p.m., M-F (academic year); 1 p.m. to 5 p.m., M-F (recess hours).

Restrictions on use: All materials must be used in the Special Collections reading room. As we are a public institution, nobody is denied access to materials.

Inclusive years represented in collection: ca. 1880 to present.

Principal years represented in collection: 1965 to present.

Primary subjects included in the collection: Underground and alternative newspapers and journals from social and political movements stemming from anti-war and student activism of the sixties and seventies, including today's activist publications. The collection embraces alternative lifestyles; left- and right-wing political ideologies and strategies; and peace and disarmament, civil rights, women's, black, environmental; gay/lesbian, Native American, and radical professional groups and movements. Also, some books, pamphlets, ephemera, and realia from various organizations.

Secondary subjects included in the collection: Approximately 2,900 Communist and Socialist pamphlets from the early to mid-twentieth century.

Formats collected: Primarily newspapers and journals. Also, pamphlets, flyers, books, some audiotapes, broadsides, posters, buttons, and other realia. Microfilm copies of some journals are purchased for the library's general microform collection.

Imprints collected: Only materials published by "alternative" publishers or organizations.

Number of volumes: 7,000 newspaper and journal titles, 5,000 books and pamphlets, and 1,700 organizational files.

Number of journals or newspapers currently on subscription: Approximately 400.

Housing considerations: All materials are housed in environmentally protected closed stacks, in the Special Collections department. Preservation of materials is assured by containing materials in acid-free containers, housed by format: newspapers are housed in acid-free folio boxes; journals are measured for acid-free phase boxes; single issues

are housed in acid-free envelopes; books are covered with acid-free dust wrappers; ephemera is housed by issuing organization in acid-free folders in approximately 50 linear feet of filing cabinets. All journal titles are arranged alphabetically by title. All books and pamphlets are arranged by locator number, assigned contiguously at the time of cataloging. Over-sized volumes are numbered separately at the end of each collection.

Bibliographic control provided: All monographs are cataloged on OCLC. Additionally, specialized card catalogs are maintained to provide additional access points: additional subject headings are assigned, using the *Alternative Press Index* and *Hennepin County Cataloging Bulletin* as guides. In addition, added entries are assigned for various organizations. Geographic headings are provided for journals and newspapers. All serial titles are added to the library's general serials list and reported to various union lists. Soon, titles will be added to OCLC and its union list component.

Published guides to the collection: Akeroyd, Richard. *Alternatives: By Which Is Introduced the Alternative Press Collection in the Special Collections Department of the Wilbur Cross Library at the University of Connecticut at Storrs.* Storrs, CT: University of Connecticut, Wilbur Cross Library, 1972. (Photocopies available, $.15 per page); Akeroyd, Richard. "Storrs: Notes on Our Alternatives." *Wilson Library Bulletin* (November 1973): 252-54; Akeroyd, Joanne. *Alternatives: A Guide to the Newspapers, Magazines, and Newsletters in the Alternative Press Collection in the Special Collections Department of the University of Connecticut Library.* 2d ed. Storrs, CT: University of Connecticut Library, 1976. (Photocopies available, $.15 per page); Gardner, Maureen. *Women's Sources: An Annotated List of Women's Periodicals Received in the Alternative Press Collection of the Homer Babbidge Library.* Storrs, CT: University of Connecticut, Homer Babbidge Library, 1986. (Free while supplies last; thereafter, photocopies at $.15 per page); Embardo, Ellen E. *Alternative Titles: A Subject Listing of Newspapers, Magazines and Newsletters Received Regularly in the Alternative Press Collection.* Storrs, CT: The University of Connecticut, Homer Babbidge Library, 1982. (Photocopies, $.15 per page.)

Other publications/services: Semi-annual listing of new acquisitions to the APC (Free). *New Views* bibliographies (citations to contemporary issues) [currently 37 bibliographies available]. (Free while supplies last; thereafter, photocopies at $.15 per page.)

Date the collection was established: 1970.

History/Description of the collection: The Alternative Press Collection at the University of Connecticut's Homer Babbidge Library was founded in 1970 as a repository of underground and alternative publications emanating from the social and political upheavals of the sixties and seventies. Four curators have built upon previous strengths, collecting and organizing the alternative press as it evolved through the seventies and into the eighties. The collection houses more than 7,000 newspaper and journal titles, 400 of which are currently on subscription; 5,000 books and pamphlets; 1,700 organizational files; and a variety of other materials written and published by individuals and groups involved in social and political activism. The APC embraces alternative lifestyles; left- and right-wing political ideologies and strategies; and peace and disarmament, civil rights, women's, black, environmental, gay/lesbian, Native American, and radical professional groups and movements.

Citation of descriptive articles about your collection: Roy, Mark J. "Rebel Publications Offer Alternative to Daily Papers." *UConn Advance* 4, no. 20 (26 February 1987): 8; Case, Patricia J. "New Left Publishing in the Seventies." *Harvest* (Fall 1979): 5; Moran, Michael, Joanne Akeroyd, Richard and Benedict Russell, eds. "A Directory of Ephemera Collections in a National Underground Network." *Wilson Library Bulletin* 48, no. 3 (November 1973): 236-54; Embardo, Ellen E. "The Alternative Press Collection, University of Connecticut." *Library Quarterly* (April 1989): 55-63.

Additional information: The curators attempt to collect comprehensively in New England, with examples of key titles throughout the United States and English-language publications from abroad. Some Spanish-language materials are added, particularly as they relate to U.S. policy in Central America.

Are you still adding materials to the collection? Yes. There is a monographs budget of approximately $2,500 per year. In addition, approximately 100 new journal subscriptions are placed each year. (With the same number ceasing publication each year, the total number of titles on subscription remains about the same.) Gifts are added regularly.

Institution: *University of Hartford*

Address: 200 Bloomfield Ave.
West Hartford, CT 06117

Phone number: (203) 243-4090

Collection name: Museum of American Political Life

Curator or contact person: Professor Edmund B. Sullivan

Public service hours: 11 a.m. to 4 p.m, T-Saturday.

Restrictions on use: None but proper credit requested.

Inclusive years represented in collection: 1789 to 198+.

Primary subjects included in the collection: Paper, textile, china, glassware, and other objects associated with American presidential campaigns.

Secondary subjects included in the collection: Related "causes" areas—protests of various movements (e.g., women's rights, abolition, anti-nuclear, peace, labor).

Number of volumes: We don't count "volumes"—rather leaflets, posters, pamphlets, and the like—approximately 60,000 campaign artifacts.

Housing considerations: When the museum was opened in the fall of 1988, there were facilities available for scholars' use: stacks, drawers, frames. We are still not readily accessible to scholars; moved into new museum in February, survived a disasterous flood, and still getting sorted out-but call anyway.

Bibliographic control provided: Standard literary procedures.

Date the collection was established: Private ownership 1922 to 1959; University of Hartford ownership 1959.

Citation of descriptive articles about your collection: Many newspaper and magazine articles over the years. For latest, Neely, Mark, and Harold Holzer. "Mementos of Politicos." *Americana* (August 1989): 23.

Additional information: A permanent exhibit entitled "Reform and Protest," focuses on the dedicated, visionary and sometimes quirky individuals and groups outside the two-party system who introduced new and often controversial themes and issues into the political arena.

Are you still adding materials to the collection? Yes.

ILLINOIS

Institution: *Special Collections Department, Northwestern University Library*

Address: 1937 Sheridan Rd.
Evanston, IL 60208-2300

Phone number: (312) 491-2895 or 491-3635

Collection name: The Women's Collections

Curator or contact person: R. Russell Maylone and Judy Lowman, assistant curator of Special Collections

Public service hours: 8:30 a.m. to 5 p.m., M-F; 8:30 to 12 p.m., Saturday (during regular school year and during summer sessions only).

Restrictions on use: All materials must be used in the department's reading room. Those materials in sufficiently good condition may be photocopied. Otherwise all materials may be photographed or microfilmed at the patron's request and expense.

Inclusive years represented in collection: 1965 to present.

Principal years represented in collection: 1970 to 1987.

Primary subjects included in the collection: Women's liberation movement and every subject in which women are, or have been, playing an active role since 1970. Academics, abortion, reproductive policies, lesbianism, lesbian ethics, women in business, law, chemistry, and science in general and many many others.

Secondary subjects included in the collection: See "History."

Formats collected: Primarily periodicals: newspapers, magazines, newsletters, etc.; also books, pamphlets, and posters.

Imprints collected: No restriction or limitation.

Number of volumes: 1,200 monographs, 5,500 subject folders, 4,000 periodical titles.

Number of journals or newspapers currently on subscription: 308.

Housing considerations: Arranged by Cutter # within alphabetical scheme. Periodicals, almost all of which are unbound, kept in acid-free containers in four size designations. Pamphlets and other fragile items in acid-free envelopes. Posters in map cases.

Bibliographic control provided: Monographs and periodicals cataloged and online in the NOTIS system. Available in RLIN; perhaps in OCLC in the future. Subject folders indexed, guide available in department.

Published guides to the collection: "Women's Collection Newsletter" through no. 15. Free upon request. Several other guides to parts of the collection and to its use; free on request or for the taking from the table at the entrance to the Special Collections department.

Other publications/services: Research consultations, class presentations, bibliographical instruction for individuals or classes.

Date the collection was established: 1970.

History/Description of the collection: The Women's Collection was initiated in 1968 by Richard L. Press, formerly assistant university librarian for Collection Develop-

ment. By 1969, he had accumulated several file drawers of periodicals, leaflets, and pamphlets about the alternative movements then gaining momentum, among them anti-Vietnam War, the women's movement, sexual freedom movement, and minority activism.

The first librarian to develop the alternative collection added many serial titles from throughout the country, Canada, and England in all of the above-mentioned areas but especially the radical antiwar movement. In addition, she began in a more systematic way to follow the growing women's movement and to add appropriate titles of periodicals, pamphlets, and books. In 1974 she published the first issue of the "Women's Collection."

A second librarian joined the department in 1974 to continue developing the alternative collections. By this time, however, the radical antiwar, sexual liberation and free speech movements, largely represented in periodical holdings, had begun to fade. Numerous, formerly underground, papers had become established legitimate alternative community papers. The *Chicago Seed* disappeared; the *Chicago Reader* remains an outstanding paper today with branches in L.A. and Washington, DC.

The emerging strength of the women's movement and declining strength of the other movements had for some time been in evidence. This gave us the opportunity to concentrate on building the Women's Collection through the addition of new serial titles, donations of large collections of women's ephemera from interested friends, faculty, and women collectors near and far. At about this time, the periodical collection of the Women's History Research Center of Berkeley, California, was given to the Women's Collection and the titles subsequently incorporated.

An aggressive acquisition policy for periodicals appropriate to the Women's Collection but not yet held has been pursued for the last 12 to 14 years. With but several exceptions the Women's Collection has pursued every aspect of the women's movement in country after country throughout the world. Through regular examination of published sources and regular gifts from a friend, the Women's Collection adds hundreds of new titles on a regular basis. Unfortunately, as many as are ordered for the Women's Collection are almost matched by those that disappear.

The assistant curator of Special Collections and head of the Women's Collection was appointed in 1987 and has continued to acquire periodicals aggressively, has published many issues of the *Women's Collection Newsletter*, been active in outreach programs within the university and beyond, and has given the Women's Collection a new clarity and focus. The library's commitment to Special Collections and the Women's Collection remains strong after twenty years of collecting, organizing, and outreach.

Additional information: Handouts available on request or in the department.

Are you still adding materials to the collection? Very much so.

Institution: *Indiana State University, Cunningham Memorial Library*

Address: Terre Haute, IN 47809

Phone number: (812) 237-2610

Collection name: [Eugene V.] Debs Collection

Curator or contact person: David E. Vancil or Robert L. Carter

Public service hours: 8 a.m. to 4:30 p.m., M-F; all year except for New Years Day, last Friday of spring break, Memorial Day, July 4th, Labor Day, Thanksgiving and day after, Christmas and day before and after.

Restrictions on use: Materials do not circulate. Photocopying permitted (except for very fragile materials).

Inclusive years represented in collection: Mid-nineteenth century through mid-twentieth.

Principal years represented in collection: 1905 to 1921.

Primary subjects included in the collection: Eugene V. Debs; American Socialist Party [parties]; U.S. labor history; socialism; U.S. radical movement; social questions; and Socialists.

Secondary subjects included in the collection: U.S. politics; U.S. history.

Formats collected: Letters, books, pamphlets, memorabilia, photographs, periodicals, microfilm, speeches (photocopies).

Imprints collected: No restrictions if subject material appropriate.

Number of volumes: ca. 1,500 books, ca. 3,600 pamphlets, and 3,800 letters to and from Debs, and ca. 2,500 speeches and articles by Debs.

Number of journals or newspapers currently on subscription: 0.

Housing considerations: Rare Books and Special Collections department is in spacious quarters recently renovated and given special climate control on third floor of main library. Books are being cataloged in Library of Congress system and are shelved accordingly. Pamphlets are slowly being cataloged and interfiled in file cabinets. Letters are arranged alphabetically by name of correspondent and housed in file cabinets. Speeches and articles (photocopies) by Debs are housed in a separate file cabinet. Memorabilia and photographs in acid-free boxes. Periodicals are cataloged (short

runs only). Pertinent microfilm materials are housed in the department and others.

Bibliographic control provided: All monographs are cataloged on OCLC. Before December 1985 a full set of cards was made and filed for all books and pamphlets cataloged. Department has own card catalog, but same cards were also filed in main public catalog on main floor. At present shelflist cards only are being filed, in department and in library's main shelflist. All newly cataloged items are being given full cataloging directly on library's electronic bibliographical system (LUIS). Terminals for public and staff access are available throughout the building and in the Department of Rare Books and Special Collections.

Published guides to the collection: Constantine, J. Robert, ed. *The Papers of Eugene V. Debs, 1834-1945: A Guide to the Microfilm Edition.* New York: Microfilming Corp. of America, 1983. The 21-reel set of microfilm and index is available for sale and may be used at Indiana State University Libraries or other libraries owning them. NOTE: This guide set does not include books and pamphlets in the collection. It indexes letters and speeches only.

Other publications/services: No publications, photocopying service available, queries answered by mail and by telephone, most of the original letters have been annotated.

Date the collection was established: 1967.

History/Description of the collection: Vancil, David E., Charles D. King, and Robert L. Carter. "The Debs Collection at Indiana State University." *Labor History* 31 (Winter-Spring 1990): 139-44.

Citation of descriptive articles about your collection: Vancil, David E., Charles D. King, and Robert L. Carter. "The Debs Collection at Indiana State University." *Labor History* 31 (Winter-Spring 1990): 139-44; Vancil, David E. *A Guide to the Department of Rare Books and Special Collections.* Terre Haute: Indiana State University, 1988.

Are you still adding materials to the collection? Yes.

IOWA

Institution: *University of Iowa*

Address: Special Collections Department
University of Iowa Libraries
Iowa City, IA 52242

Phone number: (319) 335-5921

Collection name: The Social Documents Collection

Curator or contact person: Robert A. McCown

Public service hours: 9 a.m. to 12 p.m., 1 p.m. to 5 p.m., M-F.

Restrictions on use: All materials must be used in the reading room of the Special Collections department.

Inclusive years represented in collection: ca. 1945 to the present.

Principal years represented in collection: 1955 to the present.

Primary subjects included in the collection: Right-wing, conservative, and libertarian organizations from every geographic region of the United States.

Formats collected: Periodicals, pamphlets, flyers, radio broadcast scripts, handbills, leaflets, bulletins, news sheets, correspondence, bumperstickers, newsletters, broadsides, and more.

Imprints collected: U.S. imprints only.

Number of volumes: 659 document boxes, 21 file drawers of serials publications, and 31 file drawers of non-serial publications.

Number of journals or newspapers currently on subscription: 250+.

Housing considerations: Materials are housed in a controlled stack area.

Bibliographic control provided: Material is divided into "serial" and "non-serial" publications and cataloged under author or title. "See" references are used quite frequently, but there is no descriptive cataloging of materials. There is a separate card catalog in the department.

Date the collection was established: ca. 1945.

Are you still adding materials to the collection? Yes.

KANSAS

Institution: *University of Kansas*

Address: Kansas Collection
Spencer Research Library
University of Kansas
Lawrence, KS 66045

Phone number: (913) 864-4274

Collection name: Wilcox Collection of Contemporary Political Movements

Curator or contact person: Sheryl K. Williams

Public service hours: 8 a.m. to 5 p.m., M-F; 9 a.m. to 1 p.m., Saturday during the academic year.

Restrictions on use: Materials must remain within the department.

Inclusive years represented in collection: ca. 1933 to present.

Principal years represented in collection: 1960 to present.

Primary subjects included in the collection: Approximately 60 percent of the collection is comprised of materials from the American Right and includes conservative, libertarian, anti-communist, patriotic, free-market, pro-family, and racial nationalist publications. The remainder of the collection is comprised of materials from the American Left, including socialist, communist, radical, and reform movements. The radical student movement of the sixties is also well represented.

Formats collected: The collection includes books, pamphlets, serials, audiotapes, flyers, broadsides, buttons, and other ephemera.

Number of volumes: 5,000 books and pamphlets, 4,000 serial titles, 800 audio tapes, 80,000 pieces of ephemera.

Housing considerations: Materials are housed in environmentally controlled, closed stacks in the Kansas Collection. Preservation is maintained through the use of acid-free storage boxes and folders. Materials are arranged by size and accession number.

Bibliographic control provided: The collection is being cataloged via OCLC. All materials are made available through the Wilcox card catalog in the Kansas Automated Serial system and the University of Kansas Online Catalog.

Published guides to the collection: No.

Date the collection was established: 1965.

History/Description of the collection: The Wilcox Collection of Contemporary Political Movements was established at the University of Kansas in 1965, when Mr. Laird Wilcox, a participant and observer of the protest movement of the sixties and lifelong student of the psychology of political organizations, sold his collection to the university libraries in order to foster research in this area. The collection has grown dramatically over the years as Mr. Wilcox has continued to exhaustively collect materials issued by organizations and individuals identified with both left- and right-wing political movements, and has donated these to the library.

Citation of descriptive articles about your collection: Kehde, Ned. "Lawrence: Wilcox, Left and Right." *Wilson Library Bulletin* (November 1973): 245-46.

Are you still adding materials to the collection? Mr. Wilcox continually makes donations to the library. In addition, special acquisition funds have been made available to support the collection.

LOUISIANA

Institution: *Manuscripts and Rare Books, Howard-Tilton Memorial Library Tulane University*

Address: New Orleans, LA 70118

Phone number: (504) 865-5685

Collection name: The Political Ephemera Collection

Curator or contact person: Wilbur E. Meneray and John Guidry

Public service hours: 8:30 a.m. to 5 p.m., M-F; 9 a.m. to 1 p.m., Saturday.

Restrictions on use: Cannot leave reading room of Manuscripts and Rare Books area; must register each article with receptionist.

Inclusive years represented in collection: 1868 to present.

Principal years represented in collection: 1955 to present.

Primary subjects included in the collection: The collection is divided into several sections: WWI, WWII, Louisiana, campaign literature, books, right wing, left wing, American Enterprise Institute, John Birch Society, foreign, and the right-wing microfilm collection. The collection is strongest in civil rights; general right wing—such as John Birch Society, Christian movements, gay lib, workers' literature, and WWI and WWII propaganda.

Secondary subjects included in the collection: Vietnam War, Central America, white supremacy, and conspiracy theory.

Formats collected: Primary newspapers, journals, pamphlets, books, campaign literature (mostly Louisiana). Also collected are posters, cassettes, personal papers, political science texts.

Imprints collected: "Alternative" groups, newsletters, and journals. We prefer more radicalized, less mainstream political literature.

Number of volumes: 2,790 books, monographs, 177 reels of microfilm (right wing), 5,047 organizational files (including 1,979 newspaper or newsletter titles).

Number of journals or newspapers currently on subscription: Approximately 200.

Housing considerations: Housed in environmentally protected, closed stacks, all being contained in acid-free files or boxes. Currently we have 177 reels of microfilm, 135 linear feet of books, 74 file drawers, and 31 cubic feet of boxes.

Bibliographic control provided: Collection divided as follows: books shelved alphabetically by author, John Birch Society, American Enterprise Institute, WWI, WWII, right-wing ephemera, left-wing ephemera, foreign, Louisiana, campaign, posters, and microfilm.

Published guides to the collection: None.

Other publications/services: None.

Date the collection was established: June 1970.

History/Description of the collection: Began in the sixties as the Civil Rights Collection. Expanded in 1970 to embrace all political literature. The political ephemera has its own curator, usually a graduate political science student. The PEC's files represent over 5,000 organizations and individuals, 2,000 newspaper and newsletter titles, and almost 3,000 books, monographs, and journals. Also, the PEC holds the manuscripts and research of Dr. Maurice Rees, 15 cubic feet of newsclippings, and research on communism. The collection is strongest in right-wing material, so strong that we supplied over 20,000 pages to be microfilmed for the University of Iowa's Right Wing Microfilm Collection, 177 reels, a copy of which we hold also. Currently, we are expanding the holdings on Louisiana and New Orleans.

Citation of descriptive articles about your collection: Meneray, Wilbur E. "New Orleans: Strident Segregation." *Wilson Library Bulletin* (November 1973): 247-48; Meneray, Wilbur E. "The Political Ephemera Collection." *Significa*, Tulane University Library Newsletter (July 1986): 1, 4.

Additional information: The focus of the collection is national, although we do hold a large bulk of publications from Communist countries and parties throughout the world, as well as a significant amount of European war propaganda between 1914 and 1945.

Are you still adding materials to the collection? Yes, primarily via donations and complimentary subscriptions. We have a number of patrons, who regularly send publications from around the country and we hold about 200 subscriptions currently.

MARYLAND

Institution: *Alternative Press Center*

Address: Box 33109
Baltimore, MD 21218

Phone number: (301) 243-2471

Collection name: Alternative Press Center Library

Curator or contact person: Bill Wilson, Leslie Wade, and David Schubert

Public service hours: 10 a.m. to 2:30 p.m., T-Saturday.

Restrictions on use: Must have card to borrow; anyone may use collection.

Inclusive years represented in collection: 1960 to present.

Principal years represented in collection: 1972 to present.

Primary subjects included in the collection: Alternative newspapers, magazines, and journals from the sixties to the present covering black movement, womens' movement, gay/lesbian, left groups, alternative life styles, and others.

Formats collected: Newspapers, journals, some pamphlets.

Imprints collected: Primarily materials published by alternative publishers, but also some materials published by university and mainstream publishers.

Number of volumes: Books about 2,000 volumes.

Number of journals or newspapers currently on subscription: Approximately 300.

Housing considerations: Periodicals arranged alphabetically by title; in boxes; some back issues housed in attic, pamphlets arranged by subject in file cabinets; books arranged by about 20 broad subject areas.

Bibliographic control provided: Books—in process of cataloging them; adding/changing subject headings as needed. Periodicals—catalog kept of holdings for each periodical title.

Other publications/services: *Alternative Press Index, Directory of Alternative Publications* ($3/each) published annually.

Date the collection was established: 1975.

History/Description of the collection: Collection consists primarily of periodicals that the APC has received on exchange. In its present form it covers mostly the years 1972 to present and is very complete.

Citation of descriptive articles about your collection: Getaz, Betsy. "Alternative Press Index." *SRRT Newsletter* no. 64 (July 1982): 1; "Alternative Press Index." *Show-Me Libraries* 34, nos. 1-2 (October-November 1982): 21-24; Peattie, Noel. "The Indexers." *Sipapu* 16, no. 2 (late 1985): 2-8.

Are you still adding materials to the collection? Yes.

MASSACHUSETTS

Institution: *Salem State College*

Address: Salem, MA 01970

Phone number: (508) 741-6000, ext. 2625

Collection name: Alternatives Library

Curator or contact person: Margaret Andrews

Public service hours: By appointment (due to staff shortage). (See M. Andrews.)

Restrictions on use: Magazines do not circulate. Books may be checked out by those affiliated with SSC.

Inclusive years represented in collection: 1972 to present and on.

Principal years represented in collection: 1972 to 1978.

Primary subjects included in the collection: Material that represents an "alternative" point of view to mainstream publications.

Secondary subjects included in the collection: Other paperbacks of more general interest; small press publications.

Formats collected: Serials; books (mostly paperbacks).

Number of volumes: 3,000 books.

Number of journals or newspapers currently on subscription: 40.

Housing considerations: By general subject areas (i.e., then by author).

Bibliographic control provided: Author/title catalog only.

Other publications/services: *Community Resource Directory* local human service, many "alternatives" to the established ones.

Date the collection was established: 1972.

History/Description of the collection: Established to provide an alternative to the establishment. Aim was to gather non-exploitative material to support radicalism of the time. Have adhered to basic philosophy, while widening criteria.

Are you still adding materials to the collection? In a limited way, due mainly to budget and space restrictions.

––––––

Institution: *Amherst College Library*

Address: Amherst, MA 01002

Phone number: (413) 542-2299

Collection name: Marshall Bloom Collection

Curator or contact person: John Lancaster

Public service hours: 8:30 a.m. to 4:30 p.m., M-F; 8 a.m. to 4 p.m. during June-August.

Restrictions on use: Must be used in Special Collections reading room.

Inclusive years represented in collection: 1967+.

Principal years represented in collection: 1968 to 1975.

Primary subjects included in the collection: Underground newspapers.

Formats collected: Newspapers.

Imprints collected: Limited to alternative press.

Number of volumes: ca. 2,500 titles.

Housing considerations: Closed stacks—access through staff only.

Bibliographic control provided: Title lists.

Date the collection was established: 1972.

History/Description of the collection: Consists primarily of the working files of Liberation News Service (LNS), founded by Marshall Bloom.

Are you still adding materials to the collection? Very little.

MICHIGAN

Institution: *Michigan State University Libraries, Special Collections Division*

Address: East Lansing, MI 48824

Phone number: (517) 355-3770

Collection name: American Radicalism Collection

Curator or contact person: Peter Berg

Public service hours: 9 a.m to 5 p.m., M-F; 10 a.m. to 2 p.m., Saturday (during academic year only).

Restrictions on use: Materials are used in Special Collections reading room only; satisfactory ID is required.

Inclusive years represented in collection: Mid-nineteenth century to present.

Principal years represented in collection: 1900 to present.

Primary subjects included in the collection: American Left and Right; alternative social and economic viewpoints. Strengths are in American Communist groups of the twenties-fifties, especially the CPUSA and the various Trotskyist organizations, in the New Left era, in the KKK of the twenties and thirties.

Secondary subjects included in the collection: Third World solidarity movements in the eighties.

Formats collected: Books, pamphlets, periodicals, posters, ephemera (anything in print).

Number of volumes: We do not have this broken down. Our current count is ca. 13,000 volumes, but this includes ca. 55 linear feet of vertical file material counted by file folder, along with books, pamphlets, and periodicals.

Number of journals or newspapers currently on subscription: ca. 75.

Housing considerations: Collection is housed in the Special Collections Division in a closed stack area. Most books, periodicals, and some pamphlets are cataloged; the very large ephemera collection is accessible through a card file (we are moving toward automated access to these files).

Bibliographic control provided: See above.

Date the collection was established: No clear date; first major purchase was in late fifties, significant collection development effort began in mid to late sixties.

Are you still adding materials to the collection? Yes, through purchase and through donations.

––––––

Institution: *University of Michigan*

Address: Department of Rare Books and Special Collections
711 Hatcher Library

University of Michigan
Ann Arbor, MI 48109-1205

Phone number: (313) 764-9377

Collection name: Labadie Collection

Curator or contact person: Edward C. Weber and R. Anne Okey

Public service hours: 10 a.m. to 12 p.m. and 1 p.m. to 5 p.m., M-F, 10 a.m. to 12 p.m., Saturday from September-April; 1 p.m. to 5 p.m., M-F, 10 a.m. to 12 p.m., Saturday from May-August. Closed during some holiday and intersession periods.

Restrictions on use: Open to qualified researchers, college students, and faculty.

Inclusive years represented in collection: 1790 to present.

Principal years represented in collection: 1870 to present.

Primary subjects included in the collection: Anarchism, socialism, communism, civil liberties, counterculture.

Secondary subjects included in the collection: U.S. labor history to 1940, sexual freedom (especially gay/lesbian), free thought, radical right, Spanish Civil War (1936-1939), pacifism, women's liberation, colonialism, imperialism, and national liberation movements, monetary reform, single tax, cooperatives, utopian communities, minorities, libertarianism.

Formats collected: Books, periodicals, pamphlets, manuscripts, records of organizations, microforms. Also, flyers, broadsides, posters, photographs, prints, buttons, badges, and other realia.

Imprints collected: Various.

Number of volumes: 8,000 officially cataloged monographs, 7,000 serials, 20,000 pamphlets, 450 reels of microfilm, 150 phonograph records, 200 tapes and cassettes, and 50 vertical file drawers.

Number of journals or newspapers currently on subscription: 600.

Housing considerations: All materials housed in environmentally protected closed stacks. Books in call number order. Pamphlets in database in numerical order, others still by subject arrangement. Serials shelved according to size in four alphabets.

Bibliographic control provided: Officially cataloged monographs and some serials have catalog card records and shelflist; only very recent acquisitions are in RLIN. Serials and 15,000 pamphlets are entered in the Labadie database;

subject and author checklists can be run off. Many special local indexes have been compiled over the years.

Published guides to the collection: *Manuscripts in the Labadie Collection* ($5).

Other publications/services: Some books and most microfilms may circulate on interlibrary loan. Photoduplication services are provided by the Department of Rare Books and Special Collections when the condition of the materials and copyright regulations permit.

Date the collection was established: 1911.

History/Description of the collection: Originally the personal library and gift of Joseph Labadie (1850-1933), anarchist and Michigan labor leader, the Labadie Collection was first organized and greatly expanded by his friend and fellow-anarchist, Agnes Inglis (1870-1952), the first curator. While this anarchist emphasis has made it the foremost collection on the subject in the hemisphere, it is also very strong in other fields of political radicalism and social protest, enumerated above. American materials predominate, but there is wide foreign coverage in certain areas.

Citation of descriptive articles about your collection: Stewart, Rolland C. "The Labadie Labor Collection." *Michigan Alumnus Quarterly Review* 53, no. 20 (10 May 1947): 247-53; Weber, Edward C. "The Labadie Collection." *Labor History* 23, no. 4 (Fall 1982): 575-81.

Are you still adding materials to the collection? Yes. The Labadie Collection receives yearly budget allotments for current books, continuations, and retrospective purchasing. We encourage donations.

NEW YORK

Institution: *Sarah Lawrence College*

Address: Bronxville, NY 10708

Phone number: (914) 395-2474

Collection name: Esther Raushenbush Library

Curator or contact person: Stephanie Pfaff

Public service hours: 9 a.m. to 10 p.m., M-Th; 9 a.m. to 7 p.m., F; 11 a.m. to 7 p.m., Saturday and Sunday.

Restrictions on use: Onsite, except through ILL.

Primary subjects included in the collection: Literature, women, civil liberties, multi-cultural literature.

Formats collected: Mostly monographs—also periodicals, audiocassettes.

Number of volumes: We have microfilm collections of Herstory, underground student newspapers, women's suffragette journals, and women's oral histories.

Number of journals or newspapers currently on subscription: 200 to 300.

Housing considerations: It is all cataloged and included in the general collection. A few intensive special collections.

Bibliographic control provided: Card catalog—80 percent online via OCLC and PAIS.

Published guides to the collection: No.

Other publications/services: Some bibliographic subject lists.

Date the collection was established: 1927.

History/Description of the collection: Ever since the library was established in 1927 (with the founding of the college) the collection policy has made an effort to buy "alternative" materials, some of this is directly due to the educational philosophy of the college.

Additional information: It is somewhat difficult to describe the collection as it is not separate, but collecting "alternative" material was always a normal part of our buying policy. These materials are added to our general collections.

Are you still adding materials to the collection? Yes.

———

Institution: *Elmer Holmes Bobst Library, New York University*

Address: 70 Washington Square South
New York, NY 10012

Phone number: (212) 998-2630

Collection name: Tamiment Institute Library & Robert F. Wagner Labor Archive

Curator or contact person: Dorothy Swanson

Public service hours: 10 a.m. to 5:45 p.m., M-F; evening and weekend hours vary with the academic calendar; please inquire.

Restrictions on use: All materials must be used in the Tamiment Library area. Nothing circulates; some book, periodical, and manuscript material on microfilm is interlibrary loaned. Public institution, open to all.

Inclusive years represented in collection: 1865 to present.

Principal years represented in collection: 1920s to present.

Primary subjects included in the collection: Unique center for scholarly research on labor history, socialism, communism, and anarchism. Utopian experiments, women's movements, and other radical activities are also documented in the collection. Although the focus is the United States, most of the movements documented were consciously international in outlook. Book and journal collections in particular contain many non-U.S. items.

Secondary subjects included in the collection: Labor movement outside the New York area.

Formats collected: Emphasis on manuscript collections and primary materials; newspapers, journals, and books. Pamphlets, flyers, audiotapes (Oral History of the American Left), film, posters, buttons, photographs, and other memorabilia. Microfilm collections from other institutions and commercial vendors are purchased.

Imprints collected: Left, radical organizations as well as the scholarly press, labor, trade union organizations especially NYC Local.

Number of volumes: 30,000 book titles, extensive vertical file collection containing perhaps 500,000 pamphlets, leaflets, flyers, and internal documents from labor and left organizations, 4,800 reels of microfilm.

Number of journals or newspapers currently on subscription: Approximately 600 currently received.

Housing considerations: Environmentally protected closed stacks. Journals alphabetical by title (some in acid-free folio boxes). Ephemera by issuing organization in approximately 600 linear feet of filing cabinets. Books shelved by LC number. Manuscript collections in acid-free folders and document boxes in special caged area by location code.

Bibliographic control provided: Book collection in RLIN; likewise the majority of the serials and approximately 75 percent of the manuscript collections (as well as reported to NUCMUC). Many additional in-house indexes and databases exist.

Published guides to the collection: Bell, Daniel. *The Tamiment Library.* New York: NYU Libraries, 1969. (Xerox $3.50 from us); *Guide to the Manuscript Collections of the Tamiment Library.* New York: Garland, 1977. ($24); *Socialist Collections in the Tamiment Library, 1872-1956, a Guide to the Microfilm Edition.* Sanford, NC: Microfilming Corporation of America, 1979. (Now available from UMI, Ann Arbor, MI); *Guide to the Oral History of the American Left.* New York: NYU Libraries, 1984. (Available from us $5); *Catalog of the Tamiment Institute Library of NYU.* 4

vols. Boston: G.K. Hall, 1980; *New York University Information Bulletin #8* (updated periodically). Free; *Bulletin of the Tamiment Institute Library*, nos. 1-50. New York: NYU Libraries, 1957-1984; *New York Labor Heritage.* Newsletter of the Robert F. Wagner Labor Archives, nos. 1-11. New York: NYU Libraries, 1979-1986. Free.

Other publications/services: Limited reproduction of archival material including photoprints.

Date the collection was established: 1906.

History/Description of the collection: The Tamiment Institute Library, donated to New York University in 1964 and home of the important scholarly journal *Labor History*, originated as part of the Rand School for Social Science, a worker's educational institution founded in New York City in 1906. In 1977, New York University established the Robert F. Wagner Labor Archives, as a unit of the Tamiment Library, in conjunction with the Tamiment Institute and the New York City Central Labor Council, AFL-CIO. Creating a labor archive was a natural extension of the history and collecting scope of the Tamiment Library. The collections of the Tamiment/Wagner focus on labor history, socialism, communism, anarchism, women's movements, and radical activities in the United States since 1865. Currently administratively under the head of archival collections, the staff consists of the Tamiment librarian, two processing archivists, one full-time collection assistant, and several part-time student workers.

Citation of descriptive articles about your collection: Rosengarten, Frank. "Some Notes on Library Resources for the Study of Socialist and Labor History." *Socialism and Democracy* no. 3 (Fall/Winter 1986): 83-87; Swanson, Dorothy. "Tamiment Institute/Ben Josephson Library and Robert F. Wagner Labor Archives." *Labor History* 23, no. 4 (Fall 1982): 562-67; Swanson, Dorothy. "NYU's Tamiment Library-a-Progress Report." *Workmen's Circle Call* (January-February 1975): 5-6; Akeroyd, Richard, and Russell Benedict. "A Directory of Ephemera Collections in a National Underground Network" and Swanson, Dorothy. "New York: Labor's Left," *Wilson Library Bulletin* (November 1973): 244-45. Numerous articles in various NYU publications, the *New York Times*, and once we even made the *Daily News* for Labor Day. Watstein, Sarah B. "Highlighting Women: A Profile on Library Services & Collections." *WLW Journal* (1985) [on our women's collections]: 2-5; Swanson, Dorothy. "The Tamiment Institute/Ben Josephson Library and Robert F. Wagner Labor Archives at NYU." *Library Quarterly* (April 1989): 148-61.

Are you still adding materials to the collection? Yes, especially seeking manuscript and primary materials to increase our documentation of more recent radicalism. Monographs budget of approximately $4,000 per year. But NYU libraries does regard Tamiment as one of its key unique collections and frequently purchases the major microform collections in our subject areas if there is money in the budget at the end of the year. We are also heavily dependent on gifts and actively seek grants.

OKLAHOMA

Institution: *Central State University Library*

Address: Edmond, OK 73034-0192

Phone number: (405) 341-2980, ext. 2880

Collection name: Political and Social Issues File

Curator or contact person: Carol Barry

Public service hours: 7:25 a.m. to 10 p.m., M-Th; 7:25 a.m. to 5 p.m., F; 10 a.m. to 6 p.m., Saturday; 2 p.m. to 10 p.m., Sunday; and intersessions 8 a.m. to 5 p.m., M-F.

Restrictions on use: Library use only.

Inclusive years represented in collection: 1960 to 1980 with earlier dates on runs of some periodicals.

Principal years represented in collection: Same.

Primary subjects included in the collection: Underground and alternative newspapers covering social and political issues of the sixties; right- and left-wing periodical literature; alternative lifestyles, civil rights, prisoners' rights, Native American movement; gay/lesbian causes; and antiwar activities.

Formats collected: Samples or runs of periodicals, pamphlets, broadsides, flyers, a few recordings, microfilm (underground newspaper collection).

Number of volumes: Number of items—not available; periodicals and pamphlets are stored in four file cabinets; Underground Newspapers Collection: 1963 to 1984, 446 reels.

Number of journals or newspapers currently on subscription: None.

Housing considerations: File folders arranged as follows: periodicals—alphabetically by title; organization publications—alphabetically by name of organization with "sa" from subject heading; and miscellaneous materials—by subject.

Bibliographic control provided: Brief entry card catalog containing: periodicals—title and holdings information and pamphlets, etc.—subject access.

Date the collection was established: 1974.

History/Description of the collection: There is no budget for this collection so all materials in the collection are donations received from various sources over the years. Sources: duplicates received through the Collector's Network; materials solicited through the mail from various issue-oriented groups; and a substantial donation of political extremist literature from a CSU faculty member.

Are you still adding materials to the collection? No.

PENNSYLVANIA

Institution: *Temple University*

Address: Contemporary Culture Collection
Temple University Library
Philadelphia, PA 19122

Phone number: (215) 787-8667

Collection name: Contemporary Culture Collection

Curator or contact person: Elaine Cox Clever, curator

Public service hours: 10 a.m. to 4 p.m., M-F, during academic year. Call for information at other times or to make appointment with curator.

Restrictions on use: All material must be used in the Collection reading room.

Inclusive years represented in collection: Mid-1960s to present.

Principal years represented in collection: 1969 to present.

Primary subjects included in the collection: Reform movement organizations including feminist, gay, and animal liberation; anti-nuclear, antiwar, alternative political, ecology/energy, economic and lifestyle advocates; radicals in the arts and the professions; and the output of small literary presses.

Formats collected: Newspapers, newsletters, journals, books. Flyers, announcements, other ephemera. Some posters and audiotapes. Subscribe to Bell & Howell's Underground Newspaper Microfilm Collection.

Imprints collected: Alternative publishers; small presses.

Number of volumes: 5,000 newspaper/journal titles, 6,000 books and pamphlets, 72 linear feet of ephemera.

Number of journals or newspapers currently on subscription: Approximately 400.

Housing considerations: Primarily closed stacks with small area for browsing currently received material.

Bibliographic control provided: All monographs currently being cataloged/classified. Card catalog is scheduled for closure. Access will be through library's GEAC system.

Published guides to the collection: *Alternative Press Periodicals: A Catalog of Those Periodicals Held in the Contemporary Culture Collection Which Have Been Filmed for Preservation by Temple University Libraries* (the Library, 1976) now out of print but available for consultation at the collection. Subject listings to currently received newspapers, newsletters, and journals are frequently updated and available for consultation at the collection.

Other publications/services: Periodic exhibits with accompanying bibliographies on topics of current interest. Free while supplies last.

Date the collection was established: 1969.

History/Description of the collection: Established in 1969 to preserve the output of the anti-Vietnam War movement, the collection has grown to include alternative, anti-mainstream publications of all shades and persuasions. The collection is international in scope with more than 5,000 newspaper and journal titles and over 6,000 books and pamphlets. English is the primary language although a few titles are available in Spanish and other languages.

Citation of descriptive articles about your collection: Case, Patricia J. "An Antidote to the Homogenized Library." *New Pages* (Spring 1983): 4-5; Salisbury, Stephen. "A Collection That Goes to Extremes." *Philadelphia Inquirer* (6 February 1984): 1C, 5C.

Additional information: Archival material includes the papers of poet Lyn Lifshin; records of the Liberation News Service, the Committee of Small Press Editors and Publishers, *Seven Days*, and *Health/PAC Bulletin*. In storage boxes; has received limited processing.

Are you still adding materials to the collection? Monograph budget limited. Number of serial subscriptions remains constant at approximately 400.

Institution: *La Salle University*

Address: Special Collections
Connelly Library
La Salle University
20th St. & Olney Ave.
Philadelphia, PA 19141

Phone number: (215) 951-1290

Collection name: Imaginative Representations of the Vietnam War

Curator or contact person: John S. Baky, bibliographer

Public service hours: 9:00 a.m. to 5:00 p.m., M-F and by appointment.

Restrictions on use: Some material must have written permission of author in order to quote extensively. Otherwise, no restrictions but location of use.

Inclusive years represented in collection: 1961 to present.

Principal years represented in collection: 1965 to present.

Primary subjects included in the collection: The collection is limited primarily to imaginative literature and the visual arts the subject of which is the Vietnam War. The collection is focused on fictive writing in the form of novels, short stories, poetry, drama, filmscripts, extensive examples of graphic art, painting, video, TV productions, and sound recordings.

Formats collected: Contained in this collection, and additional to the published written material itself, are unpublished manuscripts, corrected manuscripts, shooting scripts, galley proofs, page proofs (corrected and uncorrected), holograph copies, limited editions, variant editions, runs of comic books, and cartoon art. The remainder of the collection consists of carefully cataloged items of ephemera such as poetry broadsides, dealer catalogs of Vietnam War fiction, published strategy games, published software, vanity publications, and curriculum guides to teaching the war through its literature across all educational levels.

In direct support of the written and cinematic dimensions of the collection are actively developed collections of graphic arts (posters, prints, collage, ephemera, and more) featuring such material as the ten original silk screens presented to Denise Levertov during the poet's trip to Hanoi in 1972. Additionally, artifacts of a musical/sound recording nature include tapes of Hanoi Hannah, recordings of Armed Forces Radio broadcasts from Saigon and Danang, tapes of attacks in progress recorded during the onslaughter of Tet, underground tapes of G.I. music broadcasts in-country, and sound tracks of most films released about the war.

Imprints collected: Many small presses, vanity presses, self-publishers, protest groups, academic organizations.

Number of volumes: 3,000 books of fiction writing and poetry, 500 non-print items, and 300 films and videos.

Date the collection was established: 1986.

History/Description of the collection: A collection of material entitled Imaginative Representations of the Vietnam War resides in the Department of Special Collections of La Salle University, in the city of Philadelphia. The fundamental aspiration of the collection has a dual intention:

1. to discover how a discrete body of creative literature becomes mythopoeic. That is, how a complex event is interpreted through creative means; and

2. to discover how creative treatments of an event use aesthetic values to reveal both the fact and emotional essence of traumatic cultural phenomena.

Additional information: About 1,000 items reflect the protest/social awareness stances of the 1960s era.

The collection is directly supportive of research in the following areas of Vietnam War studies: American culture reflected in the war experience; autobiography as mythopoeic source; Central America becoming a new Vietnam; changing images of gender and race; commercialization of the war experience; the "enemy's" point of view; film versions of the war; gay perspectives in the war; graphic art and the Vietnam War; Hollywood and Vietnam; how the war is appropriated to other agendas; interrelationship of war, literature, and the arts; memory and the war; missionary work carried on during the war; narrative strategies in war writing; non-fiction films about the Vietnam War; pedagogy and the war; *Platoon*: the game; racial tensions among American troops; student projects for courses on the war; Vietnam and Graham Greene; Vietnam pornography; Vietnam Veterans Memorial as myth and metaphor; Vietnam War translated into commercial gaming; the war as *bildungsroman*.

Are you still adding materials to the collection? Yes, at 200 items per year.

––––––––

Institution: *Swarthmore College*

Address: Swarthmore College Peace Collection
Swarthmore, PA 19081

Phone number: (215) 328-8557

Collection name: Swarthmore College Peace Collection (SCPC)

Curator or contact person: Wendy E. Chmielewski

Public service hours: 8:30 a.m. to 4:30 p.m., M-F (when the college is in session); 9 a.m. to 12 p.m., Saturday. Closed the entire month of August. Holidays vary with the college calendar.

Restrictions on use: Collection is open to all serious researchers. Some collections have restrictions.

Inclusive years represented in collection: 1643 to date.

Principal years represented in collection: 1866 to date.

Primary subjects included in the collection: History of the peace movement, conscientious objection, pacifism, women and the peace movement, disarmament, nonviolence, internationalism, civil disobedience, and Vietnam era.

Secondary subjects included in the collection: Progressivism, black protest, feminism, civil liberties, history of social work, and related reform movements.

Formats collected: Books, manuscripts, pamphlets, serials; and, to lesser extent, realia, films, video and sound recordings.

Imprints collected: Materials dealing with our primary subject areas.

Number of volumes: Approximately 12,000 cataloged books and pamphlets; 1,400 reels of microfilm; 155 major document groups; 2,000 small collective document groups; 2,000 periodical titles; 4,500 posters; 11,000 photographs.

Number of journals or newspapers currently on subscription: 400.

Housing considerations: Ongoing conservation program to store manuscripts and other materials in appropriate acid-free housing.

Bibliographic control provided: Books and pamphlets are cataloged on OCLC. Serials are cataloged on Tri-College (Swarthmore, Haverford, and Bryn Mawr College) serials automated cataloging system. Checklists are available for about 3/4 of manuscript collections. Some non-print materials are cataloged.

Published guides to the collection: *Guide to the Swarthmore College Peace Collection* 2d ed. Swarthmore, PA: Swarthmore College, 1981. ($5); *Guide to Sources on Women in the Swarthmore College Peace Collection.* Swarthmore, PA: Swarthmore College, 1988). ($7).

Other publications/services: See above.

Date the collection was established: 1930.

History/Description of the collection: Swarthmore College Peace Collection was established in 1930, when Jane Addams of Hull House in Chicago donated her papers and books relating to peace and social justice to Swarthmore College. Since that time, the Peace Collection has gathered and preserved for scholarly research the materials of persons and organizations who have worked for nonviolent social change, disarmament, and conflict resolution between peoples and nations. The collection now contains nearly 155 major document groups, approximately 2,000 smaller collective document groups, over 12,000 cataloged books and pam-

phlets, 400 periodicals currently received, and 1,400 microfilm reels.

Citation of descriptive articles about your collection: Soderlund, Jean R. "Swarthmore College Peace Collection." *Philadelphia City Archives News Letter* (June 1986): 1-3.

Additional information: Approximately 30 of our collections have been microfilmed, and we will lend the microfilm through interlibrary loan, three reels at a time.

Are you still adding materials to the collection? Yes, we have an annual budget of $8,000 for books and periodicals. We receive records from official depositors (peace organizations) on a regular basis. We also regularly receive gifts of manuscripts and books from individuals.

RHODE ISLAND

Institution: *Rhode Island College*

Address: Special Collections
James P. Adams Library
Rhode Island College
Providence, RI 02908

Phone number: (401) 456-9653

Collection name: Social and Political Materials Collection

Curator or contact person: Sally M. Wilson

Public service hours: 9 a.m. to 12 p.m., 1 p.m. to 4 p.m., M-F.

Restrictions on use: Materials available for use in Special Collections reading room.

Inclusive years represented in collection: 1930s to 1980s.

Principal years represented in collection: 1960s to 1980s.

Primary subjects included in the collection: The collection was based on a donation from Gordon Hall, a private collector, and is a selective collection that gives an overview of political and social extremism in the United States. Groups represented advocating or opposing abortion, anti-Semitism, communism, economic problems, labor organizations, race relations and white supremacy, women's questions. There are also materials from foreign countries.

Secondary subjects included in the collection: Atheism, education, homosexuality, prisons, and radioactive pollution.

Formats collected: Newspapers, journals, pamphlets. Some books, a few tapes (audio).

Number of volumes: Approximately 2,320 titles, journals and pamphlets, 62 cataloged monographs, and others awaiting cataloging.

Housing considerations: Closed stacks in Special Collections area, materials stored in acid-free folders and boxes, and books shelved nearby.

Bibliographic control provided: Main file by name of organization or title of journal, subject file by topic, geographic file, in main library catalog are subject cards with reference to the collection, the complete files are located in Special Collections reading room.

Date the collection was established: 1975.

History/Description of the collection: The Social and Political Materials Collection was started as a teaching collection by a faculty member in history. The Gordon Hall donation formed the basis, and letters to organizations requesting examples of publications were helpful in expanding the collection.

Are you still adding materials to the collection? Yes, at a limited rate. We have also weeded material that has become more commercial and mainstream over the years.

WISCONSIN

Institution: *State Historical Society of Wisconsin*

Address: 816 State Street
           Madison, WI 53706-1482

Phone number: (608) 264-6531

Collection name: State Historical Society of Wisconsin. There is no specific collection name; rather materials are integrated into the archival and library collections.

Curator or contact person: James P. Danky

Public service hours: 8 a.m. to 9 p.m., M-Th and 8 a.m. to 5 p.m., F-Saturday when the University of Wisconsin is in session; 8 a.m. to 5 p.m., M-Saturday when not in session.

Restrictions on use: There are no special restrictions and the collections are open to all.

Inclusive years represented in collection: Nineteenth and twentieth centuries.

Principal years represented in collection: Nineteenth and twentieth centuries.

Primary subjects included in the collection: Underground.

Number of journals or newspapers currently on subscription: 8,000: A figure that includes all currently received periodicals including standard academic journals in addition to many minority and radical titles.

Housing considerations: All materials are handled in the same fashion. That is, ours is an integrated collection where nothing is segregated because of subject or opinion, books with books, periodicals with periodicals. Not a browsing collection.

Bibliographic control provided: OCLC, 1977-; full cataloging provided for all items equally. Archival materials available on RLIN, 1984-.

Published guides to the collection: *=Available for purchase. +=Available on ERIC fiche. Undergrounds: *A Union List of Alternative Periodicals in Libraries of the United States and Canada*. Madison: The Society, 1974; + *Hispanic Americans in the United States: A Union List*. Madison: The Society, 1979; + *Asian American Periodicals and Newspapers: A Union List*. 2d ed. Madison: The Society, 1979; + *Black Periodicals and Newspapers: A Union List*. 2d ed. Madison: The Society, 1979;* *Native American Periodicals and Newspapers*. Westport, CT: Greenwood, 1984;* *Women's History: Resources at the State Historical Society*, 4th ed. Madison: The Society, 1982;* *Social Action Collections at the State Historical Society of Wisconsin, a Guide*. Madison: The Society, 1983;* *Women's Periodicals and Newspapers, from the 18th Century to 1982*. Boston: G.K. Hall, 1982.

Additional information: Akeroyd, Richard, and Russell Benedict, eds. "A Directory of Ephemera Collections in a National Underground Network." *Wilson Library Bulletin* 48, no. 3 (November 1973): 236-54.

Are you still adding materials to the collection? The society's library has continued to collect comprehensively in the areas of radical reform, minority, women's, peace, and related literatures since its founding in the mid-nineteenth century. The collection is national in scope and includes Canada.

CANADA

Institution: *Canadian Women's Movement Archives*

Address: PO Box 128
           Station P
           Toronto, Ontario M5S 2S7
           Canada

Phone number: (416) 597-8865

Collection name: Canadian Women's Movement, 1960 to present

Curator or contact person: Nancy Adamson or Debbie Green

Public service hours: 6 p.m. to 9 p.m., Th; 10 a.m. to 2 p.m., Saturday; and by appointment.

Restrictions on use: All materials must be used in our reading room. Some organizational collections require permission of the group before we can grant access. Names of living individuals can only be used in research or articles with the permission of those individuals.

Inclusive years represented in collection: 1960 to present.

Principal years represented in collection: 1970 to present.

Primary subjects included in the collection: The organizations that make up the Canadian Women's Movement. Our collection includes approximately 1,500 organizational files; we also have some files on individuals. We also have approximately 750 periodicals from the Canadian Women's Movement—newsletters, broadsheets, and so on. We have a large collection of lesbian material. Also a small library.

Formats collected: Primarily organizational records; buttons, posters, T-shirts, ephemera. Books and pamphlets published in Canada by women or about women. Small collection of photographs and slides. Also collect cassette or reel-to-reel tapes of women's meetings.

Number of volumes: 1,750 organizational files, 250 individual files, 750 newspaper and journal titles, 200 cassette tapes, 1,000 buttons, and 250 posters.

Number of journals or newspapers currently on subscription: Approximately 350.

Housing considerations: All journal and newspaper titles are arranged alphabetically by title and are housed in acid-free boxes. All organizational files are arranged in alphabetical order by name of organization. These are filed in regular legal size folders in filing cabinets. Buttons in plastic containers. Posters in mylar.

Bibliographic control provided: Organizational files and journals and newspapers are cataloged on card catalogs. Specialized card catalogs and finding aides exist for our lesbian holdings. The entire collection is indexed and cross-referenced on a microcomputer (IBM).

Date the collection was established: 1975.

History/Description of the collection: The Canadian Women's Movement Archives was founded in 1975 by a collective of feminists. We are now incorporated as a non-profit organization and exist as an independent archives. Our collection, the largest of its kind in Canada, contains many manuscript collections of records of women's organizations in Canada, as well as the largest collection of the publications of the women's movement in Canada.

Citation of descriptive articles about your collection: Zaremba, Eve. "CWMA: Collective Collections." *Broadside: A Feminist Review* 6, no. 5 (March 1985): 4-5; Brown, Sylvia. "Women and Archiving." *Status of Women News* (Winter 1984): 10-13; Thomson, Aisla. "Interview: The Canadian Women's Movement Archives Collective." *Women's Education des Femmes* (Winter 1986): 18-23.

Are you still adding materials to the collection? Yes. Many groups donate their records on an ongoing basis and we are constantly getting new donations. We receive approximately 350 journals each year.

————

Institution: *W.A.C. Bennett Library, Simon Fraser University*

Address: Burnaby, British Columbia
Canada V5A 1S6

Phone number: (604) 291-4626

Collection name: Contemporary Literature Collection

Curator or contact person: Eugene E. Bridwell, Special Collections librarian; Charles Watts, assistant for Special Collections

Public service hours: 12:30 p.m. to 4:30 p.m., M-F.

Inclusive years represented in collection: 1908 to present.

Principal years represented in collection: 1948 to present.

Primary subjects included in the collection: Modern and post modern poetry and poetics including strong representation from the Black Mountain movement, the San Francisco Renaissance, the Beats, the New York school, and the Canadian *Tish* group, as well as the seminal writers Pound, Williams, Olson, Stein, and H.D. Also included are the "language-centered" writers, Jack Kerouac School of Disembodied Poetics, and the long poem in Canada and the United States.

Secondary subjects included in the collection: The sixties in the United States and Canada; the underground literary and political movements in journalism; the ecology movements of the sixties and seventies in the United States and Canada; "fine press" printing and publication; regional movements in literature, Zen Buddhism and other eastern religions in recent and current literature.

Formats collected: Monographs, serials, broadsides, ephemera, audio reel-to-reel and cassette recordings. (Monographs range from finely printed letterpress editions, handbound, to stapled photocopied or mimeographed sheets.) The CLC also houses several manuscript and press archives.

Number of volumes: Monographs 14,000, journals 1,600 titles, manuscripts 75 metres, broadsides 650+, and sound recordings 800.

Number of journals or newspapers currently on subscription: 185 continuing subscriptions.

Housing considerations: The Contemporary Literature Collection is housed in the Special Collections, a separate room on the library's fourth floor. All materials are housed in environmentally protected closed stacks in Special Collections. Monographs are shelved alphabetically by author, journals alphabetically by title. Broadsides are stored flat in map cases. Tapes are shelved on wooden shelves and rewound periodically. Manuscript archives are housed in acid-free boxes; some materials are deacidified and encapsulated in mylar.

Bibliographic control provided: All acquisitions, whether current or out of print, are processed by the library's monographs or serials acquisitions department; are assigned serial numbers; and are entered along with primary bibliographic information and vendor information on the library's GEAC Marc Records Management System. All monographs are cataloged on the library's in-house GEAC system. Serials and journals are also cataloged on GEAC. Also, we maintain a Special Collections card catalog with cross-references for critical works, contributions to magazines, multiple author anthologies and critical works, bibliographies, and more.

Published guides to the collection: Groves, Percilla. "Archival Sources for Olson Studies." *Line* no. 1 (Spring 1983): 94-102. (Available from *Line, a Journal of Contemporary Writing and Its Postmodern Sources*, c/o English Dept., Simon Fraser University, Burnaby, B.C. V5A 1S6.) We have developed a computerized inventory of our manuscript holdings and are putting our holdings online in the MARC

format. In addition, complete analytical and descriptive inventories of the CLC's Ezra Pound archives and *Northwest Review-Coyote's Journal* archive have been done and will be available on request at $.20 per page for photocopying.

Other publications/services: *Line, a Journal of Contemporary Writing and Its Postmodern Sources*, edited by Roy Miki at Simon Fraser University and published at S.F.U., features one of CLC's manuscript archives each issue, publishing historical notes, facsimile manuscript pages, and so on. A recent issue has an article on the publishing history of *The Northwest Review-Coyote's Journal*. See also "The Contribution of Special Collections as Evidenced by Articles, Books and Theses," photocopy, 6 leaves.

Date the collection was established: 1965.

Citation of descriptive articles about your collection: "SFU Special Collections Becoming More Special All the Time." *SFU Week* 14 (August 1984): 1; Peterson, Leslie. "SFU in for a Pound." *The Vancouver Sun* (24 June 1981): F1; "Library to Boost Collection with $21,000 Federal Grant." *SFU Week* 21 (10 September 1981): 1; Sullivan, Nancy. "A Look at University Collections." *University Affairs* 17 (October 1976): 4-7; Donald, Alan. "Cracking Books in Special Collections; Plotting the Past in Archives: Alan Donald Reveals All." *Afterthoughts: SFU Alumni* (Spring 1976): 3-6; "Grants Boost Special Collections." *SFU Week* 45 (21 September 1989): 3.

Are you still adding materials to the collection? Yes. There is a current monographs approval plan with Small Press Distribution, a West Coast supplier of small press books and magazines, with purchases of about $1,500 per year; grants from the Social Sciences and Humanities Research Council of $21,000 and $25,000 have enabled us to purchase out-of-print items over the past six years. New manuscript archives have been purchased with the aid of extraordinary grants from the Social Science and Humanities Research Council of Canada and the university library.

DIRECTORY 2: GAY AND LESBIAN SPECIAL COLLECTIONS LIBRARIES
(IN ORDER BY STATE, THEN COLLECTION)

CALIFORNIA

Institution: **Alternative Research Center**

Address: PO Box 28977
            Santa Ana, CA 92799-8977

Phone number: (714) 751-2856

Collection name: Alternative Research Center [formerly Lavender Archives]

Curator or contact person: Daniel C. Tsang

Public service hours: By appointment only.

Restrictions on use: Non-circulating collection.

Inclusive years represented in collection: 1960s to present.

Principal years represented in collection: 1970s to present.

Primary subjects included in the collection: Anti-surveillance collection: including periodicals, monographs, pamphlets, videos, sound recordings, clippings, leaflets, posters, declassified documents. Lavender Archives: Lesbian and gay male materials, including periodicals, monographs, pamphlets, videos, sound recordings, clippings, leaflets, organizational press releases, posters, declassified documents, with focus on sexual minorities within the lesbian and gay movements, Third World people, and international materials. Alternative press collection: periodicals, monographs, dissertations, pamphlets, sound recordings, clippings, leaflets, organizational press release, and book announcements, posters, declassified documents.

Formats collected: Monographs, serials, pamphlets, posters, clippings, audio-cassette recordings, VHS videocassettes.

Other publications/services: Publishes *Alternative Collections* (1991-). Published *Gay Insurgent* nos. 6-7 (1980-1981).

Date the collection was established: 1980 as Lavender Archives; 1989 as Alternative Research Center.

Citation of descriptive articles about your collection: Silberman, Steven. "Librarian Follows FBI's Anti-gay Trail." *Orange County Register* (10 October 1990): B1, B7; Tsang, Daniel C. "Homosexuality Research Collections." In *Libraries, Erotica, Pornography*, ed. by Martha Cornog, [199]-210. Phoenix: Oryx Press, 1991.

––––––––

Institution: *A Project of Connexxus*

Address: June Mazer Lesbian Collection
626 N. Robertson Blvd.
West Hollywood, CA 90069

Phone number: (818) 783-7348

Collection name: June Mazer Lesbian Collection

Curator or contact person: Degania Golove

Public service hours: 6 p.m. to 10 p.m., W; 11 a.m. to 5 p.m., Sunday; and by appointment M-Th.

Restrictions on use: All materials must be used at the JMLC.

Inclusive years represented in collection: Twentieth century.

Principal years represented in collection: 1970 to present.

Primary subjects included in the collection: Lesbiania and feminist materials, including books, periodicals, lesbian organization papers, lesbian- and women-owned business files, flyers, art works (lesbian and non-lesbian women), ephemera and realia from the women's movement and lesbian activities.

Secondary subjects included in the collection: General issues of interest to women. Very limited material, (e.g., some periodicals) with a focus on gay men.

Formats collected: Books, newspapers, journals, periodicals, newspaper clippings, posters, buttons, T-shirts, dissertations, organization files, audiotapes, videotapes, flyers, fine art works, manuscripts (published and unpublished), personal letters, photographs.

Number of volumes: 2,500 books, 250 lesbian periodicals, and 300 more feminist periodicals.

Bibliographic control provided: Items are cataloged, following our own guidelines.

Published guides to the collection: A variety of flyers, position papers, and collection development guidelines are available.

Date the collection was established: 1981 in Oakland, California, under the name The West Coast Lesbian Collections. The WCLC was moved to Los Angeles, California, in 1987 when the name was changed to the June L. Mazer Lesbian Collection.

History/Description of the collection: As part of its goal of providing resources and services to women of the greater Los Angeles area, the June L. Mazer Lesbian Collection was brought to Los Angeles by Connexxus Women's Center—Centro de Mujares in April 1987.
    Originally known as The West Coast Lesbian Collections, its doors opened December 1981 in Oakland. The goal of the coordinating committee was to establish a credible community-based lesbian archives for the West Coast.

Additional information: Also included is a large collection of manuscripts; including papers from Daughters of Bilitis & Ladder files; Martin/Lyon LESBIAN/WOMAN files; Diana Press archive; Telewoman archive; Betsy York's WMDC archive—history of women's music; Margaret Cruikshank papers; Lillian Faderman papers; Ruth Reid & Kent Hyde papers; Sue Prosin papers; Joanne Parrent papers—history of Feminist Economic Network; Roma Guy papers; Betsy Callaways papers; and others.

Are you still adding materials to the collection? Yes.

––––––––

Institution: *Lesbian/Gay Archives of San Diego*

Address: PO Box 4186
San Diego, CA 92104

Phone number: (619) 260-1522

Collection name: Lesbian/Gay Archives of San Diego

Curator or contact person: R "Jess" Jessop

Public service hours: Not yet open to public. Collection currently housed in private homes. Use by appointment only. We are currently looking for a public facility.

Restrictions on use: Materials may be used on premises only.

Inclusive years represented in collection: Fifties to present for photographs, posters, newspapers, memorabilia. Some history books cover periods from B.C. to modern times.

Principal years represented in collection: 1960s to 1980s.

Primary subjects included in the collection: AIDS, lesbian/gay persons in military, liberation movement, lesbian/gay pride, sports, art, local and national lesbian/gay leaders.

Formats collected: Photographs, slides, audiotapes, videotapes, posters, periodicals, proclamations, clippings files, books, framed art, and newsletters of local and national lesbian/gay organizations.

Number of volumes: Approximately 300.

Number of journals or newspapers currently on subscription: 200.

Housing considerations: All newspaper clippings copied on 100 percent cotton (acid free) paper and placed in page-protectors in three-ring binders. Organized by year and subdivided by subject within each year set. Periodicals are stored in shelf-file boxes in chronological order of appearance, and subdivided by region. The collection is currently housed in private homes.

Bibliographic control provided: This has not been done yet. (We are young and small.)

Published guides to the collection: None.

Other publications/services: None.

Date the collection was established: December 1987.

History/Description of the collection: The lesbian and gay archives of San Diego was founded in 1987 by concerned San Diegans to combat the great information deficit on lesbian/gay issues by uncovering, preserving, and teaching lesbian/gay history. The contributions of lesbians and gay men to regional and world culture shall be elucidated through the following programs: establishment of a library of printed, audio, and video materials that document lesbian/gay history; collection of lesbian/gay liberation movement memorabilia and artifacts; teaching of lesbian/gay history through a variety of speaking engagements, seminars, and exhibits;

collection and display of lesbian/gay art; research of local lesbian/gay history; and establishment of archival service to local lesbian/gay organizations.

Citation of descriptive articles about your collection: Fitzsimmons, Barbara. "Local Archives May Make Life Easier for Lesbians, Gays." *San Diego Union* (21 May 1989): D2.

Additional information: The focus of the collection is on materials that illustrate lesbian/gay contributions to world culture.

Are you still adding materials to the collection? Yes.

FLORIDA

Institution: *The Naiad Press, Inc.*

Address: PO Box 10432
Tallahassee, FL 32302

Phone number: (904) 539-5965

Collection name: Lesbian Archives of the Naiad Press

Curator or contact person: Barbara Grier

Public service hours: None, per se, use by application, and hours are simply arranged to meet the needs of the researcher.

Restrictions on use: Serious research as opposed to look for the joy of it.

Inclusive years represented in collection: 1870 to present.

Principal years represented in collection: 1910 to present.

Primary subjects included in the collection: Lesbian literature, gay male literature fiction, drama, poetry, essays, biography, and autobiography are the major fields but there are several thousand works of lesbian non-fiction and gay male non-fiction.

Secondary subjects included in the collection: Women's literature loosely in the field of feminist or women's liberation materials...but the collection in this area is very very wide ranging and covers books by and about women from all over the world.

Formats collected: Primarily books. The enormous periodicals archive accumulated from 1955 through 1988 was turned over to the June Mazer Lesbian Collection in Los Angeles in 1988 and all incoming periodicals are being sent to them on a regular basis. About 500 magazines are being maintained here, primarily the very early major magazines (not newspapers) from the first 10-15 years of the current phase of the lesbian and gay liberation movements. Some videos, recordings, about eight large files of clippings (again from early years).

Imprints collected: Impossible question...we have about all known lesbian titles in the English language...this obviously means hundreds of publishers are represented.

Number of volumes: 12,000 lesbian titles, about 10,000 gay male titles, about 7,000 women's liberation (feminist) related titles.

Number of journals or newspapers currently on subscription: 300 gay and lesbian periodicals are sent to us on some kind of exchange basis.

Housing considerations: The main four collections (lesbian hardback, lesbian paperback, gay male hardback, and gay male paperback) are housed alphabetically on shelves (alphabetically by author). The gay male and lesbian mixed non-fiction is simply alphabetized as well (primarily because I know the authors by heart).

Bibliographic control provided: No active processing except shelving has taken place since 1968 when I became editor of *The Ladder*, and with the demands of Naiad Press it looks like that will have to wait until I am a very old lady.

Date the collection was established: 1946. I began collecting lesbian literature at age 13...I am 56. It's a lifework.

History/Description of the collection: The collection simply grew...collecting lesbian literature and then gay male literature was my first "movement" activity. Simply an outgrowth of a literate childhood. Then I worked in the publishing of *The Ladder*, the oldest lesbian magazine (save one...called *Vice Versa*), for 16 years and now have been running the oldest and largest lesbian publishing company for 17, soon to be 18 years...the collection is just an obvious part of this.

Citation of descriptive articles about your collection: There are some, I have no time at present to go into them, that is to look them up to send to you, sorry.

Additional information: Call me at (904) 539-5965, if I can provide any other information.

Are you still adding materials to the collection? Yes, each year we add all the published material in lesbian literature that we are aware of. We stopped actively searching for gay male material in 1968, but we acquire a great deal anyway. I still dream of being able to do another edition of the lesbian in literature someday...if I live long enough.

————

Institution: *The Stonewall Library & Archives*

Address: c/o Metropolitan Community Church
330 S. W. 27th St.
Ft. Lauderdale, FL 33315

Phone number: (305) 462-2004

Collection name: The Stonewall Library & Archives

Curator or contact person: Jerry Mitchell

Public service hours: 12 p.m. to 3 p.m., second Saturday each month; 10 a.m. to 12 p.m., every Sunday.

Restrictions on use: Out-of-print books and periodicals for reference only. All others can be checked out.

Inclusive years represented in collection: Early 1900s to present.

Principal years represented in collection: 1970 to present.

Primary subjects included in the collection: Gay & lesbian fiction, non-fiction, and periodicals.

Secondary subjects included in the collection: Related materials to gay and lesbian issues.

Formats collected: Books, records, video, magazines, periodicals, records of gay and lesbian organizations, and also clippings.

Imprints collected: Memorabilia—T-shirts, buttons, and others from gay and lesbian functions.

Number of volumes: 3,000 books (hardback and paper); 200 cartons of periodicals, magazines, and clippings.

Number of journals or newspapers currently on subscription: Approximately 30.

Housing considerations: Hardback and paperbacks on shelves. Periodicals and magazines on shelves and in boxes.

Bibliographic control provided: Cataloged on computer. Circulation is controlled on checkout form. Printed copy of catalog is available for use in the library.

Published guides to the collection: No.

Other publications/services: Heritage of Pride—a program of gay and lesbian speakers in May of each year giving an oral history of the speaker's involvement in the community. These programs are on video for reference and research.

Date the collection was established: 1970 to 1971.

Citation of descriptive articles about your collection: None available.

Additional information: We are a not-for-profit corporation.

Are you still adding materials to the collection? Yes.

GEORGIA

Institution: *Atlanta Lesbian Feminist Alliance*

Address: PO Box 5502
Atlanta, GA 30307

Phone number: (404) 378-9769

Collection name: Southeastern Lesbian Archives

Curator or contact person: Library Committee

Public service hours: By appointment.

Restrictions on use: Most materials do not circulate. Books circulate to members only. Will copy materials for small fee.

Inclusive years represented in collection: 1972 to present.

Principal years represented in collection: 1972 to present.

Primary subjects included in the collection: Women, lesbianism, feminism, and lesbian-feminism.

Formats collected: Periodicals, books, and manuscripts.

Number of volumes: ca. 850 to 1,000.

Number of journals or newspapers currently on subscription: Total of 450 titles, both current and ceased publications.

Housing considerations: Presently stored in building under renovation. No temperature or humidity control. Metal file cabinets and metal and wooden shelving.

Bibliographic control provided: Periodicals checked into kardex and filed alphabetically. Card catalog for books, which are accessed through a topical cataloging system.

Other publications/services: *Atalanta*, newsletter of the Atlanta Lesbian Feminist Alliance.

Date the collection was established: 1972.

History/Description of the collection: ALFA is a lesbian-feminist organization open to all lesbians. We welcome women to participate in and work on ALFA-sponsored social, political, educational, cultural, and recreational activities and events. We are concerned with the entire spectrum of lesbian-feminist issues, which includes, but is not limited to, the liberation of women; eliminating discrimination based on sexual orientation, ending racial, anti-Semitic, and economic oppression; eliminating nuclear weapons and reducing the threat of war; creating a positive, enabling environment for fat and differently abled women; and ensuring that the world's living and non-living resources are used in a responsible manner for the benefit of all and not exploited for the profit of a few. ALFA allows a lesbian to meet and get together with other lesbians who share her interests. We welcome lesbians of all races, religions, political orientations, economic status, occupations, and degrees of openness. When you become a member you will receive our monthly newsletter *Atalanta*, may borrow books from our large library (local members only), may vote in monthly meetings, and receive a discount on certain ALFA events at the house. Your name and address are kept confidential.

Are you still adding materials to the collection? Yes.

ILLINOIS

Institution: *Henry Gerber-Pearl M. Hart Library*

Address: 3352 North Pauline
Chicago, IL 60657

Phone number: (312) 883-3003

Collection name: Henry Gerber-Pearl M. Hart Library, the Midwest Lesbian & Gay Resource Center

Curator or contact person: Bill Schwesig

Public service hours: 7:30 p.m. to 10:00 p.m., Th; 12:00 p.m. to 4:00 p.m., Saturday.

Restrictions on use: Open to the public for reference. Members may borrow books for which we hold more than one copy.

Inclusive years represented in collection: ca. 1890 to date.

Principal years represented in collection: 1945 to date.

Primary subjects included in the collection: Gay men and lesbians in the United States, their social and legal status, political activity, history, literature, religion, psychology, family and interpersonal relationships; the gay liberation movement; gay and lesbian fiction, poetry, and drama; general information about AIDS; government AIDS policy.

Secondary subjects included in the collection: Feminism.

Formats collected: Books, periodicals, newsletters, microfilm, pamphlets, dissertations, course syllabi, ephemera, archives and manuscripts, organization records, realia (buttons, T-shirts, novelties, picket signs, and more), posters, prints, photographs, videos, films, audio recordings.

Imprints collected: American, Canadian, and British.

Number of volumes: 5,000 books, 50 videos, 100 linear feet of periodicals, 20 linear feet of archives, and 1 reel microfilm.

Number of journals or newspapers currently on subscription: ca. 75.

Housing considerations: Books on open stacks, divided into reference, non-fiction (by title), fiction, poetry, plays (by author), anthologies, AIDS, government documents (by source), biography. Bound periodicals in stacks, unbound periodicals and newsletters in file cabinets (all by title). AIDS clippings, general clippings, and archives in file cabinets.

Bibliographic control provided: Computer-produced author/title book catalog; subject catalog under development. Authority list for clippings file headings.

Published guides to the collection: None.

Other publications/services: Photocopying. Irregular newsletter.

History/Description of the collection: Established in 1981 by the late historian Greg Sprague and members of the Midwest Gay Academic Union, whose collections were merged with that of the Gay Horizons Library. Opened in its current location in 1986.

Governed by a board of directors, managed by male and female co-librarians and an archivist, operated by volunteer staff. The library relies on donations and review copies for almost all acquisitions.

Additional information: Special collections include Chicago gay periodicals, Metis Press archives, Black Maria (non-defunct lesbian collective) archives. Volunteer staff includes five professional librarians.

Are you still adding materials to the collection? Yes.

KENTUCKY

Institution: *Kentucky Collection of Lesbian Her-Story*

Address: PO Box 1701
Louisville, KY 40203

Phone number: (502) 895-3127

Collection name: Kentucky Collection of Lesbian Her-Story

Curator or contact person: Iandras Moontree

Public service hours: Not open to the public until funding permits.

Restrictions on use: For lesbians and wimmin. Not all material can be removed or checked out.

Inclusive years represented in collection: Late 1960s to present.

Principal years represented in collection: 1970s and 1980s to present.

Primary subjects included in the collection: Lesbian cultural areas such as music, art, politics, religion/spirituality.

Formats collected: Various.

Number of volumes: Approximately 1,000 books, 400 newspapers and journals, and 100 organizational files.

Number of journals or newspapers currently on subscription: 50.

Housing considerations: Books grouped into general sections: feminist literature, fiction, non-fiction, autobiographies, women's movement, spirituality, lesbian periodicals and journals. Subject file categories in alphabetical groupings.

Other publications/services: Clearinghouse of information for lesbians.

Date the collection was established: 1980.

Are you still adding materials to the collection? Yes.

Institution: *Kentucky Gay & Lesbian Archives*

Address: 1464 S. Second St.
Louisville, KY 40208

Phone number: (502) 636-0935

Collection name: Kentucky Gay & Lesbian Archives

Curator or contact person: David Williams

Public service hours: By appointment.

Restrictions on use: Materials cannot be loaned out at present except by special arrangement. Archives are open to general public.

Inclusive years represented in collection: 1950s to present.

Principal years represented in collection: 1980 to present.

Primary subjects included in the collection: Magazines, newspapers, newsletters, videotapes, newspaper clippings of a gay and lesbian nature.

Secondary subjects included in the collection: T-shirts, posters, buttons, matchbooks, other memorabilia.

Formats collected: Newsmagazines and books.

Imprints collected: Only materials published by "alternative" publishers or organizations.

Number of volumes: 100 books; 50 newspaper and journal titles; and 300 newsclipping files.

Number of journals or newspapers currently on subscription: 5.

Housing considerations: No special arrangements possible at present.

Bibliographic control provided: General typed listings only.

Published guides to the collection: None.

Date the collection was established: 1982.

History/Description of the collection: Contains comprehensive collection of gay/lesbian newspapers and materials from throughout Kentucky as well as Indiana and Ohio. Also contains materials from throughout the United States and other countries.

Citation of descriptive articles about your collection: None.

Additional information: Long-term goal is to become the regional repository of gay and lesbian materials for Kentucky, Indiana, and Ohio.

Are you still adding materials to the collection? All the time.

MINNESOTA

Institution: *Quatrefoil Library*

Address: 1619 Dayton Ave., #325
St. Paul, MN 55104

Phone number: (612) 641-0969

Collection name: Quatrefoil Library

Curator or contact person: David D. Irwin, executive director

Public service hours: 7 a.m. to 9:30 p.m., M-Th; 12 p.m. to 4:00 p.m., Saturday; and by appointment.

Restrictions on use: Anyone can use resources. To check out books, must be member.

Inclusive years represented in collection: Late nineteenth century to date.

Principal years represented in collection: 1953 to date.

Primary subjects included in the collection: Gay and lesbian fiction, non-fiction, biography, and periodicals.

Number of volumes: 5,000, includes videos, audiotapes, records, games, clippings file, newsletter file, AIDS file, art, and memorabilia.

Number of journals or newspapers currently on subscription: Approximately 30.

Bibliographic control provided: Materials listed on computer.

Published guides to the collection: No.

Date the collection was established: 1983—open to public February 1986.

History/Description of the collection: The Quatrefoil Library is a dream-come-true for David Irwin, a gay bookworm. In the mid-1970s both he and Dick Hewetson started collecting gay books. In 1977 they moved into a large condominium, combining collections in a linen closet. But as David continued to buy even more books, the collection soon outgrew the "closet." When the two parted in 1984 their more than 1,500 volumes remained united.

David and Dick's long-time dream of starting a lending library came true when Quatrefoil Library was incorporated as a not-for-profit organization in 1983. Late in 1985, the Minnesota Civil Liberties Union purchased a building in North Minneapolis and invited Quatrefoil to be a tenant. The dream library quietly went public on 4 February 1986.

During its first year, the collection and the use of the library grew so rapidly, it was soon apparent more space was needed. Thanks to the timely renovation of the Richards Gordon School in St. Paul, the library found a new and larger home. The library re-opened on 6 June 1987, with more than 4,000 volumes and over 300 gay and lesbian periodicals.

The library currently receives local, national, and international periodicals and houses a vast collection of memorabilia, clippings, historical erotica, and periodicals going back to the fifties.

Are you still adding materials to the collection? Yes.

NEW YORK

Institution: *National Museum of Lesbian & Gay History*

Address: 208 West 13 Street
New York, NY 10011

Phone number: (212) 620-7310

Collection name: Gay & Lesbian Center Archives

Curator or contact person: Rich Wandel, archivist

Public service hours: 8:00 p.m. to 10:00 p.m., T and Th; or by appointment.

Restrictions on use: Restrictions vary from collection to collection.

Inclusive years represented in collection: 1950 to present. Bulk is in the 1970s and 1980s.

Primary subjects included in the collection: Lesbian and gay history.

Secondary subjects included in the collection: AIDS.

Formats collected: All formats except books. We include many periodicals and newsletters, as well as one-of-a-kind organizational and personal papers. We also have audio and video tapes.

Bibliographic control provided: Standard archival methods and finding aids are used.

Date the collection was established: Spring 1990.

Are you still adding materials to the collection? Yes.

Institution: *L.H.E.F Inc.*

Address: PO Box 1258
New York, NY 10116

Phone number: (212) 874-7232

Collection name: "Lesbian Herstory Archives," formally Lesbian Herstory Educational Foundation, Inc.

Curator or contact person: Deborah Edel

Public service hours: By appointment. We are all volunteers so try calling evenings as well. We return long distance calls.

Restrictions on use: No material on loan—some materials have access restrictions because of issues of confidentiality.

Inclusive years represented in collection: Full scope of lesbian presence throughout history.

Principal years represented in collection: Later nineteenth and twentieth century.

Primary subjects included in the collection: All aspects of lesbian lives, history, culture, and literature.

Secondary subjects included in the collection: Feminist and gay men's material.

Formats collected: All forms: books, pamphlets, manuscripts, clippings, fliers, unpublished papers, diaries, letters, newsletters, journals and magazines, monographs, audio and visual tapes, records, graphics, posters, T-shirts, photographs, and other ephemera...etc.

Imprints collected: All material by and or about lesbian culture, lesbian life.

Number of volumes: As of 1986: 5,500+ books, 537 organizational files—648 subject files, 1,269 biographical files, plus manuscript and special collections as well as unpublished documents.

Number of journals or newspapers currently on subscription: As of 1986: 309 lesbian titles, 648 gay titles, 497 feminist titles, and 301 others.

Housing considerations: Housed in an apartment where two women live as well—takes up most of the large apartment. Material housed in acid-free boxes, permalife file folders, and mylar binders, on steel shelving and in file cabinets. Clippings often photocopied on acid-free paper. Alphabetized by women's first name. Storage units house additional materials. Graphics and audio tapes at second location.

Bibliographic control provided: We have developed our own subject headings in conjunction with Clare Potter of the Circle of Lesbian Indexes Project and other lesbian and gay archives and libraries. We have some materials on library cards and an increasing listing on computer (PC file database system). We will always maintain cards as well as printouts of computer listings for access. We publish occasional bibliographies.

Published guides to the collection: Newsletters 1-8 contain large bibliographic listings covering various aspects of the collection (at cost of photocopy and postage). We have published separate bibliographies. Computer printouts of subject headings and some other listings.

Other publications/services: L.H.A. Newsletter's "Preserving Your Individual and Community History" by Judith Schwarz.

Date the collection was established: 1974 as L.H.A.

History/Description of the collection: The "Lesbian Herstory Archives" is a resource and information center on all aspects of lesbian culture. Founded in the mid-1970s and incorporated in the late seventies as the Lesbian Herstory Educational Foundation, Inc., we function as a mixture of a library and a family album, a concrete expression of a people's refusal to lose their memory. In addition to housing the collection of materials, the LHEF, Inc. does speaking engagements and slide shows in order to share the cultural history with the community at large. It is and has always been staffed by volunteers.

Citation of descriptive articles about your collection: Descriptions of the LHEF, Inc. have appeared in many lesbian, gay, & feminist journals and magazines.

Are you still adding materials to the collection? Always.

OREGON

Institution: *Douglas County Gay Archives*

Address: PO Box 942
Dillard, OR 97432

Phone number: (503) 679-9913

Collection name: Douglas County Gay Archives

Curator or contact person: Billy Russo

Public service hours: None, by appointment only.

Restrictions on use: None.

Inclusive years represented in collection: 1950s to present.

Principal years represented in collection: 1981 to present.

Primary subjects included in the collection: Newsletters, magazines, letters, pamphlets, and articles stemming from gay/lesbian activism and homophobia. Includes 1/2" VCR video interviews with locals and photo albums depicting gay/lesbian life in rural Oregon.

Secondary subjects included in the collection: AIDS-related materials.

Formats collected: Primarily newsletters and magazines. Also articles about gay/lesbian lifestyle printed in local mainstream press.

Number of volumes: 125 newsletter and magazine titles, 10 floppy disks (PC), 25 1/2" VCR videos, 150 additional files.

Number of journals or newspapers currently on subscription: Approximately 100.

Housing considerations: Reading room of Gay & Lesbian Community Center, Rosebury, Oregon; Mixed Company, Myrtle Creek, Oregon; Ruby House, Dillard, Oregon; Trillium Valley Farm, Winston, Oregon.

Other publications/services: Ruby House Foundation Quarterly Report.

Date the collection was established: 1986.

History/Description of the collection: Established to archive relevant information regarding homophile movement in rural Oregon. Began in 1981 as a committee of Gay & Lesbian Alliance (Rosebury). We filed for incorporation in 1986.

Citation of descriptive articles about your collection: None.

Additional information: We are intent on collecting the materials. We have not established any procedures at this time.

Are you still adding materials to the collection? Yes.

TEXAS

Institution: *Dallas Gay/Lesbian Historic Archives*

Address: 6146 St. Moritz
Dallas, TX 75214

Phone number: (214) 821-1653

Collection name: Dallas Gay/Lesbian Historic Archives

Curator or contact person: Phil Johnson

Public service hours: Appointment only.

Restrictions on use: Nothing leaves this archives.

Inclusive years represented in collection: 1944 to present day.

Principal years represented in collection: Same.

Primary subjects included in the collection: Anything pertaining to gay and lesbian history especially as it pertains to Dallas area.

Secondary subjects included in the collection: The Lee Worshim Collection: Hollywood and Theatre Collection.

Formats collected: Books, magazines, buttons, T-shirts, posters, pamphlets, photographs, phonograph records, sculpture, oral history, newspaper clippings on anything about gays and lesbians. Also homophobic materials—remember Anita Bryant.

Number of journals or newspapers currently on subscription: 6.

Housing considerations: The archives is located in my home. Most of it is upstairs, some in my living room, and some in my office.

Bibliographic control provided: To save space, books are arranged according to height. Magazines according to name. Newspapers according to name. Buttons and T-shirts in a box. Posters in the attic. Photographs and slides in boxes. Sculpture and paintings on the walls. Newspaper clippings according to subject matter and date.

Published guides to the collection: No guides, no purchases.

Other publications/services: All is available for research. We also have a narrative, song, dance, slide, humor presentation called *The History of Gay and Lesbian Texans*, which travels around the state on occasion.

Date the collection was established: Informally, 1944.

History/Description of the collection: Growing up in the 1930s and 1940s I *never* heard of the words "homosexual" and "gay." Like millions of others, I thought I was "The only one in the world." Well, that shit has come to an end. Books, despite book burners and censors, have outlived empires. Truth will out. But if it is to do so, our history must be collected and handed down. Word of mouth won't do. Until recently, we had no history. Now we have. I started collecting things during World War II. Been collecting ever since.

Additional information: If one reads the history of the gay movements, one assumes that it exists on both coasts. Are there no homosexuals in middle America? In Texas? The purpose of this archives is to record gay Texas history.

Are you still adding materials to the collection? Yes.

———

Institution: *Metropolitan Community Church (of Houston)*

Address: 1919 Decatur
Houston, TX 77007

Phone number: (713) 861-9149

Collection name: Metropolitan Community Church (MCC) Library

Curator or contact person: Charles Botts

Public service hours: 9 a.m. to 6 p.m., M-F; 10 a.m. to 1 p.m., Sunday; special arrangements can be made for night access.

Restrictions on use: All books can be checked out, but only one at a time. Periodicals can be checked out if the library has a duplicate copy. Archival materials usually cannot be removed from the premises unless the circumstances warrant it.

Inclusive years represented in collection: Ancient Greek to present.

Principal years represented in collection: Twentieth century.

Primary subjects included in the collection: Gay/lesbian topics.

Secondary subjects included in the collection: Theology, Jungian psychology, and self-help psychology.

Formats collected: Books, periodicals, pamphlets, flyers, records, posters, buttons, artwork, obituaries, mailing lists, newsletters, files on gay/lesbian organizations and persons, photographs, audiotapes, videotapes, and newspaper clippings.

Number of volumes: 9,000 books and pamphlets on gay/lesbian topics; 4,000 books on theological topics; 500 books on self-help psychology and Jungian psychology; and thousands of periodicals, films, clippings, and the like.

Number of journals or newspapers currently on subscription: None. All of the library's periodicals are obtained from third-party sources.

Housing considerations: The theology collection is housed in the church's fellowship hall. The gay/lesbian material is housed in an adjacent room. Periodicals are stored in acid-free storage boxes. Posters are stored in a special storage bin. Buttons are mounted on a burlap covered board. Filing cabinets are used for other collections.

Bibliographic control provided: A cataloging system was devised on a MacII system using Hypercard.

Published guides to the collection: The library can generate printouts of the entire inventory of the collection. A self-published bibliography and index may at some point in the future be mailed out to various collectors and institutions. The only two guides that are currently mailed out are duplicate periodicals from the MCC collection available for deaccession and trade and duplicate books from the MCC collection available for deaccession and trade.

Other publications/services: The parent organization publishes a newsletter.

Date the collection was established: 1977.

History/Description of the collection: For several years there were two rival gay/lesbian archives in Houston. The smaller of the two collections was called The Gay/Lesbian Archives of Houston. It originated in 1971 in Fort Worth and was called The Aura Library. It was acquired, or rather it merged, in 1986 with the MCC Collection. There are too many war stories about the library's history to relate in the space provided.

Citation of descriptive articles about your collection: Darbonne, Sheri Cohen. "Expansion of Houston's Gay and Lesbian Archives May Lead to Move." *The New Voice* (12-15 April 1991): 2; Darbonne, Sheri Cohen. "Vast Array of Gay Literature Available at MCCR Library." *Montrose Voice* (16 December 1986): 5.

Additional information: The library is interested in trading duplicate archival material with other interested institutions, deaccession lists will be exchanged for other deaccession lists.

Are you still adding materials to the collection? Yes, the library acquires ten new titles to the gay/lesbian collection each week. Numerous periodicals are received weekly.

CANADA

Institution: *Canadian Gay Archives*

Address: Box 639
Station A
Toronto, Ontario, Canada M5W 1G2

Phone number: (416) 921-6310

Collection name: Canadian Gay Archives

Curator or contact person: Harold Averill, president

Public service hours: 7:30 p.m. to 10 p.m. and by appointment, T-Th.

Restrictions on use: Some of the holdings of archival materials are restricted by the donors.

Inclusive years represented in collection: c. 1880 to present.

Principal years represented in collection: 1970 to present.

Primary subjects included in the collection: Materials in any format relating to lesbians and gays, with an emphasis on Canada but including other countries.

Secondary subjects included in the collection: Pornography, censorship, transsexualism, and transvestism.

Formats collected: Records of organizations and papers of individuals, periodicals, books, pamphlets, posters, newspapers and other printed material, audio and video tapes, microform; artifacts including buttons and banners, matchbook covers, uniforms, T-shirts, and so on.

Imprints collected: Anything published by gay and lesbian organizations and presses, or by non-gay/lesbian organizations and presses about lesbians and gays.

Number of volumes: James Fraser Library contains about 3,500 books, 600 pamphlets, over 2,000 titles of lesbian and gay journals; material about lesbians and gays from about 1,500 non-lesbian/gay publications; clippings from Canadian daily press from across Canada.

Number of journals or newspapers currently on subscription: About 200 lesbian/gay journals on subscription.

Housing considerations: Books are cataloged according to a system worked out in Los Angeles for lesbian/gay libraries; lesbian/gay periodicals and non-lesbian/gay periodicals are filed in alphabetical order by title, press clippings are filed chronologically, all in acid-free containers, records/papers of gay and lesbian individuals and organizations are arranged by accession number according to archival principles and in acid-free files and containers; vertical files are filed by country in filing cabinets.

Bibliographic control provided: See above for books, pamphlets are filed by accession number, with card indexes for both being produced; accession files, provenance cards, basic cross-reference cards, and finding aids are produced for archival materials as time permits, Kardex is produced for lesbian/gay periodical titles.

Published guides to the collection: Canadian materials have been listed in *Homosexuality in Canada: A Bibliography*, 2d ed., comp. by William Crawford. (1984); lesbian and gay periodicals are presently being listed in an anthology of lesbian and gay periodicals; materials in the archives also entered in other publications by the archives and periodically referred to in our newsletter, the *Gay Archivist*.

Other publications/services: *Gay Archivist* (newsletter, published occasionally). List of publications includes the following: *Homosexuality in Canada: A Bibliography*. Comp. by Alex Spence. (1979), 85; *The Genetic Imperative: Fact and Fantasy in Sociobiology*. Comp. by Alan V. Miller. (1979), 107; *Ian Young: A Bibliography (1962-1980)*. (1981), 58; *Lesbian Periodical Holdings in the Canadian Gay*

Archives. Comp. by Alan V. Miller. (1981), 15. Out of print; *Lesbian and Gay Heritage of Toronto.* (1982), 12. Out of print; *Homosexuality in Ancient Greek and Roman Civilization.* Comp. by Beert C. Verstraete. (1982), 14. Out of print; *Gays and Acquired Immune Deficiency Syndrome (AIDS): A Bibliography.* Comp. by Alan V. Miller. 1st ed. (November 1982), 21; 2d ed. (May 1983), 67. Out of print; Fraser, James A., and Harold A. Averill. *Organizing an Archives: The Canadian Gay Archives Experience.* (1983), 68. 3d printing, (1989); *Homosexuality in Canada: A Bibliography.* 2d ed. Comp. by William Crawford (1984), 378; *Medical Social and Political Aspects of the Acquired Immune Deficiency Syndrome (AIDS) Crisis.* Comp. by Donald W. McLeod and Alan V. Miller. (1985), 314. Out of print; *The Writings of Dr. Magnus Hirschfeld: A Bibliography.* Comp. and introduced by James D. Steakley. (1985), 54; *Our Own Voices: Lesbian and Gay Periodicals Through Time.* Comp. by Alan V. Miller. (September 1989).

Date the collection was established: 1973.

History/Description of the collection: Begun in 1973 as the records of *The Body Politic*; created one of the divisions of Pink Triangle Press, 1975; incorporated independently, 1980; charitable status granted, 1981.

Citation of descriptive articles about your collection: The following feature articles: Bebout, Rick. "Stashing the Evidence." *The Body Politics* 55 (August 1979): 21-22, 26; MacDonald, Stephen. "Diggers." *The Body Politic* 108 (November 1984): 35-36; Stuart Timmons, "The Future of the Past: Who Controls Gay History?" *Advocate* (27 May 1986), has a section (pp. 30-33) on Gay/Lesbian Archives, including the CGA.

Additional information: Douglas, John W.A. "Gay Archives: The Canadian Gay Archives: For Lesbians and Gay Men."*TGA Bulletin* 83, no. 6 (1983): 16; numerous reviews of our publications, including Robert French's review of Fraser, James A., and Harold A. Averill. "Organizing an Archives: The Canadian Gay Archives Experience." *Archives and Manuscripts* 13, no. 1 (May 1985): 63-64.

Are you still adding materials to the collection? Yes.

———

Institution: *Homophile Association of London Ontario (HALO Club)*

Address: 649 Colburne St.
London, Ontario Canada
N6A 3Z2

Phone number: (519) 433-3762

Collection name: HALO Library

Curator or contact person: Richard Hudler

Public service hours: 7 p.m. to 10 p.m., M.

Restrictions on use: Materials may not be removed from the building. A photocopier is available at $.05 a copy.

Inclusive years represented in collection: 1970 to present.

Primary subjects included in the collection: Gay/lesbian.

Formats collected: Books, newsletters, pamphlets, correspondence, some audiotapes and videotapes.

Number of volumes: Unknown.

Housing considerations: Filing cabinet, boxes, and shelving.

Bibliographic control provided: Very poor.

Other publications/services: HALO newsletter.

Date the collection was established: 1970.

History/Description of the collection: Files and records of the HALO Club since its beginning are The Homophile Association of The University of Western Ontario in 1970. The Homophile Association of London Ontario (HALO Club) is a membership operated, non-profit organization incorporated by letters patent in the Province of Ontario, (corporate $2919151) 16 July 1974. The objects of the association are to provide services and facilities to meet the social, cultural, psychological and spiritual needs to the members of the homophile community; to act as a referral source to the members of the homophile community with medical, legal, psychological, and spiritual problems; and to provide a program to assist in the integration through education of individuals of different sexual orientations.

Are you still adding materials to the collection? Yes.

———

Institution: *Winnipeg Gay/Lesbian Resource Centre*

Address: Box 1661
Winnipeg, Manitoba, Canada, R3C 2Z6
or 1 - 222 Osborne St. South
Winnipeg, Manitoba, Canada, R3L 1Z3

Phone number: (204) 284-5208

Collection name: Winnipeg Gay/Lesbian Resource Centre Library and Manitoba Gay/Lesbian Archives

Public service hours: 7:30 a.m. to 10 p.m., M-F; other hours change with seasons; call for further information.

Restrictions on use: No one is denied access. Books lent for three-week periods. Archive materials must be used on premises; some donors impose restrictions.

Inclusive years represented in collection: 1950 to present.

Principal years represented in collection: 1972 to present.

Primary subjects included in the collection: Homosexuality, lesbianism, sexuality, gay liberation, and homosexuality in Manitoba.

Secondary subjects included in the collection: AIDS/STDS.

Formats collected: Books, newspapers, pamphlets, flyers, buttons, banners posters, audiotapes, videotapes, and artifacts.

Imprints collected: Any gay- or lesbian-related materials.

Number of volumes: Books—3,000; periodicals—60 meters; archival records—20 meters; audiotapes—200 hours; and videotapes—450 hours.

Number of journals or newspapers currently on subscription: About 40.

Housing considerations: Books, periodicals, files are given locator numbers/accession numbers. Storage controls are minimal, it has been decided that the acid content of the paper makes it impossible to conserve collection in present form. As the material is relatively new, microfilming or a similar storage means will be necessary in the future.

Bibliographic control provided: All materials are catalogued according to the classification system of the International Gay/Lesbian Library/Archives Index. Computer-generated card catalogues are filed in a Master Index. As we are a small collection, controls are of low importance.

Published guides to the collection: No, only in-house finding aids and guides are available.

Other publications/services: Professional research services are available for hire. Books are lent via mail to persons in adjoining provinces.

Date the collection was established: 1972.

History/Description of the collection: The Winnipeg Gay/Lesbian Resource Centre Collection was begun in 1972 at the University of Manitoba by a group called Gays For Equality. In 1983, it was moved to the Winnipeg Gay Community Centre, where the collection was expanded to include the records of additional local gay organizations and book collections of two other organizations. In 1988, the Winnipeg Gay/Lesbian Resource Centre was established, on the dissolution of the Winnipeg Gay Centre, to house and preserve the collection. The collection is recognized locally to be a significant collection in its documentation of civil rights and social history of the province.

Citation of descriptive articles about your collection: Sorry, we can't say at the moment. We don't keep a running list, although we do collect them—the few that there are.

Additional information: Materials originating in Manitoba are our main interest. This is followed by Canada, North America, and Europe.

Are you still adding materials to the collection? Yes, gifts are added regularly. No annual budget is allotted for purchases but rather as materials are identified as significant to the collection.

DIRECTORY 3: NON-RESPONDENTS
(IN ORDER BY STATE, THEN COLLECTION)

CALIFORNIA

Center for Research & Education in Sexuality
San Francisco State University
San Francisco, CA 94132

Contemporary Issues Collection
Department of Special Collections
University of California Library
Davis, CA 95616

Gay History Film Project
PO Box 77043
San Francisco, CA 94107

International Gay/Lesbian Archive
Natalie Barney/Edward Carpenter Library
Box 38100
Los Angeles, CA 90038

Meiklejohn Civil Liberties Library
Box 673
Berkeley, CA 94701

Midpeninsula Nonviolent Library
457 Kingsley Street
Box 1001
Palo Alto, CA 94301

National Clearinghouse on Marital Rape and Women's
History Research Center
2325 Oak Street
Berkeley, CA 94708

One Institute, Inc.
3340 Country Club Drive
Los Angeles, CA 90019

San Francisco Bay Area Gay/Lesbian Historical Society
Box 42332
San Francisco, CA 94191

CONNECTICUT

Institute of Social Ethics
1 Gold Street, #22-ABC
Hartford, CT 06103

KANSAS

T.S. Library
2425 Indiana
Box 1144
Topeka, KS 66601

LOUISIANA

Homosexual Information Center Library
115 Monroe Street
Bossier City, LA 71111

MASSACHUSETTS

New Alexandria Lesbian Library
Box 402, Florence Station
Northampton, MA 01060

Science for the People
897 Main Street
Cambridge, MA 02139

Vocations for Social Change
353 Broadway
Cambridge, MA 02139

MICHIGAN

Alternative Press Collection
Oakland University Library
Rochester, MI 48063

MONTANA

Out in Montana Resource Center
Box 7223
Missoula, MT 59807

NEVADA

Baker Archives
350 S. Center Street, #350
Reno, NV 89501

NEW MEXICO

The University of New Mexico
General Library
Albuquerque, NM 87131
(Collection is unprocessed; prefers not to be included in the
directory as yet.)

NEW YORK

Buffalo Women's Oral History Project
255 Parkside Avenue
Buffalo, NY 14214

Center for Lesbian & Gay Studies
c/o Center for the Study of Women in Society
Graduate Center
City University of New York
33 West 42nd Street
New York, NY 10036

Gay Alliance of the Genesee Valley Library
713 Monroe Avenue
Rochester, NY 14607

Human Sexuality Collection
(includes Mariposa Foundation Archives)
101 Olin Library
Cornell University
Ithaca, NY 14853-5301

Latina Lesbian History Project
Box 627, Stuyvesant Station
New York, NY 10009

Mattachine Society
59 Christopher St.
New York, NY 10014

Moncada Library
434 5th Avenue
Brooklyn, NY 10018

Washington Square Library for Social Change
133 West 4th Street
New York, NY 10012

Wason-Echols Collection
107-E Olin Library
Cornell University
Ithaca, NY 14853-5301

NORTH CAROLINA

The Feminist Library
c/o Y.W.C.A.
809 Rector Street
Durham, NC 27707

OHIO

Committee on Social Movements and May 4th Collection
Archives Department
Kent State University Library
Kent, OH 44242

PENNSYLVANIA

Black Gay Archives
Box 30004
Philadelphia, PA 19103

Gay & Lesbian Library/Archives of Philadelphia
3500 Lancaster Avenue
Box 15748
Philadelphia, PA 19103

SOUTH CAROLINA

Right/Left Collection
Information Files
Robert Scott Small Library
College of Charleston
Charleston, SC 29401

TENNESSEE

Tennessee Lesbian Archives
c/o Hornsby
6401 Nightingale Lane, N.107
Knoxville, TN 37909

TEXAS

Gay & Lesbian Archives of Texas
201 Peach Street
Denton, TX 76201

WASHINGTON, DC

Triangle Institute
Box 2296
Washington, DC 20013

CANADA

Archives Gaies du Quebec
CP 395 succ Place du Parc
Montreal, Quebec H2W 2N9

Gay Archives Collection
Box 3130, MPO
Vancouver, British Columbia V6B 3X6

Hamilton-Wentworth Gay Archives
Box 44, Station B
Hamilton, Ontario L8L 7T5

Lesbian and Gay History Group of Toronto
Box 639, Station A
Toronto, Ontario M5W 1G2

Womansline Books
711 Richmond Street
London, Ontario N6A 3H1

PRESERVING THE U.S. UNDERGROUND AND ALTERNATIVE PRESS OF THE 1960S AND '70S: HISTORY, PROSPECTS, AND MICROFORM SOURCES

Daniel C. Tsang

Tsang is a social sciences bibliographer and lecturer at the University of California, Irvine. He is a volunteer indexer for the *Alternative Press Index*, and indexed the first twelve issues of *Covert Action Information Bulletin*, as well as two biographies by former CIA officers. His review of anti-surveillance periodicals in *Library Journal* was the only material released from his CIA file; the remainder of his dossier remains classified for national security reasons. He reviews Asian American and lesbian and gay periodicals for *Magazines for Libraries*, edits *Alternative Collections* and *UCInsider*, and heads the Lesbian and Gay Declassified Documentation Project. He serves on the editorial boards of *Journal of Homosexuality* and *Paidika*.

Acknowledgment: This article is based in part on research first conducted at the University of Michigan (Tsang, 1977). Thanks to the following for their assistance: Elaine Clever and Tom Whitehead, Temple University; Kathy Ratliff, UMI; Bill Walker, Gay and Lesbian Historical Society of Northern California; Keith McKinney, New York Public Library; Jim Danky, State Historical Society of Wisconsin; Chuck Eckman and Bill Roberts, University of California, Berkeley; Sara Eichhorn, Kevin Fredette, and Eric MacDonald, University of California, Irvine; and UCI student assistants Jonathan Bloomfield and Eddie Lee for their cheerfulness in providing research help. Errors are the author's responsibility, of course. Please report any errors, missing microform titles, or new titles as they are filmed, to the author at 380 Main Library, University of California, PO Box 19557, Irvine, CA 92713; (714) 856-4978, dtsang@uci.edu.

What constitutes the underground or alternative press of the 1960s and 1970s is a matter of dispute. Various compilers or observers have defined the press in different ways. Robert H. Muller subtitled his classic two-volume study, *From Radical Left to Extreme Right*, as follows: "A bibliography of current periodicals of protest, controversy, advocacy, or dissent...."[1] The *Alternative Press Index* in 1969 was subtitled: "An index to the publications which amplify the cry for social change and social justice."[2] Danky, in his introduction to *Undergrounds: A Union List...*, noted that "no two definitions are likely to be the same."[3] Lutz preferred "alternative press," since the periodicals attempted to "present an alternative to the establishment press."[4] In a subsequent edition of what he continued nonetheless to call *Underground Press Directory*, Lutz dismissed "underground" as a "poor word" to describe the publications, since they are "certainly very open and above ground."[5] Furthermore, Cook, in a critical essay, argued that the "underground press of the late 1960s...was not written for workers," but instead "appealed primarily to middle-class youth who had the money and leisure time to explore 'lifestyles' that posed alternatives to the 'nine to five' work week that threatened to engulf them." The term was "an inaccurate name used mostly for its romantic connotations," according to Cook.[6] What seems clear is that underground press, as contemporaries defined it, applied to the publications generated by the social and political upheavals that erupted in the 1960s; Spiers argued that before 1965 the underground press just did not exist.[7] It did, of course, but not in the way we later understood it. Zald and Whitaker have gone even further, arguing that, in the United States, the underground press of the Vietnam era never existed, since the publishers were not "secretive, covert organizations," except for the Weather Underground.[8]

In this essay, the focus is on social change or radical publications in the United States published during the 1960s and 1970s. Unlike most studies of the period that betray a cultural bias by focusing only on papers edited by white men, I will aim to be more ecumenical and include among the underground and alternative press those published by and for ethnic, feminist, and gay communities.

THE CASE FOR MICROFILMING THE UNDERGROUND AND ALTERNATIVE PRESS

Why should one attempt to preserve the underground or alternative press in microform? Very simply it is because film, under archival conditions, lasts much longer than newsprint. But that answer, of course, is inadequate. Is the press *worth* preserving?

Xerox University Microfilms [now University Microfilms International] apparently felt that some of the underground press material of the time was "in poor taste" and initially stopped microfilming it, according to then-UMI official Stevens Rice, who was an instructor of reprography at the University of Michigan when he made this remark. Indeed, Muller has noted that:

> A great obstacle is the traditional concern of librarians about quality. The main purpose of book selection, in professional rhetoric, is to choose the good, screen out the shoddy, and build up a "choice" collection that will educate and elevate the public by offering them the "best." Yet, considerations of "quality" may be inappropriate when it comes to choosing polemic tracts. How important, after all, is the style in which an opinion is expressed? What if a viewpoint be printed on poor paper, with bad typography, many errors in spelling, inelegant language, and much profanity? What if the reasoning be illogical? The drawings lacking in artistry? What if this viewpoint so shoddily tricked out is, furthermore, read eagerly by only a few hundred or a few thousand people? A tract, though half-literate, is still a document. If it puts forward myths or lies, with intent to deceive, should it be excluded? On such grounds many librarians reject astrology, numerology, palmistry, descriptions of dubious medical cures, etc. It is hard to know where to draw the line. What a librarian should avoid is excluding a point of view because he is offended by the way in which it is presented.[9]

It is incumbent upon librarians and other library workers of today not to act as censors of what future generations may want to read. What is good or poor taste, after all, is a variable across time and among people. Taste should not be the criterion to base a decision on whether or not one should preserve the underground and alternative press. Who are we to prevent future historians from studying the protest movements of the 1960s and its associated ephemera, just because we happen to be hung up over quality? Nor should political correctness dictate our decisions in collection development or preservation.[10] Our role as library workers is to preserve research materials for posterity and to provide service—in public libraries as in academic libraries—to all patrons, whether serious researchers or not. Our role is definitely not to act as guardians of morality or of establishment views.

Several dozen libraries already maintain special collections of underground or alternative publications [11,12,13] and students and faculty have used these resources for casual reading or serious study.[14] Additional community-based movement archives abound, especially those collecting lesbian and gay periodicals.[15,16] The fact that only a limited number of academic libraries maintain such collections underscores the need for improved access to the material. Ease of access can be facilitated if these materials are preserved and microform copies distributed.

Judith F. Krug, who directs the American Library Association's Office for Intellectual Freedom, was quoted (in an undated Bell and Howell advertisement for the Underground Newspaper Microfilm Collection circulating in the 1970s) as follows: "In the long run, the newspapers will have great historical and research value. Unfortunately, the stock on which they are printed is not of the best quality, and immediate attempts to preserve them must be made. If this is not done, the whole period of turmoil that we are currently experiencing will be lost to history." In the same brochure, Herbert Finch, curator and archivist at Cornell University, was quoted as saying:

> I think that a compilation of these newspapers, easily available on microfilm, should become an outstanding source of information for scholars who wish to study in this era of student unrest and rebellion which has been so influential on contemporary history. Since these papers, even at the time of publication, are very difficult to acquire through ordinary channels, I think that it is most important that you try to make your filmed set as comprehensive as possible.

The fact that many institutions of higher education have deemed it important to collect and preserve such "ephemera" attests to the necessity of preserving such material on film, as well as facilitating access to the material (through sale and loan of film).

Beyond preservation and ease of access, there are several more reasons why the alternative press should be microfilmed. In those libraries that currently subscribe to such publications, space can be a problem, which would be partly resolved by keeping the material on film. A more important factor would be that wear and tear will cause the material to deteriorate. Another major consideration is the risk of loss, through fire, damage, or theft. A microfilm master of a periodical, stored safely, will thus ensure that the serial is not lost forever.

The passion of the underground and alternative press has also been preserved, so to speak, in sporadic reprint editions, or in collected essays. The 1991 facsimile edition of the *San Francisco Oracle* is a welcome development, but many other alternative titles have been reprinted in full runs or in selected anthologies (see appendix A).

Finally it is often suggested that maintaining microfilmed copies rather than hard copies of a run of periodicals will be less costly,[17] especially taking into consideration the cost of binding the latter. These days, one would not want to recommend binding newsprint. Big business, however, will not be rushing to microfilm the alternative press, unless it can make a profit off the product. When I enquired of UMI in 1980 if it was interested in filming a publication I edited, *Gay Insurgent*, the response was: UMI was interested in indexed titles with "high circulation" in libraries. Otherwise, "we ask that a list of customers and their firm orders be provided so that we can determine whether a real need exists to justify the cost of filming."[18] The title *did* get filmed for the Underground Press Collection, but it is not available separately on film.

Marshall suggests that if profit-making is the only reason big business is willing to microfilm these titles, then library workers need to take action and organize to pressure the American Library Association to do the preservation work.[19]

PROGRESS TO DATE

What has been done in the microreproduction on film of the underground and alternative press? Two contrasting projects are illustrative.

Underground Press Collection (Bell & Howell/UMI)

The first, indeed massive, attempt to microfilm the alternative press was undertaken in the late 1960s by the Microphoto Division of Bell and Howell. Its Underground Newspaper Microfilm Collection [subsequently called Underground Press Collection, see appendix B] was heralded as an "unbiased view of the '60s and '70s" in its promotional literature, and comprised initially some 600 titles. However, reviewers to a person panned the initial release of the collection.

The basic criticism was over the lack of a system. Ed Weber, longtime curator of the University of Michigan's Labadie Collection, believes the firm apparently at the time filmed only what they could get their hands on. He had spent two days examining some rolls from the collection, borrowed from the Center for Research Libraries. The notes he took at that time, preserved in the Labadie Collection, give ample proof to the charge that the collection was haphazardly compiled. A number of titles were thrown together in a roll, and some titles only were represented by one issue. Indeed, the circulation librarian for the Center for Research Libraries felt impelled to issue a memo (dated 8 February 1971) stating:

> A few words of explanation might save you from the utter confusion (of) the microfilm of the Underground Newspaper Collection. The holdings for each title are very incomplete and appear on different roles (sic).

Despite the firm's claim that "an exhaustive effort was made by both Bell & Howell and the office of the Underground Press Syndicate in an attempt to find any and all missing issues and titles," it was clear that the firm merely filmed what the syndicate happened to have available.[20] Ed Weber found that the Labadie Collection had more complete runs of some of the titles initially filmed sporadically in the B&H Collection.

It was also found that in spite of a claim of maintaining "the highest possible quality of readability," one reviewer had to constantly refocus the microfilm reader.[21] Weber found the first page of the *Baltimore Free Press* (roll 5) to be "very black, no volume or number distinguishable." Pages appeared to be missing, and it was unclear if this was due to an error in filming, or if the pages were actually missing from the original. Obviously the absence of explanatory targets (e.g., PAGES LACKING) compounded the problem.

In a devastatingly critical review titled "Bawl & Howl,"[22] Marshall blasted the poor quality of the filming, the gaps in long runs, sparsely represented number of titles, and the total absence of any subject access. She levelled her sharpest barbs against B&H for trying to place profit over quality. Indeed, the entry for her review in the index to volume one of *Booklegger* says it all: PUBLISHING—MICROFORM RIP-OFFS.

The reviewer for *Microform Reviews*, while congratulating B&H for undertaking the project, pointed out similar flaws in the collection, including missing issues and pages. Dorothy Martin concluded by calling the collection "both expensive and frustrating."[23]

The table of contents provided with the collection did not provide sufficient ease of access. Later, various attempts were made to index titles in the collection, to supplement titles already indexed in the *Alternative Press Index*.

In 1970 B&H had made an effort to provide subject access to the collection through the indexing efforts of the volunteers who were then compiling the *Alternative Press Index*. The bid did not succeed, as Mary McKenney of the index staff subsequently reported:

> [t]he problem was that the publications they microfilmed weren't necessarily the ones we indexed. So they had another bright idea: we could microfilm them, and *then* "give" away the Index with the package. When we asked what we were to get out of the deal, they said, we'd get *not only* all that good (?) publicity for being connected with them, but also a free copy of the film! This was supposed to make up for all the extra expense of printing enough copies of the Index to accommodate them...and we knew no one would benefit from the deal except B&H.[24]

Subsequently, the American Library Association's Social Responsibilities Round Table was solicited by B&H to produce a subject index to the collection. Space was provided at the ALA convention to solicit volunteers. Dependent as it was on unpaid labor, the indexing never materialized. Marshall blames B&H for not wanting to spend the money to index the collection, citing Block in his letter to the Bay Area SRRT: "We find that librarians sometimes forget that organizations like ours must answer to a corporate entity. The name of what we are trying to do here is 'make profit'."[25]

Overall, while the number of titles microfilmed is impressive, the fact that individual titles are not available for purchase (in addition to the flaws already described) reduces the usefulness of the collection.

In the 1990s with Bell & Howell having taken over UMI, and with UMI distributing this collection, supplementing it with additional titles, and filling in gaps, such as with issues from the Hoover Institution and from the University of Missouri holdings, there is some optimism that a renewed effort to preserve these emphemeral materials is again upon us. UMI has also begun filming a new set, Alternative Press Collection, with issues dating from 1986. Fortunately, the problems that plagued the earlier B&H collection appear to have been largely resolved today; the technical quality should be greatly improved, now that UMI is filming it. Some libraries, however, especially those belonging to the Association for Research Libraries, already subscribe to many if not most of the titles in the new collection, and may not feel they can justify expending more money to acquire this set. At one ARL institution, the University of California, Irvine, the majority of the 1980s titles were already in the collection, often backed up with individual microfilm subscriptions. However, in 1991, the University of California, Santa Cruz, acquired the Alternative Press Collection through the UC-system's shared acquisitions program, meaning the collection will be loanable among UC-campuses and Stanford, with access via reel guides placed on all campuses.

Harvester Press Collections

Although this essay focuses on the underground and alternative press in the United States, a look at what has occurred abroad is appropriate here. In contrast to what has happened in the United States, from England has emerged a very different microfilming enterprise, the filming of current and retrospective runs of Britain's underground and alternative press. The project was everything (almost) that the B&H project was not. Every attempt was made to locate the materials, and separate fiches or roll films are used for separate titles. Explanatory targets are utilized, and an external finding aid (including location designations and a bibliographic essay) is provided. The collection resides mostly on silver halide standard microfiche, with some parts on 35mm silver halide roll film, where merited by reduction size.

The relevant collection included *The Underground and Alternative Press in Britain since 1961* and its various updates, *The Left in Britain*, *The Anarchist Press in Britain*, and *Sexual Politics in Britain*, containing publications of the women's and gay liberation movements.

Reviewers have consistently praised the collection. "Harvester Press has performed the Herculean task of collecting and assembling a comprehensive set of "underground" newspapers, which it has made available in a well-packaged microform edition. An exemplary bibliographical guide, including an illuminating introductory essay by John Spiers, testifies to the richness and diversity of the assortment," wrote Koss in *Microform Review*.[26]

Martin was likewise effusive in his praise of Harvester Press for "the comprehensiveness...(and) meticulous work evident in the production of this microform collection of British underground and alternative newspapers. Congratulations, Harvester Press, for a job well done!"[27]

Indeed, the Harvester Press collections appear to be many times superior to the original B&H collection, with its usefulness enhanced by the bibliographic guide compiled by Spiers.[28] The ability to acquire individual titles, without purchasing the set, is another attractive feature. It is not surprising that Harvester was given the Queen's Award for Export Achievement in 1986.[29]

Other Projects

A brief comment is appropriate here about other projects. Women's liberation movement publications have been preserved in the massive Herstory Collection (see appendix C), produced by the Women's History Research Center in Berkeley. The initial release of the collection merited a congratulatory review by Piddington in *Microforms Review*, who called it a "remarkably complete collection," although excitement at the availability of such a comprehensive source (especially of U.S. women's liberation periodicals) was tempered by frustration at the inadequate finding aids.[30] Access was improved subsequently with the cataloging of titles in the supplements to this collection.[31] Related microform collections produced by the Women's History Research Center comprise *Women and Law* and *Women and Health/Mental Health*. The National Women's History Project (7738 Bell Road, Windsor, CA 95492), is currently handling distribution of these collections.[32]

Other micropublishers have engaged in filming radical publications dating from even before the 1960s turmoil, and "underground press" materials are often included in their collections, as is the case with *Radical Periodicals in the United States, 1880-1960* (Greenwood Press) and *Socialist Party of America Papers* (Microfilming Corporation of America) both released in 1975. Greenwood also has released *Black Journals: Periodicals Resources for Afro-American and African Studies*, in 1971. Furthermore there are projects filming special collections at libraries. Clearwater and MCA filmed Native American periodicals at various libraries (UPA now distributes them); a selection appears in appendix D. Right-wing titles from 1918-1977 were filmed at the University of Iowa by University Microfilm Corporation of America, as the *Right Wing Collection*; and radical pamphlets have been filmed at the University of Michigan (see below). Finally, individual contracts have been made with individual alternative press publishers to micropublish their titles.

Among libraries or archives with active microfilming programs concerning radical periodicals, the State Historical Society of Wisconsin is without peer. In fact, it is the only major library to aggressively seek out, collect, and preserve underground and alternative press material, all over the United States, and has done so since 1967.[33] A clue to its holdings can be found in its publication, *Periodicals and Newspapers Acquired by the State Historical Society of Wisconsin Library*.[34] The periodicals listed are accessible by subject (e.g., "Alternatives") with an indication as to whether it is filmed by the society (see appendix E). Individual titles on microform are also cataloged on OCLC.

The University of California is another institution that has participated in efforts to preserve these publications, especially Chicano movement publications, those of the lesbian/gay liberation movement, and leaflets distributed on the Berkeley campus. The holdings of Berkeley's Chicano Studies Library have been filmed by Library Microfilms of Sunnyvale, California (see appendix F). Quotes for individual reels are available.

Further, as a result of a joint project between the university and the Gay and Lesbian Historical Society of Northern California, Bay Area lesbian and gay periodicals have been preserved on microfilm by the university library on the Berkeley campus. The latter project was supported with the university system's shared acquisitions funds, and the film is shareable among UC and Stanford campuses and beyond.[35] (Berkeley's holdings of these lesbian and gay titles are most accessible through its GLADIS catalog, now searchable by remote access. The UC-system catalog, MELVYL, also contains the records. MELVYL is also accessible remotely. The full Chicano Studies Library serials collection, however, is not on MELVYL.)

UC Berkeley's University Archives has also microfilmed its "Sather Gate Handbill Collection," which includes leaflets passed out on the Berkeley campus during the Free Speech Movement in 1964 through the turmoil of the Vietnam War protests. The five-reel collection is available for purchase.[36,37] While not microfilmed, selected issues of periodicals from the period also form part of the Bancroft Library's Social Protest Collection at UC Berkeley, according to the finding aid for the collection.[38]

The Labadie Collection at the University of Michigan has microfilmed its pamphlets on anarchism and communism, including those published in the 1960s and 1970s. The microform sets form part of a series, *Radical Pamphlets in American Collections*, produced by Chadwyck Healey.

The New York Public Library is well known among connoisseurs of the genre for its select collection of erotica, acquired from nearby 42nd Street magazine dealers during regular forays by librarians into the neighborhood. Selections of these magazines, many from the 1960s and 1970s, have been microfilmed for posterity and are accessible through its catalog and on RLIN.[39,40] In addition, at the initiative of Keith McKinney, periodicals librarian at NYPL, a project was begun to microfilm selected lesbian and gay periodicals from around the United States and abroad.[41] With the imminent arrival of Father Timothy Healy as NYPL president, the fear that his anti-gay record (while he was Georgetown University president) would put an end to the project resulted in the staff reportedly scurrying to finish the project before that happened.[42,43]

Of course, research libraries routinely back up newsprint material on microform, but locating what has been filmed is a difficult task, unless the library itself issues microforms holdings lists. Since not all libraries notify the office of the National Register of Microform Masters about their filming, there is, in effect, no central directory that lists all library-filmed serials. *Guide to Microforms in Print* remains an indispensable source, and more and more libraries are cataloging their microform serials on OCLC or RLIN. Micropublishers also need to be more concerned about bibliographic control of microform sets, and seek better ways of having their microform masters registered.[44]

Because there is no consensus on subject cataloging of even individual serials in microform, title access is often the only way to locate these holdings. Searching by series title (e.g., "San Francisco Bay Area Lesbian and Gay Periodicals Collection") is another option where there are distinct series tracings. As more and more libraries opt for local computerized cataloging systems, title access should continue to be provided for the alternative press that form part of microform sets. Subject access needs to be improved, but in the meantime the best printed guide to a library's print and film holdings of underground, alternative, and ethnic periodicals is one put out by John Liberty at California State University Library in Sacramento: entries in his *Journals of Dissent and Social Change* take up 518 pages.[45] It is a worthy project even in these days of online catalogs.

Temple University's Contemporary Culture Collection has preserved on film some of the alternative titles for which it could not get commercially filmed copies,[46] including a number of gay titles[47] (see appendix G). Quotes on individual reels are also available. But as budget woes affect more and more research collections, the monies available to do preservation microfilming are fast disappearing.

Empirical Findings

In a mid-1970s attempt to compile data on the extent of micropublishing of alternative media, publications indexed by the Alternative Press Centre (leaving out earlier indexed titles, but including titles listed in its *Alternative Press Index* for 1975, which had just appeared) were compared with titles reported as being available for purchase in microform, using standard sources. Of the 151 titles then being indexed by the center, only 66, or 44 percent, were found to be available individually in microform.[48] (Titles in the B&H Collection, for instance, were not counted.)

More recent research undertaken for this article indicates that less than a third of the approximately 240 titles indexed in the October/December 1989 issue of *Alternative Press Index* are preserved as individually available microfilmed titles. Interestingly, the findings indicate that most publications are being microfilmed by UMI, despite its earlier apparent abhorrence of "bad taste."

HOW ALTERNATIVE PUBLICATIONS CAN GET TO BE PRESERVED

A brief biographical digression may be illustrative here. This author's graduate education at the University of Michigan in Ann Arbor in the 1970s was intertwined with passionate participation in the radical student and alternative press movements. Those were days of turmoil, as striking teaching assistants practically closed down the university in a month-long walkout, and Third World students took over the administration building and camped out for days in the president's office. In those heady times, I was freelancing for and then employed regularly as a reporter by the weekly *Michigan Free Press* (until it stopped paying its writers). I edited *Gay Space* and also the *Midwest Gay Academic Journal*, which became *Gay Insurgent*. My immersion in the Ann Arbor-Detroit alternative scene placed me in the unique position to witness the fall and demise of a number of important alternative publications, including *Gay Liberator, The Ann Arbor Sun, Michigan Free Press*, and *Her-self*.

How have these titles fared, preservation-wise? *Gay Liberator* is contained in UMI's Underground Press Collection, but the title cannot be purchased individually from UMI. However, the New York Public Library has preserved the entire run of the *Gay Liberator* on microfilm; portions were also preserved on film by Temple University.

The *Sun* and *Gay Insurgent* (issues 4-7) are also part of the Underground Press Collection, but the latter title is not available for individual purchase on film. The *Sun* was also filmed by UMI as a separate title. In the interest of full disclosure, I will reveal I did get a few dollars in royalty payments from the Alternative Press Syndicate, which had arranged for the filming of *Gay Insurgent* by UMI. While I was at *Michigan Free Press*, I arranged to have copies of the weekly sent to UMI to be microfilmed, but UMI declined to sell the title until enough libraries requested it. Being defunct, the title is no longer listed by UMI as currently available in the latest *Serials in Microform*, but it is still listed in *Guide to Microforms in Print*.[49] Even though I was refused a microfilm copy in return, I also lent the State Historical Society of Wisconsin a complete run of the *Michigan Free Press*, including its short-lived "Mid-Michigan edition," to be filmed. That the society did, and the paper copies were mailed back to me. It is now available from the society. *Her-self* is, of course, available as part of the Herstory Collection and also incompletely filmed separately by UMI. Most of the defunct titles were indexed in the *Alternative Press Index*. As for *Michigan Free Press*, which I did begin indexing for the *Alternative Press Index*, it never made it into print—the paper was already defunct. *Gay Space* was never filmed, nor was *Midwest Gay Academic Journal*. New York Public Library planned to microfilm *Gay Insurgent* as well as *Midwest Gay Academic Journal*, but as of this writing that has not come to pass.

Subsequently, while working as an adult reference librarian at the Free Library of Philadelphia, a question I raised at a staff meeting as to why local gay papers were not acquired led to the immediate decision to microfilm three such titles, one defunct, with help from the local gay archive. It helped that the National Newspapers Program was being implemented locally, but elsewhere, alternative newspapers are not likely to have been included in the program. Alternative publishers and micropublishers need to be reminded of the urgency to preserve these materials, and if they fail to do that, library workers, libraries, or activists must take "direct action" to see that it is done.

MICROFILMING PRIORITIES

Very few places have complete runs of the titles indexed in the *Alternative Press Index*, and every attempt should be made to microfilm titles—especially those on newsprint—that have been indexed by the *Alternative Press Index* before they disintegrate or disappear. University Microfilms International can be commended for filming the bulk of the titles indexed by the *Alternative Press Index*, which are available for individual purchase. Most noteworthy is the title's notation in *Serials in Microform* indicating it is indexed in the *Alternative Press Index*. If any priorities need to be set, it would make sense to attempt to microfilm material that is already indexed, giving that material a priority over and above other alternative publications. But many important, if obscure or controversial titles never even get indexed; the contemporary explosion of "zines" and other alternative papers, as documented by the listings in such serials as *Factsheet Five, Anarchy, Feminist Collections*, or the activist *MSRRT Newsletter* from the Minnesota Social Responsibilities

Round Table, exposes the lie behind the myth that the alternative press has died. It is, in fact, flourishing in the Bush era, with a panel on 'zines packing a standing-room audience at the March 1991 Outwrite conference in San Francisco.

In a recessionary period, additional attempts should be made to increase the sharing of the work of preserving such publications, with the University of California-system shared acquisition filming of the San Francisco area lesbian and gay periodicals a good prototype. A number of union lists have been published,[50,51] but none specifically on microform collections of such material. After all, it is unlikely that libraries would lend their hard copies of the *Black Panther* to other libraries, but a microform copy would be more likely to circulate.

In reference to the national foreign newspaper microfilming program, Cole has written, "The most efficient means of making a greater number of titles available is to concentrate resources on the microfilming of titles never before filmed, rather than on producing duplicate positive copies for a number of institutions."[52] In the case of such ephemeral publications as the alternative press, his advice is even more relevant.

Because there are a number of collections of such publications in libraries, it would make sense for libraries to agree to microfilm specific titles. Cole thinks that "librarians prefer to encourage microfilming by a library or a research institution" rather than a commercial micropublisher. It will, I think, depend on which micropublisher is involved. A library may not have the technical expertise to film, but a micropublisher may not have the same concern for bibliographic control as a library. Apart from its pamphlet collection, the bulk of the Labadie Collection's materials has not been microfilmed because of shortage of staff, according to its curator, even though the University of Michigan runs its own small microfilming operation.

COPYRIGHT CLEARANCES

It is of course incumbent for copyright clearances to be secured from any alternative or underground publisher (where locatable) before engaging in any microfilming project. An earlier attempt by Bell and Howell to film major portions of alternative titles in Temple University's Contemporary Culture Collection was aborted when it "turned out that such clearances were in many cases impossible to obtain, largely because of the fugitive nature of many of the publications." In addition, B&H lawyers were "concerned that some of the publications might be libellous and result in damage suits. For these reasons, the contract was cancelled."[53] Subsequently, the library did its own preservation on film of selected titles.

More successful was the University of California's recent project to film northern California lesbian and gay periodicals. While a number of titles were not able to be filmed, some 61 (including partial runs) were successfully filmed after obtaining copyright clearances.[54]

REDUNDANCY OR NOT?

To avoid duplication of effort, libraries (and micropublishers) owning masters should have them cataloged in OCLC or RLIN, or reported to *Guide to Microforms in Print* and the office of the National Register of Microform Masters at the Library of Congress (which is now being published in the *National Union Catalog*). Appendix H lists additional microforms of underground and alternative press titles of the 1960s and 1970s that are available for individual purchase. Care should be taken to ensure that coverage is complete (or if incomplete, to find out what is missing). Duplication of effort is wasteful if another library or commercial firm has already created an archivally sound microform master for the run of the desired title. Such was the case with the gay paper, *The Advocate*, which I discovered was being sent out for filming by my library, even when the University of Southern California was already doing a better job preserving it on microfilm. Purchasing the USC microform edition meant we did not need to claim missing issues or seek to replace defaced issues for filming.

However, some redundancy is appropriate, since titles available as parts of microform sets are usually not available individually. In such a case, individual serial titles can justifiably be filmed. In addition, if there is no guarantee that microform masters are being kept in archival conditions, or that the original filming was done to preservation standards, then another master should be made. In addition, what happens to the masters when the firms go under (or are taken over)? A microform master that is not preserved according to exacting archival standards does not deserve the name.[55]

In her overview of Women's Studies materials on microform, Patterson notes the trend against large-scale microform projects, with micropublishers now opting for small projects such as papers of individuals.[56] Marshall's early concern about big business rip-offs is worth keeping in mind.[57] Although UMI is now marketing a new series on the alternative press in microform, a more productive (and economically feasible) route to follow is suggested by the University of California project to film lesbian and gay periodicals of northern California. That project is worth emulating, for it took advantage of alternative periodicals archived by a local resource (Gay and Lesbian Historical Society of Northern California), systemwide collection development monies were spent on funding the filming, and the resulting microforms will be shareable, findable through online catalogs.

In a recessionary period of the New World Order, it is perhaps not so bad to "think small." Regional and local preservation efforts are perhaps the best way to tackle such alternative and ephemeral serials. The National Newspaper Program, funded by the National Endowment for the Humanities, is not likely to include much of alternative materials, given the uproar over funding of controversial art and artists by its sister organization, National Endowment for the Art.

As a federally funded research librarian on Temple University's Alternative Acquisitions Project in the late 1970s, I believe one should not be overly dependent on government grants; I was unemployed for a year after the "soft" money dried up. Those of us who believe in library activism, and in social change, must reach out into our communities and organize alternative publishers to preserve their publications, utilizing local resources, especially local libraries, library workers, and community activists.

The moral panic over taboo sex and its related paraphernalia has resulted in the enactment of poorly but hastily written federal and state legislation banning what is deemed today to be "child pornography," including its possession and reproduction. The most recent federal incarnation of this type of repressive legislation assaulting the First Amendment continues to mandate burdensome recordkeeping procedures for "producers" of any sexually explicit material, whatever the age of the person portrayed.[58,59,60,61]

Although the American Library Association and the Freedom to Read Foundation are leading the legal battle against these recordkeeping regulations, the library profession has yet to take up the battle against the possession and duplication provisions of these statutes, refusing for the most part to acknowledge their potentially devastating impact on libraries. It is especially worrisome that the federal statute does not exempt libraries or legitimate researchers from these provisions. According to U.S. Justice Department officials, this omission is intentional. One official, Doug Tillet, could not understand why libraries should be allowed to possess illegal material: "Describe for us if you can what legitimate research purpose is served," he asked.[62] First Amendment attorney David Ogden, who has represented the ALA and the Freedom to Read Foundation in many legal fights, is not at all confident libraries are immune. He compares the illegal possession of pornography to that of illegal drugs and states: "I can certainly see how there might be some risk for libraries...and the penalties are astronomical."[63] However, ALA and its legal arm are waiting for a case to happen before taking any action. They may not have long to wait.

Libraries such as New York Public Library, which have been routinely microfilming erotica titles (which included "child pornography"), remain at high risk of being hauled into court, just as Cincinnati's Contemporary Arts Center was prosecuted for exhibiting Robert Mapplethorpe's photographs of naked minors. Even more vulnerable are the community-based lesbian and gay archives that dot the landscape; many contain erotic periodicals of the 1960s and 1970s now banned by state or federal law.[64,65] Today's preservation library worker needs not only an open mind but also education in what is legally permissible to reproduce (or even admit to possessing) so that one does not end up in jail or place the employing institution at risk of a police raid. Ironically, it is in the 1990s that a truly underground press is developing, one that is banned, ex post facto, by law.

Activists are rarely archivists and much of what they put out will be lost to their contemporaries and to future generations unless a systematic attempt is made, especially by those of us in the library profession, to preserve the periodicals and other ephemera of the underground and alternative press, while speaking out for the right to challenge and dissent from the establishment.

NOTES

1.   Robert H. Muller, Theodore J. Spahn, and Janet M. Spahn, *From Radical Left to Extreme Right*, 2d ed., rev. and enlarged. (Vol. I, Ann Arbor, MI: Campus Publishers, 1970; vol. II, Metuchen, NJ: Scarecrow Press, 1972).

2.   *Alternative Press Index*. (Northfield, MN: Radical Research Center, 1969).

3.   James P. Danky, comp., *Undergrounds: A Union List of Alternative Periodicals in Libraries of the U.S. and Canada*. (Madison: State Historical Society of Wisconsin, 1974).

4.   William D. Lutz, *Underground Press Directory*, 2d ed. (Stevens Point, WI: Counterpoint, 1969).

5.   William D. Lutz, *Underground Press Directory*, 4th ed. (Stevens Point, WI: Counterpoint, 1970).

6.   John Cook, "The 'Underground' Press: Once in Its Heyday Is Now in Decline," *Guardian* [New York] (14 March 1973): 8.

7.   John Spiers, *The Underground and Alternative Press in Britain: A Bibliographic Guide with Historical Notes*. (Hassocks, England: Harvester Press, 1974).

8.   Anne E. Zald and Cathy Seitz Whitaker, "The Underground Press of the Vietnam Era: An Annotated Bibliography," *Reference Services Review* 18, no. 4 (Winter 1990): 77-96.

9.   Muller, Spahn, and Spahn, vol. I, xxii-xxiii.

10.   Daniel Tsang, "Censorship of Lesbian and Gay Materials by Library Workers," in *Gay and Lesbian Library Service*, ed. by Cal Gough and Ellen Greenberg. (Jefferson, NC: McFarland, 1990), 166-70.

11.   Richard Akeroyd and Russell Benedict, eds., "A Directory of Ephemeral Collections in a National Underground Network," *Wilson Library Bulletin* 48, no. 3 (November 1973): 236-54.

12.   Patricia J. Case, comp., "Collections of Contemporary Alternative Materials in Libraries: A Directory," in *Alternative Materials in Libraries*, ed. by James P. Danky and Elliott Shore. (Metuchen, NJ: Scarecrow Press, 1982), 122-49.

13.   Ellen Embardo, "Directories of Special Collections on Social Movements Evolving from the Vietnam Era," *Reference Services Review* 18, no. 3 (Fall 1990): 59-98.

14.   Roger C. Palmer, "Alternative Research Center, a Proposal." (Washington, DC: ERIC Clearinghouse on Library and Information Science, 1973). ED 072 830.

15.   Embardo, 59-98.

16.   Daniel Tsang, "Homosexuality Research Collections," in *Libraries, Erotica, Pornography*, ed. by Martha Cornog. (Phoenix: Oryx, 1991), 199-210.

17.   Jutta R. Reed, "Cost Comparison of Periodicals in Hard Copy and on Microform," *Microform Review* 5, no. 3 (July 1976): 185-92.

18.   Rachel R. Bacon, letter to the author, 11 February 1980. Bacon was UMI serials project coordinator.

19.   Joan K. Marshall, "Bawl & Howl," *Booklegger* 1, no. 5 (July/August 1974): 25.

20. Marshall, 23.

21. Marshall, 22.

22. Marshall, [21]-25.

23. Dorothy Martin, "Underground Newspapers [sic] Microfilm Collection," *Microform Review* 1, no. 4 (October 1972): 311-14.

24. Marshall, 23.

25. Marshall, 24.

26. Stephen Koss, "The Underground and Alternative Press in Britain since 1961," *Microform Review* 4, no. 3 (July 1975): 222-23.

27. Dorothy Martin, "The Underground and Alternative Press in Britain—1973 Update," *Microform Review* 6, no. 2 (March 1977): 116-17.

28. Spiers, *The Underground....*

29. "Harvester Receives Queen's Award," *Microform Review* 15, no. 4 (Fall 1986): 206.

30. Pamela Piddington, "Herstory," *Microform Review* 2, no. 1 (January 1973): 48-49.

31. "Herstory Cataloging Project," *Microform Review* 7, no. 2 (March 1978): 76.

32. "Items of Note," *Feminist Collections* 12, no. 1 (Fall 1990): 36. (Item on Herstory collection)

33. James Danky and Eleanor McKay, "Not So Silent," *Wilson Library Bulletin* 48, no. 5 (January 1974): 383-84. (Letter responding to Akeroyd and Benedict; see note 11)

34. James P. Danky and Clifford W. Bass, eds., *Periodicals and Newspapers Acquired by the State Historical Society of Wisconsin Library, July 1974-December 1985.* (Madison: The Society, 1986). *January-June 1986 Supplement* (June 1986).

35. Bill Walker, *Lesbian and Gay Periodicals of Northern California: A Guide to the Microfilm Collection.* (Berkeley: The University of California and San Francisco: The Gay and Lesbian Historical Society of Northern California, forthcoming).

36. J.R.K. Kantor, "Sources in the Streets: The Sather Gate Handbill Collection of the University of California Archives," *California Historical Quarterly* 55, no. 3 (Fall 1976): [270]-73.

37. William M. Roberts, letter to the author, 1 May 1990. Roberts is university archivist at University of California, Berkeley.

38. *The Social Protest Collection, 1960-1982: Collection Number 86/157 c.* (Berkeley: The Bancroft Library, University of California, n.d.), 6.

39. Gwendolyn L. Pershing, "Erotica Research Collections," in *Libraries, Erotica, Pornography*, ed. by Martha Cornog. (Phoenix: Oryx, 1991), 196.

40. Tsang, "Homosexuality...," 201-2.

41. Keith McKinney, letter to Bill Walker, 5 January 1988. Attachments included RLIN printouts.

42. Alisa Solomon, "Scholar or Bigot? Is Father Healy Fit to Run Our Public Library?" *Village Voice* (28 March 1989): 11.

43. Tsang, "Homosexuality...," 202.

44. Shirley W. Leung, "Bibliographic Control of Microform Sets: Some Recent Accomplishments and Concerns," *Microform Review* 18, no. 2 (Spring 1989): 74.

45. John Liberty, comp., *Journals of Dissent and Social Change: A Bibliography of Titles in the California State University, Sacramento, Library*, 6th ed. (Sacramento: California State University, Sacramento, Library, 1986).

46. See Elliott Shore, "Microfilming Project," *Temple University Libraries Special Collections Newsletter* 2, no. 1 (May 1976): 7 and *Alternative Press Periodicals: A Catalog of Those Periodicals Held in the Comtemporary Culture Collection Which Have Been Filmed for Preservation by Temple Universities Libraries.* (Philadelphia: Temple University Libraries, 1976).

47. Daniel Tsang, "The Gay Press," *Gay Insurgent*, nos. 4 and 5 (Spring 1979): 18-21.

48. Daniel Tsang, "The Alternative Press in Microform." (Washington, DC: ERIC Clearinghouse on Library and Information Science, 1977). ED 143 340.

49. *Guide to Microforms in Print.* (Westport, CT: Meckler, 1990).

50. Danky, *Undergrounds*....

51. Joanne V. Akeroyd, *Alternatives, a Guide to the Newspapers in the Alternative Press Collection in the Special Collections Department of the University of Connecticut Library*, 2d ed. (Storrs: University of Connecticut Library, 1976).

52. John Y. Cole, "Developing a National Foreign Microfilming Program," in *Microforms in Libraries: A Reader*, ed. by Albert James Diaz. (Weston, CT: Microform Review, 1975), [298]-310.

53. *Alternative Press Periodicals*....

54. Chuck Eckman, telephone conversation with author, 5 March 1991.

55. Robert DeCandido, "Considerations in Evaluating Searching for Microform Availability," *Microform Review* 19, no. 3 (Summer 1990): 116-18.

56. Elizabeth Patterson, "Women's Studies Resources in Microform: An Update," *Microform Review* 18, no. 2 (Spring 1989): 94-97.

57. Marshall, [21]-25.

58. Daniel Tsang, "Broad New Porn Laws Planned," *Update: Southern California's Gay Newspaper* [San Diego] no. 313 (23 December 1987): A1, A3, A14.

59. Neil A. Lewis, "Publishers, Artists and Librarians Challenge New Pornography Law," *The New York Times* (24 February 1991): 14.

60. "Librarians in Court, Again," *The Washington Post* (26 February 1991): A20. Editorial.

61. Allan Parachini, "Child Pornography Law Won't Be Pressed—for Now," *Los Angeles Times* (Orange County ed.) (27 February 1991): F5, F9.

62. Bill Andriette, "New Weapons for the Sex Police," *The Guide: Gay Travel, Entertainment, Politics, & Sex* (Boston) 11, no. 2 (February 1991): 24.

63. Andriette, 24.

64. Andriette, 24.

65. Tsang, "Homosexuality...," 205-6.

BIBLIOGRAPHY

I. Union Lists, Directories, Bibliographic Guides, and Indexes

Access. Syracuse, NY: Gaylord, 1975- .

Akeroyd, Joanne V. *Alternatives, a Guide to the Newspapers in the Alternative Press Collection in the Special Collections Department of the University of Connecticut Library*. 2d ed. Storrs: University of Connecticut Library, 1976.

Akeroyd, Richard, and Russell Benedict, eds. "A Directory of Ephemeral Collections in a National Underground Network." *Wilson Library Bulletin* (November 1973) 48, no. 3: 236-54.

Alternative Press Index. Baltimore: Alternative Press Centre, 1969- .

Alternative Press Periodicals: A Catalog of Those Periodicals Held in the Contemporary Culture Collection Which Have Been Filmed for Preservation by Temple Universities Libraries. Philadelphia: Temple University Libraries, 1976.

Case, Patricia J., comp. "Collections of Contemporary Alternative Materials in Libraries: A Directory." In *Alternative Materials in Libraries*, ed. by James P. Danky and Elliott Shore, 122-49. Metuchen, NJ: Scarecrow Press, 1982.

Center for Research Libraries. "Underground Press." In *Handbook 1990*. Chicago: The Center, 1990.

Danky, James P., comp. *Undergrounds: A Union List of Alternative Periodicals in Libraries of the U.S. and Canada*. Madison: State Historical Society of Wisconsin, 1974.

Danky, James P., and Clifford W. Bass, eds. *Periodicals and Newspapers Acquired by the State Historical Society of Wisconsin Library, July 1974-December 1985*. Madison: The Society, 1986. *January-June 1986 Supplement*, June 1986.

Danky, James, and Eleanor McKay. "Not So Silent." *Wilson Library Bulletin* 48, no. 5 (January 1974): 383-84. (Letter responding to Akeroyd and Benedict, 1973, above)

Dodson, Suzanne Cates, ed. *Microforms Research Collections: A Guide*. 2d ed. Westport, CT: Meckler, 1984.

Embardo, Ellen. "Directories of Special Collections on Social Movements Evolving from the Vietnam Era." *Reference Services Review* 18, no. 3 (Fall 1990): 59-98.

Guide to Microforms in Print. Westport, CT: Meckler, 1990.

Herstory Microfilm Collection. Berkeley: Women's History Library, n.d.

Herstory Microfilm Collection Title Listing. Sacramento: California State University, 1985.

An Index to Microform Collections. Ed. by Ann Niles. Vol. 2. Westport, CT: Meckler, 1987.

Liberty, John, comp. *Currents on the Left: An Annotated Bibliography of Radical and Left-Wing Journals*. Sacramento: California State University Library, 1974.

Liberty, John, comp. *Facing Right: An Annotated Bibliography of Conservative and Right-Wing Journals*. Sacramento: California State University Library, 1977.

Liberty, John, comp. *Journals of Dissent and Social Change: A Bibliography of Titles in the California State University, Sacramento, Library*. 6th ed. Sacramento: California State University, Sacramento, Library, 1986.

Library Microfilms 1989-1990. Sunnyvale, CA: Bay Microfilm Incorporated, n.d.

Lutz, William D. *Underground Press Directory*. 2d ed. Stevens Point, WI: Counterpoint, 1969.

Lutz, William D. *Underground Press Directory*. 4th ed. Stevens Point, WI: Counterpoint, 1970.

Malinowsky, H. Robert. *International Directory of Gay and Lesbian Periodicals*. Phoenix: Oryx Press, 1987.

Muller, Robert H., Theodore J. Spahn, and Janet M. Spahn. *From Radical Left to Extreme Right*. 2d ed. Rev. and enlarged. Vol. I. Ann Arbor: Campus Publishers, 1970. Vol. II. Metuchen, NJ: Scarecrow Press, 1972.

New Periodicals Index. Boulder, CO: Mediaworks, 1977-1980.

Nilan, Roxanne-Louise, comp. *The Woman Question: An Annotated Guide to the Women's Pamphlet Collection in the Department of Special Collections*. Irvine: University Library, University of California, 1976.

Popular Periodical Index. Camden, NJ: The Index, 1973- .

Reichmann, Felix, and Josephine M. Tharpe. "Appendix 4: A Microform Bibliography." In *Bibliographic Control of Microforms*, [55]-249. Westport, CT: Greenwood Press, 1972.

Reel Guide to Herstory Supplementary Set I... Berkeley: Women's History Research Center, 1976.

Reel Guide to Herstory Supplementary Set II... Berkeley: Women's History Research Center, 1976.

The Right Wing Collection of the University of Iowa Libraries, 1918-1977. Glen Rock, NJ: University Microfilm Corporation of America, 1978.

The Social Protest Collection, 1960-1982: Collection Number 86/157 c. Berkeley: The Bancroft Library, University of California, n.d.

Spiers, John. *The Underground and Alternative Press in Britain: A Bibliographic Guide with Historical Notes*. Hassocks, England: Harvester Press, 1974.

Tsang, Daniel. "The Gay Press." *Gay Insurgent*, nos. 4-5 (Spring 1979): 18-21.

Underground Newspaper Collection. Annotations by Alan Kimbel. Columbia: University of Missouri Libraries, n.d.

Underground Press Collection: A Guide to the Microfilm Collection, Hoover Institution Supplement. Ann Arbor, MI: University Microfilms International, 1988.

Underground Press Collection: Listing of Contents, 1963-1985. Ann Arbor, MI: University Microfilms International, 1986.

A Union List of Microform Holdings in Ohio State-Assisted Universities. Comp. by Irene Schubert and Alice Weaver. Toledo, OH: University Libraries, 1972.

A Union List of Selected Microforms in Libraries in the New York Metropolitan Area, 1979. 3d ed. New York: New York Metropolitan Reference and Research Library Agency, 1980.

UPA Research Collections 1991. Bethesda, MD: University Publications of America, 1990.

Walker, Bill. *Lesbian and Gay Periodicals of Northern California: A Guide to the Microfilm Collection*.

Berkeley: The University of California and San Francisco: The Gay and Lesbian Historical Society of Northern California, forthcoming.

Whitehead, Thomas M. "Temple of (Underground) Culture." *Wilson Library Bulletin* 48, no. 5 (January 1974): 384. (Letter responding to Akeroyd and Benedict, 1973, above)

Zald, Anne E., and Cathy Seitz Whitaker. "The Underground Press of the Vietnam Era: An Annotated Bibliography." *Reference Services Review* 18, no. 4 (Winter 1990): 77-96.

II. Reviews

Kantor, J.R.K. "Sources in the Streets: The Sather Gate Handbill Collection of the University of California Archives." *California Historical Quarterly* 55, no. 3 (Fall 1976): [270]-73.

Koss, Stephen. "The Underground and Alternative Press in Britain since 1961." *Microform Review* 4, no. 3 (July 1975): 222-23.

Marshall, Joan K. "Bawl & Howl." *Booklegger* 1, no. 5 (July/August 1974): [21]-25.

Martin, Dorothy. "The Underground and Alternative Press in Britain—1973 Update." *Microform Review* 6, no. 2 (March 1977): 116-17.

Martin, Dorothy. "Underground Newspapers [sic] Microfilm Collection." *Microform Review* 1, no. 4 (October 1972): 311-14.

Piddington, Pamela. "Herstory." *Microform Review* 2, no. 1 (January 1973): 48-49.

III. Articles and Personal Communication

Andriette, Bill. "New Weapons for the Sex Police." *The Guide: Gay Travel, Entertainment, Politics, & Sex* (Boston) 11, no. 2 (February 1991): 21-27.

Bacon, Rachel R. Letter to Daniel C. Tsang 11 February 1980. Bacon was UMI serials project coordinator.

Cole, John Y. "Developing a National Foreign Microfilming Program." In *Microforms in Libraries: A Reader*, ed. by Albert James Diaz, [298]-310. Weston, CT: Microform Review, 1975.

Cook, John. "The 'Underground' Press: Once in Its Heyday Is Now in Decline." *Guardian* [New York] (14 March 1973): 8.

___. "Underground Press: Behind the Decline." *Guardian* (21 March 1973): 8.

DeCandido, Robert. "Considerations in Evaluating Searching for Microform Availability." *Microform Review* 19, no. 3 (Summer 1990): 116-18.

Eckman, Chuck. Personal communication on the telephone 5 March 1991, Berkeley.

"Harvester Receives Queen's Award." *Microform Review* 15, no. 4 (Fall 1986): 206.

"Herstory Cataloging Project." *Microform Review* 7, no. 2 (March 1978): 76.

Holley, Robert P. "The Preservation Microfilming Aspects of the United States Newspaper Program: A Preliminary Study." *Microform Review* 19, no. 3 (Summer 1990): 124-32.

"Items of Note." *Feminist Collections* 12, no. 1 (Fall 1990): 36. (Item on Herstory collection)

Leung, Shirley W. "Bibliographic Control of Microform Sets: Some Recent Accomplishments and Concerns." *Microform Review* 18, no. 2 (Spring 1989): 71-76.

Lewis, Neil A. "Publishers, Artists and Librarians Challenge New Pornography Law." *The New York Times* (24 February 1991): 14.

"Librarians in Court, Again." *The Washington Post* (26 February 1991): A20. (Editorial)

McKinney, Keith. Letter to Bill Walker 5 January 1988. (Attachments included RLIN printouts)

Palmer, Roger C. "Alternative Research Center, a Proposal." Washington, DC: ERIC Clearinghouse on Library and Information Science, 1973. ERIC ED 072 830.

Parachini, Allan. "Child Pornography Law Won't Be Pressed—for Now." *Los Angeles Times* (Orange County edition) (27 February 1991): F5, F9.

Patterson, Elizabeth. "Women's Studies Resources in Microform: An Update." *Microform Review* 18, no. 2 (Spring 1989): 94-97.

Pershing, Gwendolyn L. "Erotica Research Collections." In *Libraries, Erotica, Pornography*, ed. by Martha Cornog, [188]-98. Phoenix: Oryx, 1991.

Reed, Jutta R. "Cost Comparison of Periodicals in Hard Copy and on Microform." *Microform Review* 5, no. 3 (July 1976): 185-92.

Roberts, William M. Letter to Daniel C. Tsang 1 May 1990. (Roberts is university archivist at University of California, Berkeley)

Shore, Elliott. "Microfilming Project." *Temple University Libraries Special Collections Newsletter* 2, no. 1 (May 1976): 7.

Solomon, Alisa. "Scholar or Bigot? Is Father Healy Fit to Run Our Public Library?" *Village Voice* (28 March 1989): 11.

Tsang, Daniel. "The Alternative Press in Microform." Washington, DC: ERIC Clearinghouse on Library and Information Science, 1977. ERIC 143 340.

___. "Broad New Porn Laws Planned." *Update: Southern California's Gay Newspaper* [San Diego] no. 313 (23 December 1987): A1, A3, A14.

___. "Censorship of Lesbian and Gay Materials by Library Workers." In *Gay and Lesbian Library Service*, ed. by Cal Gough and Ellen Greenberg, 166-70. Jefferson, NC: McFarland, 1990.

___. "Homosexuality Research Collections." In *Libraries, Erotica, Pornography*, ed. by Martha Cornog, [199]-210. Phoenix: Oryx, 1991.

Appendix A: Anthologies or Reprint Editions of the U.S. Underground and Alternative Press of the 1960s-1970s

Aphrodisiac: Fiction from Christopher Street. New York: G. P. Putnam's, 1980.

Are We There Yet? A Continuing History of Lavender Woman, a Chicago Lesbian Newspaper, 1971-1976. Edited by Michal Brody. Iowa City, IA: Aunt Lute, 1985.

The Best of the Realist. Edited by Paul Krassner. Philadelphia: Running Press, 1984.

Blacklisted News, Secret History: From Chicago, '68, to 1984: The New Yippie! Book. New York: Bleecker Publications, 1983.

First Love/Last Love: Non-Fiction from Christopher Street. Michael Denneny, Charles Ortleb and Thomas Steele. New York: G. P. Putnam's, 1980.

Gay Sunshine Interviews. Edited by Winston Leyland. San Francisco: Gay Sunshine Press, Vol. 1, 1978, Vol. II, 1982.

Gidra...The XXth Anniversary Edition. Montebello, CA: Gidra, 1990.

How a Satirical Editor Became a Yippie Conspirator in Ten Easy Years. Paul Krassner. New York: Putnam, 1971.

How Old Will You Be in 1984?: Expressions of Outrage from the High School Free Press. Diane Divoky. New York: Avon, 1969.

The Ladder 1-16 (1956-1972). 16 vol. Reprint ed. New York: Arno Press, 1975.

The Lavender Herring: Lesbian Essays from The Ladder. Edited by Barbara Grier and Coletta Reid. Baltimore: Diana Press, 1976.

Lesbiana: Book Reviews from The Ladder, 1966-1972. Barbara Grier and Coletta Reid. Reno: Naiad Press, 1976.

The Lesbians Home Journal: Stories from The Ladder. Edited by Barbara Grier and Coletta Reid. Baltimore: Diana Press, 1976.

Lesbians Lives: Biographies of Women from The Ladder. Edited by Barbara Grier and Coletta Reid. Baltimore: Diana Press, 1976.

The Living Underground: An Anthology of Contemporary American Poetry. Edited by Hugh Fox and Sam Cornish. S.l. : s.n., 1969.

Mattachine Review 1-12 (1955-1966). Reprint ed. 12 vol. in 5. New York: Arno Press, 1975.

Notes from the New Underground: An Anthology. Edited by Jesse Kornbluth. New York: Viking Press, 1968.

Our Time: An Anthology of Interviews from the East Village Other. Compiled and edited by Allen Katzman. New York: Dial Press, 1972.

Our Time Is Now: Notes from the High School Underground. John Birmingham. New York: Praeger, 1970.

Outlaws of Amerika: Communiques from the Weather Underground. New York: Liberated Guardian, 1971.

Peattie, Noel. *A Passage for Dissent: The Best of Sipapu, 1970-1988.* Jefferson, NC: McFarland, 1989.

The San Francisco Oracle 1 (1966-1968). Ed. by Allen Cohen. Facsimile ed. Berkeley: Regent Press, 1991.

Seeds of Liberation. Edited by Paul Goodman. New York: George Braziller, 1964.

Seeing Through the Shuck. Edited by Richard Kostelanetz. New York: Ballantine Books, 1972.

The Student Voice, 1960-1965: Periodical of the Student Nonviolent Coordinating Committee. Edited by Clayborne Carson. Westport, CT: Meckler, 1990.

Underground Press Anthology. Edited by Thomas King Forcade. New York: Ace Books, 1972.

The Underground Reader. Edited by Mel Howard and Thomas King Forcade. New York: New American Library, 1972.

Youth Liberation: News, Politics, and Survival Information Put Together by Youth Liberation of Ann Arbor. Washington, NJ: Times Change, 1972.

Appendix B: Underground Press Collection (UMI): 1960s-1970s U.S. Titles

A A P A Newspaper, Berkeley, CA
A B A S, Newark, NJ
Abdala El Futuro Sera Nuestro, Elizabeth, NJ*
About Face, Los Angeles, CA
Activist, The, Buffalo, NY*
Activist, The, Oberlin, OH#
Access, Washington, DC
Adult Reporter, The, Culver City, CA*
Adventures of FUB, The, Oakland, CA*
Advocate, The, Los Angeles, CA*
Aft, San Francisco, CA*
Against the Grain, Stanford, CA*
Ahisma, Malaga, NJ#
A I M, New Haven, CT
A I M S Newsletter, New York, NY#
Ain't I a Woman, Iowa City, IA
Akwesasne Notes, Rooseveltown, NY
    Marvin, SD
Alaska Free Press, Anchorage, AK#
Albany Liberator, The, Albany, NY
Alchemist, Manhattan, KS
Alice, Blacksburg, VA
All Together, Chicago, IL
All You Can Eat, New Brunswick, NJ
Ally, The, Berkeley, CA
Alternative, Beverly Shores, IN
Alternative, Naperville, IL
Alternative, The, Long Beach, CA
Alternative Features Service, Berkeley, CA
Alternative Journalism Review, The, New York, NY
Alternative Magazine, The, Indianapolis, IN

Alternative Media, New York, NY
Alternative Newspaper, The, Santa Barbara, CA
Alternative Sources of Energy, Milaca, MN
Alternatives Journal, Los Angeles, CA
Altus, Atlanta, GA
Amazing Grace, Tallahassee, FL
American Avatar, Boston, MA
    New York, NY
American Civil Liberties Union News, San Francisco, CA#
American Communist, Oakland, CA#
American Dream, Tempe, AZ
Anarchos, New York, NY
Andromeda, Stillwater, OK*
Andy Warhol's Interview, New York, NY#
Anemic Traveler, The, Woodside, NY
Ann Arbor Argus, Ann Arbor, MI
Ann Arbor Sun, Ann Arbor, MI
    Detroit, MI
Anti Fascist Front, Oakland, CA*
Anti-Brass, Los Angeles, CA*
Antiwarrior, Washington, DC
Anvil, The, Sacramento, CA*
Appalachian Lookout, Prestonsburg, KY*
Appalachian Student Press, Greeneville, TN*
Appleseed, New York, NY
Appleseed Weekly Bulletin, New York, NY
Aquarian, Temple Terrace, FL
Aquarian Arts Weekly, Fairfield, NJ
    Montclair, NJ
    Passaic, NJ

Aquarian Age, the Albany, NY
Aquarius, Berkeley, CA#
Arab Student Bulletin, East Lansing, MI*
Arena, The, Stanford, CA#
Argo, Isla Vista, CA
    Santa Barbara, CA
Argo, Pomona, NJ
As You Were, Fort Ord, CA
Aspects, Eugene, OR#
Asterisk, Omaha, NE
Athens News, Athens, OH
Atlanta Gazette, Atlanta, GA
Atlantis, Dayton, OH
Atlantis News, The, Saugerties, NY
Attica News Service, Buffalo, NY
Attitude Check, Vista, CA*
Austin Sun, Austin, TX
Avatar, Boston, MA
    New York, NY
Aware, Los Angeles, CA
AWIN Newsletter, Atlanta, GA
A W O L, Lawrence, KS
    Manhattan, KS
    Kansas City, MO
Ball & Chain Review, Berkeley, CA*
Baltimore Free Press, Baltimore, MD
Bandersnatch, Tucson, AZ
Basta Ya!, San Francisco, CA*
Bauls, West Lafayette, IN
Berkeley Barb, Berkeley, CA
Berkeley Citizen, Berkeley, CA
Berkeley Facist, Berkeley, CA#
Berkeley Monitor, The, Berkeley, CA
Berkeley Tribe, Berkeley, CA
Big Muddy Gazette, Carbondale, IL
Big River News, Mendocino, CA
Big Us, Cleveland, OH
Black and Red, Kalamazoo, MI
Black Circles, West Somerville, MA
Black Collegian, St. Louis, MO#
Black Fire, San Francisco, CA*
Black Liberator, The, Chicago, IL
Black-Out, Columbia, MO#
Black Panther, San Francisco, CA
Black Politics, Berkeley, CA
Black Star, Evanston, IL
    Milwaukee, WI
Black Vanguard, The, Danville, IL
Blade, The, Oshkosh, WI
Blimp, New York, NY
Blue Bus, The, Newton Square, PA
Blue-Tail Fly, Lexington, KY*
Bolinas Hit, The, Bolinas, CA#
Bond, New York, NY
Borrowed Times, Missoula, MT

Boston Phoenix, Boston, MA
Both Sides Now, Jacksonville, FL
Boulder, Boulder, CO*
Bragg Briefs, Fort Bragg, NC
Bread, Peace, and Land, Cleveland, OH*
Briarpatch, Reno, NV*
Broadside, New York, NY
Broadside & The Free Press, Cambridge, MA
Broken Barriers, New Orleans, LA
Brother, Berkeley, CA
Brown Shoes, Norfolk, VA
Buddhist Third Class Junk Mail Oracle, Cleveland, OH
Buffalo Chip, Omaha, NE
Buffalo Insighter, Buffalo, NY
Bugle, The, Milwaukee, WI
Bugle American, Milwaukee, WI
Bull Shit Review, The, Denver, CO
Bulletin, New York, NY*
Bullshit and Society, Berkeley, CA*
Burning River News, Cleveland, OH
Call, The, Bell Gardens, CA*
Call, The, Madison, WI
Callaloo, Lexington, KY
Calypso, Phoenix, AZ
Camp News, Chicago, IL
Campaigner, The, New York, NY#
Campus Underground, Cedar Falls, IA
Candle, Ann Arbor, MI
Capitalism Stinks, Berkeley, CA*
Captain's Log, The, Newport News, VA
Carbunkle Review, Connecticut Valley, MA*
Carolina, Chapel Hill, NC
Carolina Plain Dealer, Durham, NC
Catholic Radical, The, Milwaukee, WI#
Cauldron, The, Hartford, CT
Cause, Chicago, IL
Caveat Emptor, Coatsville, PA
Challenge, East Hanover, NJ
Challenge-Desafio, Brooklyn, NY*
Challenge to Socialism, Chevy Chase, MD#
Changes, New York, NY#
Chaparral, Stanford, CA*
Chapel Hill Sun, The, Chapel Hill, NC
Cherokee Examiner, Pasadena, CA
Chicago Express, Chicago, IL
Chicago Seed, The, Chicago, IL
Chicanismo, Stanford, CA*
Chicano Student Movement, Los Angeles, CA#
Chinook, Denver, CO
Christian Anti-Communist Crusade, Long Beach, CA#
    Le Chronic, Roxbury, MA
Chrysalis, Des Moines, IA
Citizen, The, Berkeley, CA#
City Free Press, The, Brooklyn, NY*
Class Struggle, Wollaston, MA*

Classified Flea Market, Oakland, CA#
Coalition News, Berkeley, CA*
Collage, New York, NY*
Collected Artists Worksheet 1965, The, Detroit, MI
College Press Service, Denver, CO
Colonist, Stanford, CA*
Colorado Daily, The, Boulder, CO*
Columbia Missouri Free Press, Columbia, MO#
Columbus Free Press, Columbus, OH
Come Unity, St. Petersburg, FL
Common Ground, Los Angeles, CA#
Common Sense, Bloomington, IN
Common Sense, San Francisco, CA
Common Sense, Springfield, MA
Common Sense, Washington, DC
Communique for New Politics and Left Out News,
    Berkeley, CA#
Communities, Stelle, IL
        Louisa, VA
Community Press Service, Cambridge, MA
Community Sun, Columbia, MO#
Congress Watcher, The, Washington, DC
Connections, Madison, WI
Connections, Washington, DC
Connexions, Oakland, CA
Conspiracy, The, San Francisco, CA*
Continental Magazine, San Diego, CA#
Corpus, New York, NY
Counter Attack, New York, NY#
Counterdraft, Los Angeles, CA#
Counterpoint, Stevens Point, WI
Courier, Oakland, CA*
Coyote, Tucson, AZ
Creative Loafing, Atlanta, GA
Creem, Birmingham, MI
        Detroit, MI
Critical Mass, Washington, DC
Critical Mass Bulletin, Washington, DC
Critical Mass Energy Journal, Washington, DC
Croatian Times, The, Omaha, NE#
Crocodile, The, Gainesville, FL
Cross Currents, Palo Alto, CA*
C S M/Chicano Student Movement, Los Angeles, CA
Cuervo International, Hollywood, CA
Current, The, Newburyport, MA
Daily Blotter, State College, PA
Daily Bruin, Los Angeles, CA*
Daily California, Berkeley, CA*
Daily Planet, Coconut Grove, FL
        Miami, FL
Daily Rag, Washington, DC
Daily Reveille, The, Baton Rouge, LA#
Daily World, New York, NY*
Dallas News, Dallas, TX
Dallas Notes, Dallas, TX

Damascus Free Press, Damascus, MD
Dawn, Wichita Falls, TX
D.C. Gazette, Washington, DC
Deathburger, Baltimore, MD*
Delaware Alternative Press, Newark, DE
Delaware Free Press, Newark, DE
Deserted Times, The, San Francisco, CA
Despite Everything, Berkeley, CA
Detroit Gay Liberator, Detroit, MI
Detroit Liberator, The, Detroit, MI
Digger Papers, The, San Francisco, CA#
Dine' Baa Hani', Fort Defiance, AZ
Direct Action, Voluntown, CT*
Dispatcher, The, San Francisco, CA#
Distant Drummer, The, Philadelphia, PA
Dock of the Bay, San Francisco, CA#
Doing It!, Worthington, OH
Door, San Diego, CA
Door to Liberation, San Diego, CA
Dragon, Berkeley, CA
Dragon Seed, Baltimore, MD
        Lutherville, MD
Dreamshore, Bloomington, IN
Druid Free Press, The, Tempe, AZ
Drummer, The, Philadelphia, PA
Duck Power, San Diego, CA*
Earth, San Francisco, CA#
East Village Eye, New York, NY
East Village Other, New York, NY
Edcentric, Washington, DC
        Eugene, OR
Eden, Fountain Valley, CA
Eggman, The, Monterey Park, CA
Electric Newspaper, Salt Lake City, UT
Employee's Organize, Stanford, CA*
Enlisted Times, San Francisco, CA
Eugene Augur, Eugene, OR
Every Other Weekly, The, Berkeley, CA*
Exit Nine, New Brunswick, NJ*
Exponent, Huntsville, AL
Express, Hicksville, NY
        Merrick, NY
Extra, Providence, RI
Eye of the Beast, Tampa, FL*
Eyes Left, San Francisco, CA
Faculty Peace News, Columbus, OH
Family Voice, Elmhurst, NY
Feraferia, Altadena, CA
Fertilizer, Charleston, IL
Fifth Estate, Detroit, MI
Finger, New Orleans, LA
Fire, Chicago, IL
Firing Line, The, Chicago, IL
First Issue, Ithaca, NY
First Issue, The, Brattleboro, VT

Flag in Action, New Providence, TN
Flambeau, Tallahassee, FL
Flatlands, The, Oakland, CA#
Flint Voice, Burton, MI
Flint Women's Press, Flint, MI
Florida Free Press, Jacksonville, FL
Florida Observer, Tallahassee, FL
Focal Point, Santa Monica, CA*
Focus, Des Moines, IA
Focus, Garden Grove, CA
Focus, Oakland, CA*
Folly, Bethlehem, PA
Food Monitor, Mineola, NY
    New York, NY
Fordham Ram, The, Bronx, NY
A Four Year Bummer, Champaign, IL
Fox Valley Kaleidoscope, Oshkosh, WI
F P S/Youth Liberation News Service, Ann Arbor, MI
Fred, Chicago, IL
Free Aquarian, The, Hackensack, NJ
Free Campus News, Washington, DC*
Free For All, Madison, WI
Free Pagna Press, Kansas City, KS
Free Palestine, Washington, DC
Free Press, Philadelphia, PA#
Free Press Boston, Boston, MA
Free Press of Springfield, Springfield, MA
Free Press of U.C. Davis, Davis, CA*
Free Press Underground, Columbia, MO
Free Ranger Intertribal News Service, New York, NY
Free Spaghetti Dinner, Santa Cruz, CA
Free Spirit, Brooklyn, NY
Free Statesman, The, St. Cloud, MN
Free Student, Los Angeles, CA
Free Student, New York, NY
Free University of Berkeley, Berkeley, CA*
Free Valley Advocate, Amherst, MA
Free Venice Beachhead, Venice, CA
Free You, Menlo Park, CA
    Palo Alto, CA
Free You, Minneapolis, MN
Freedom, Hollywood, CA*
Freedom News/East Bay Bridge, Richmond, CA
Fresh Air, Freeport, IL
Front Line, Washington, DC
Front Range/People's Press, Boulder, CO
F T A, Fort Knox, KY
F T E, Los Angeles, CA
Fun City, Bloomington, IN
Fuse, The, Oneonta, AL
Fusion, Boston, MA
La Gaceta Chibcha, New York, NY
Gambit, Tempe, AZ
Gar, Austin, TX
El Gaucho, Santa Barbara, CA*

Gay Insurgent, Philadelphia, PA
Gayzette Adz, San Francisco, CA*
Gazette Guide, The, Washington, DC
GE Registor, Philadelphia, PA*
Gentle Strength, Berkeley, CA*
Gest, Southfield, MI
Getting Together, San Francisco, CA*
Ghent Free Press, Norfolk, VA
GI Press Service, New York, NY
Gidra, Los Angeles, CA*
Gigline, El Paso, TX
Glyptodon News, Austin, TX
Gold Coast Free Press, Coconut Grove, FL*
Golden Bear, The, Berkeley, CA*
Good Morning Teaspoon, San Diego, CA
Good Times, San Francisco, CA
Goodbye to All That, San Diego, CA
Goodfellow Review of Crafts, The, Berkeley, CA
Gothic Blimp Works, New York, NY
Grafiti, Philadelphia, PA
Granpa, New York, NY
Grapevine, Palo Alto, CA*
Grass Roots, Washington, DC
Grass Roots Forum, San Gabriel, CA
Grass Roots Gazette, Vallejo, CA
Great Speckled Bird, Atlanta, GA
Greece Today, Chicago, IL
Green Egg, St. Louis, MO
Green Fuse, Chattanooga, TN
Green Revolution, Freeland, MD
    Louisa, VA
    York, PA
Green Solution, Brookville, OH
Greenfeel, Barre, VT
Greenhouse, Kansas City, MO
Grinding Stone, Terre Haute, IN
Growing Seasons, Lincoln, NE
La Guardia, Milwaukee, WI
Guardian, New York, NY
Guatemala!, York, PA
Guerrila, Detroit, MI
Gulf Coast Fish Cheer, Pensacola, FL
Haight Ashbury Tribune, San Francisco, CA
Hair, Minneapolis, MN
Harambee, Los Angeles, CA
Harbinger, Columbia, SC
Harbinger, New York, NY
Harbinger, San Francisco, CA#
Harbinger, The, Sebastopol, CA
Hard Core, The, New York, NY
Hard Times, Washington, DC
Harry, Baltimore, MD
Hartford Advocate, Hartford, CT
Hartford's Other Voice, Hartford, CT
Harvard Today, Cambridge, MA*

Health Rights News, Chicago, IL*
Heathen Science Monitor, Minneapolis, MN
Helix, Seattle, WA
Henderson Station, State College, PA
Her-self, Ann Arbor, MI
Here We Go Again, Stanford, CA*
Heretics Journal, Seattle, WA
Heterodoxical Voice, Newark, DE
High Gauge, Tuscaloosa, AL
High School Independent Press, New York, NY
High Times, New York, NY
Home Cookin, Oklahoma City, OK
Honky Times, San Antonio, TX
Hooka, Dallas, TX*
Horseshit, Hermosa Beach, CA*
Hot Potato, Indianapolis, IN
Humantis, Los Angeles, CA
Humboldt Independent News, Humboldt County, CA
Hundred Flowers, Minneapolis, MN
Iconoclast, Dallas, TX
Illustrated Paper, The, Mendocino, CA
Image, New York, NY
Imola News, The, Imola, CA
Impact, Danville, IL
In Arcane Logos, New Orleans, LA
In These Times, Chicago, IL
In Between, Hamilton, OH
Independent American, The, New Orleans, LA*
Independent Californian, The, Berkeley, CA*
Independent Eye, The, Cincinnati, OH
Indian Head, Santa Ana, CA
Indianapolis Free Press, The, Indianapolis, IN
Indigena, Berkeley, CA
Indochina Chronicle, Washington, DC
Indochina Crisis, Philadelphia, PA*
Indochina Issues, Washington, DC
Industrial Worker, Chicago, IL
      Washington, DC
Inferno, San Antonio, TX
Informed Source, New York, NY
Inner City Light, New York, NY
Innovator, Los Angeles, CA
Inquisition, Charlotte, NC
Instant News Service, Berkeley, CA#
Institute for the Study of Nonviolence, Palo Alto, CA#
Inter View, New York, NY#
Iron Cage, Mendocino, CA
I. S./International Socialist, Berkeley, CA
Island Surfing, Lindenhurst, NY
Israel Horizons, New York, NY
Issue, Columbia, MO*
Issues in Radical Therapy, Springfield, IL
It Ain't Me Babe, Berkeley, CA
Jewish Radical, The, location unknown
Joint Issue, Lansing, MI

Journal, The, Rochester, NY
Journal of Socialist Party in Illinois, Skokie, IL
Ka Huliau, Honolulu, HI
Kaleidoscope, Hazleton, PA
Kaleidoscope, Madison, WI
      Milwaukee, WI
Kaleidoscope, Omaha, NE
Kaleidoscope Chicago, Chicago, IL
Kansas Free Press, Lawrence, KS*
Kelsie, Reno, NE
Kerista Tribe, San Francisco, CA*
Know, Pittsburgh, PA
Korythalia, Altadena, CA#
Kudzu, Jackson, MS
Labor Newsletter, San Francisco, CA
Labor Notes, Detroit, MI
Lancaster Free Press, Lancaster, PA
Lancaster Independent Press, Lancaster, PA
Lansing Star, Lansing, MI
Las Vegas Free Press, Las Vegas, NV
Lebanon Free Press, Lebanon, PA
Left Face, Washington, DC
Left Speak Out, Peoria, IL
Leviathan, San Francisco, CA
      New York, NY
Liar, The, St. Petersburg, FL
Liberated Guardian, New York, NY
Liberation, New York, NY
Liberation News Service, Washington, DC
      Montague, MA
      New York, NY
Liberator, The, Morgantown, WV
Libertarian, San Antonio, TX
Lifestyle, Unionville, OH
Lightning, Storrs, CT*
Lincoln Gazette, Lincoln, NE
Little Free Press, The, Minneapolis, MN*
Long Beach Free Press, Long Beach, CA
Long Island Free Press, Westbury, NY
Looking Glass, Ann Arbor, MI
Los Angeles Free Press, Los Angeles, CA
Los Angeles Image, The, Los Angeles, CA
Los Angeles News Advocate, Sherman Oaks, CA
Los Angeles Underground, Los Angeles, CA
Los Angeles Weekly News, Los Angeles, CA
Love, Reno, NV
Lux Verite, Lafayette, IN
Madison Kaleidoscope, Madison, WI
Maggie's Farm, Stanford, CA#
Majority Report, The, Chicago, IL*
Majority Reports, New York, NY
El Malcriado, Keene, CA*
Marijuana Information Transfer News Service, Los
      Angeles, CA
Marijuana Monthly, Panorama City, CA

Marijuana Review, Buffalo, NY
Marijuana Review, The, Mill Valley, CA
Marijuana Review, The, San Francisco, CA
Mass Pax News, Cambridge, MA#
Match, Tucson, AZ
Maverick, Santa Clara, CA*
Max, New York, NY
Mc Kees Rocks, Mc Kees Rock, PA
M D S Newsletter, New Orleans, LA
M D S/Movement for a Democratic Society/Newsletter,
    New York, NY
Measure, New York, NY*
Mega Middle Myth, Beloit, WI
Merip Reports, Washington, DC
        Cambridge, MA
        New York, NY
Metro, The, Detroit, MI
Metro, The, Scranton, PA
Miami Free Press, Coconut Grove, FL
        Miami, FL
Michigan Voice, Burton, MI
Middle Earth, Iowa City, IA
Middle Earth Free Press, Greenville, SC
Midnight Special, New York, NY*
Midpeninsula Observer, The, Palo Alto, CA
Mile High under Ground, Denver, CO
Militant, The, New York, NY
Mill Hunk Herald, The, Pittsburgh, PA
Mindfucke, Washington, DC
Minisink Bull, Dingman's Ferry, PA
Minne Ha! Ha!, Minneapolis, MN
Minneapolis Flag, The, Minneapolis, MN
Minority Report, Dayton, OH
Mississippi Freelance, Greenville, MS#
Missouri Valley Socialist, Sioux City, IA
        Omaha, NE
Mockingbird, Houston, TX
Modern Times, New Haven, CT*
Modern Utopian, Berkeley, CA
Mom...Guess What!, Sacramento, CA
Momma, Venice, CA
Moniebogue Press, Westhampton, NY
Morning Desert Free Press, University of Nevada-
        Reno, Reno, NV*
Morning Star, Oshkosh, WI
Mother Earth News, Madison, OH
Mother of Voices, Amherst, MA
Motive, Nashville, TN
Mountain Free Press, Denver, CO
Mountain Gazette, Denver, CO
Mountain Liberator, Morgantown, WV
Mountain Life & Work, Clintwood, VA
Mountain News Real, Tucson, AZ
Movement, The, San Francisco, CA
Movin' Together, New York, NY*

Los Muertos Hablan, Laredo, TX
Muhammad Speaks, Chicago, IL*
Nashville Breakdown, Nashville, TN
Nation, The, Los Angeles, CA
National Strike Information Center, Waltham, MA*
National Underground Review, New York, NY
National Weed, New York, NY
Natty Dread, La Jolla, CA
Needle, The, New York, NY
Network, Tucson, AZ
Neuk, Princeton, NJ
New Advocate, The, Staten Island, NY
New Almanac, Bloomington, IN
New America, New York, NY*
New American Movement, Minneapolis, MN*
New Approach, Haverstown, PA#
New Banner, The, Columbia, SC
New Citizen, The, Schenectady, NY
New City Free Press, New York, NY
New Democrat, The, New York, NY#
New England Free Press, Boston, MA*
New Frontier, Laurel Springs, NJ
New Hard Times, St. Louis, MO
New Haven Advocate, New Haven, CT
New Humanist, The, Washington, DC
New Indicator, The, La Jolla, CA
New Left Notes, Boston, MA*
New Left Notes, Chicago, IL
New Mobilizer, Washington, DC
New Morning, The, Berkeley, CA*
New Paper, The, Providence, RI
New Patriot, Ithaca, NY
New Patriot, The, Chicago, IL
New Penelope, Phoenix, AZ
New Prairie Primer, The, Cedar Falls, IA
New Roots, Amherst, MA
        Greenfield, MA
New Solidarity, New York, NY*
New Sos News, San Francisco, CA
New South Student, The, Nashville, TN
New Times, Rock Island, IL
New Times, Tempe, AZ
New Times Weekly, Phoenix, AZ
New Unity, Springfield, MA
New University, Irvine, CA*
New Voice, Chester, PA
New York City Star, New York, NY
New York Daily Planet, New York, NY
New York Free Press, New York, NY
New York High School Free Press, New York,
        NY
New York News Service, New York, NY
New York Review of Sex and Politics, New York, NY
New York Roach, The, Great Neck, NY*
News and Letters, Detroit, MI#

News from Nowhere, Dekalb, IL
News Notes, Philadelphia, PA#
News Project, The, Flushing, NY
Newsfront International, Oakland, CA
Newsletter, New York, NY#
Newspaper, The, New Orleans, LA
Newsreal, Tucson, AZ
Nexus, Santa Barbara, CA*
Nickel Review, Syracuse, NY
1984, Alternative News for Naptown, Indianapolis, IN
N M A & M Conscience, Las Cruces, NM
Nola Express, New Orleans, LA
Nomad, New York, NY
North Carolina Anvil, The, Durham, NC
North Country Anvil, Millville, MN
North Star, Del Mar, CA
  La Jolla, CA
North Valley Free Press, Chico, CA
Northcoast Ripsaw, The, Eureka, CA
Northern Sun News, Minneapolis, MN
Northwest Passage, Bellingham, WA
  Seattle, WA
Notes from the Underground, Dallas, TX
Nova Media, Lafayette, IN
Nova Vanguard, Brooklyn, NY
N U C Newsletter, Chicago, IL#
Nuclear Opponents, Allendale, NJ
Observation Post, New York, NY
Observer, Annadale-on-Hudson, NY
Ocean Beach Rag, Ocean Beach, CA
Ocooch Mountain News, The, Gillingham, WI
  Richland Center, WI
off our backs, Washington, DC
Old Market Press, The, Paducah, KY
Old Mole, Cambridge, MA
OM, Washington, DC
OP, Olympia, WA
Open City, Los Angeles, CA
Open City Press, San Francisco, CA#
Open Door, Milwaukee, WI
Open Process, San Francisco, CA
Option, Los Angeles, CA
Oracle, San Francisco, CA
Oracle of Southern California, Los Angeles, CA
Oscar's Underground Chetto Press, Madison, WI
Osmosis, Tulsa, OK
Other Other, The, Brooklyn, NY
Other Scenes, New York, NY
Our Daily Bread, Minneapolis, MN
Out City, Berkeley, CA
Out of the Ashes Flashfood Service, Portland, OR
Outlaw, St. Louis, MO
Outlaw, San Francisco, CA
Overthrow, New York, NY
Ozark Digest, Eureka Springs, AR

Pac-O-Lies, New York, NY
Pack Rat, Berkeley, CA
Pamoja Venceremos, East Palo Alto, CA*
Pandora, Seattle, WA
Paper, The, East Lansing, MI
Paper, The, Mendocino, CA
Paper, The, Santa Cruz, CA*
Paper Highway, Schenectady, NY
Partisan, New York, NY
Patriot Peoples News Service, The, New York, NY*
Pax, New York, NY
Peace & Democracy News, New York, NY
Peace & Freedom News, Baltimore, MD
Peace Baloon, Santa Ana, CA
Peace News Letter, Syracuse, NY
Peacemaker, The, Cincinnati, OH#
Peninsula Bulletin, The, East Palo Alto, CA*
Peninsula Metro Reporter, San Francisco, CA*
Peninsula Observer, Palo Alto, CA
Penny Press, Jacksonville, FL
People & Energy, Washington, DC
People & Taxes, Washington, DC
People's Press, The, Springfield, IL
People's Tribune, Chicago, IL*
People's Weekly, Waterbury, CT*
People's Witness, Sacramento, CA
People's World, San Francisco, CA
Petal Paper, The, Fairhope, AL*
Phaque, Gary, IN
Philadelphia Action Report, Philadelphia, PA*
Philadelphia Free Press, Philadelphia, PA
Phoenix, San Francisco, CA
Phoenix, The, Nashville, TN
Pittsburgh Fair Witness, Pittsburgh, PA
Pittsburgh Peace & Freedom News, Pittsburgh, PA
Pittsburgh Point, Pittsburgh, PA
Plain Dealer, Philadelphia, PA
Plain Rapper, Palo Alto, CA
Plain Truth, The, Champaign, IL
Planet, San Francisco, CA#
Planet People, San Francisco, CA
Plowshare Press, The, Palo Alto, CA*
Polar Star, Fairbanks, AK
Post Amerikan, Bloomington, IL
  Normal, IL
Prairie Sun, Peoria, IL
  Rock Island, IL
Preview, Lawrence, MA
Prick, Tempe, AZ
Primo Times, Bloomington, IN
  Indianapolis, IN
Primo Times, Terre Haute, IN
Probe, Santa Barbara, CA
Progressive, The, Madison, WI
Progressive Platter, Boston, MA

Progressive Review, The, Washington, DC
Prospectus, Charleston, IL
Protean Radish, Chapel Hill, NC
Protos, Chicago, IL*
    Los Angeles, CA*
Provincial Press, Spokane, WA
Provo, Los Angeles, CA
Pterocactyl, Grinnell, IA
Public Citizen People & Taxes, Washington, DC
Public Eye, The, Chicago, IL
    Washington, DC
Public Occurance, Burlington, VT
Punch, The, Worcester, MA
Punk Research, San Diego, CA
Questionable Cartoons, New York, NY
Quicksilver Times, Washington, DC
Rabid One, The, Berkeley, CA
Radical America, Somerville, MA
Radical Rag, The, Palo Alto, CA*
Radicals in the Profession, Ann Arbor, MI
Rag, Austin, TX
    Guadalupe, TX
Rage, Jacksonville, NC*
Raisin Bread, Minneapolis, MN
Ramparts Wall Poster, The, Chicago, IL
Rap!, Columbus, GA*
Raritan Peace News, New Brunswick, NJ
Rat, New York, NY
La Raza, Los Angeles, CA
Razzberry, The, Dayton, OH
Razzberry Street Sheet, Dayton, OH
Real Fun, Philadelphia, PA
Real News, The, Stanford, CA*
Real Paper, Cambridge, MA
Real Times, Bloomington, IN
Real Times Weekly, Bloomington, IN
Realist, New York, NY
Rebirth, Phoenix, AZ
Reconstruction, Topeka, KS
Reflector, Jackson, MS
Reliable Source, New York, NY
Renaissance, Santa Barbara, CA
Renewable Energy News, Harrisville, NH
    Syracuse, NY
RE/Search, San Francisco, CA
Resist, Somerville, MA
Resister, Philadelphia, PA*
Resistance, Boston, MA
RE:Sources, Washington, DC
Resurrection, Tucson, AZ
Revolution, Chicago, IL*
Revolution, New York, NY
Revolution, San Diego, CA
Revolutionary Youth Movement, Chicago, IL#
R F D, Bakersville, NC

Richmond Chronicle, Richmond, VA
Right On!, Berkeley, CA*
Right-on Post, Seaside, CA*
Rising Tide, The, Washington, DC*
Rising Up Angry, Chicago, IL
River City Review, Memphis, TN
River City Sun, Austin, TX
River Courant, Oshkosh, WI
Roach, Eau Claire, WI
Roach, Great Neck, NY
Roach, Haleiwa, HI
Rochester Patriot, Rochester, NY
Rochester Peoples Paper, Rochester, MI*
Rocket, The, Seattle, WA
Roosevelt Torch, Chicago, IL
Root, Memphis, TN
Rough Draft, Norfolk, VA
Route One Gazette, College Park, MD*
R T, West Somerville, MA
Ryder, The, Bloomington, IN
R Y M, Chicago, IL
Sabot, Seattle, WA
Sagebrush, Reno, NV*
Sagebrush Chronicle, Reno, NV*
St. Louis Free Press, St. Louis, MO
Saint Louis Today, St. Louis, MO
San Antonio Gazette, San Antonio, TX
San Diego Door, San Diego, CA
San Diego Door to Liberation, San Diego, CA
San Diego Free Door, San Diego, CA
San Diego Free Door to Liberation, San Diego, CA
San Diego Free Press, San Diego, CA
San Francisco Bay Guardian, San Francisco, CA*
San Francisco Dock of the Bay, San Francisco, CA
San Francisco Express Times, San Francisco, CA
San Francisco Gay Free Press, San Francisco, CA*
San Jose Maverick, San Jose, CA*
San Jose Red Eye, San Jose, CA
Sanity Now, La Puente, CA
Sansculottes, New York, NY
Santa Barbara News & Review, Santa Barbara, CA
Satirist, Chicago, IL
Schuylkill River Express, Philadelphia, PA*
Science for the People, Cambridge, MA
Scimitar, Ithaca, NY
Screw, The, Kansas City, MO
Search and Destroy, San Francisco, CA
Searcher, The, Wellesley, MA
Second City, Chicago, IL
Second City, Indianapolis, IN
Second Coming, Ypsilanti, MI
Second Page, The, San Francisco, CA*
Sedition, San Jose, CA
Seed, The, Chicago, IL
Seer's Catalogue, Albuquerque, NM

See's, Albuquerque, NM
Serve the People, location not listed*
Seventy-Nine Cent Spread, Carmel, CA
S.F. Oracle, San Francisco, CA#
Shelter, Kansas City, MO
Shelterforce, East Orange, NJ
Shmate, Berkeley, CA
Short Times, The, Columbia, SC
Sierra Review, Quincy, CA*
Sipapu, Winters, CA
Socialist Action, San Francisco, CA*
Socialist Forum, New York, NY*
Socialist Voice, New York, NY*
Something Else, Ann Arbor, MI
Son of Jabberwock, The, New York, NY
S O S News, Oakland, CA*
South Baltimore Voice, Baltimore, MD*
South End, The, Detroit, MI
Southeast Asia Chronicle, Berkeley, CA
Southern Agitator, New Orleans, LA
Southern Flyer, Dunedin, FL
Southern Free Press, Carbondale, IL
Southern Libertarian Messenger, The, Florence, SC
Southern Patriot, The, Louisville, KY
Southern Struggle, Atlanta, GA
Space City, Houston, TX
Space City News, Houston, TX
Spark, Boston, MA*
Spark, Takoma, MD
Spartacist West, Berkeley, CA#
Speak Easy, Attleboro, MA
Spectator, The, Berkeley, CA
Spectator, The, Bloomington, IN
Spectrum, Little Rock, AR
Spinal Column, Davenport, IA
Spirit, Nashville, TN
Spokane Natural, Spokane, WA
Spotlight, The, Washington, DC*
S R A Federation Bulletin, San Francisco, CA
Staff, The, Hollywood, CA*
Stanford Daily, The, Stanford, CA*
Star Spangled Pentangle, The, New Orleans, LA*
Star Toot, Redway, CA
Store Front Classroom, The, San Francisco, CA
Storrs Weekly Reader, Storrs, CT*
Straight Creek Journal, Boulder, CO
        Denver, CO
Strategic Hamlet, Santa Barbara, CA*
Strawberry Fields, Miami, FL
Street Journal, San Diego, CA
Street Wall, Journal, Stanford, CA*
Strike, Chapel Hill, NC
Strike Newspaper, New Haven, CT*
Struggle, Boston, MA*
Student Action, San Bernadino, CA#

Student Mobilizer, The, Chicago, IL
        New York, NY
        Washington, DC
Student Nonviolent Coordinating Committee, San Francisco, CA*
Subersive Scholastic, Columbus, OH
Sun, Ann Arbor, MI
        Detroit, MI
Sun, The, Chapel Hill, NC
Sun Flower, The, Richmond, VA
Sun Rise, Macob, IL
Sunburst, Tucson, AZ*
Sundaze, Santa Cruz, CA
Sun/Evening Sun, Albuquerque, NM
Supplement, The, Santa Fe, NM
Survival Press Review, Boulder, CO*
Swamp Erie Pipe Dream, Cleveland, OH
Sweet Fire, Albany, NY
Synapse, Ithaca, NY
Tablet, Kansas City, KS
Take Over, Madison, WI
Takin' Union, Takoma Park, MD
Tapestry, Maryland, MA
Tartuffles, Madison, WI
Task Force, San Francisco, CA*
Tasty World, Athens, GA
Teaspoon & the Door, San Diego, CA
Temple Free Press, Philadelphia, PA#
Tenants Rising, Berkeley, CA*
Testube, Columbus, OH
Texas Observer, The, Austin, TX*
Third Paper, The, Shreveport, LA
Third World News, Davis, CA*
Thorn, New York, NY
Thrust, Pittsburgh, PA
Thursday's Drummer, Morgantown, WV
Times Change, Columbus, OH
Tin Drum, Washington, DC*
Together, Palo Alto, CA
Top Secret, Cambridge, MA
Torch, Chicago, IL
Trashman, Berkeley, CA
Tri-County Clarion, Yakima, WA
Tribal Messenger, The, Albuquerque, NM
True Free Press, Indio, CA*
Trumpet, The, Goleta, CA
Trumpet, The, Rockford, IL
Tucson Teen, Tucson, AZ
Tulsa Free Press, Tulsa, OK
Turning Point, State College, PA
Twentieth Century Anonymous, Cincinnati, OH
Ultimate Weapon, Philadelphia, PA
Under Current, Buffalo, NY
Underground Digest, New York, NY
Underground Flick, Southfield, MI

Ungarbled World, The, New Orleans, LA
Universal Life, Modesto, CA*
University Review, New York, NY
Up Against the Wall Street Journal, Ann Arbor, MI*
Up Front, Los Angeles, CA
U P S News Service, New York, NY
U R, New York, NY
Urban Underground, New York, NY
Utopian Classroom, The, San Francisco, CA
Utopian Eyes, San Francisco, CA
Valley Advocate, Amherst, MA
    Hartford, CT
Valley Advocate / Springfield Edition, Springfield, MS
Vanguard, San Francisco, CA
V D R S V P, San Francisco, CA
Venceremos, Palo Alto, CA*
Venceremos, Redwood City, CA*
Veteran Stars & Stripes for Peace, Chicago, IL
Viet Report, New York, NY
Vietnam GI, Chicago, IL
Vieux Carre Courier, New Orleans, LA*
View from the Bottom, New Haven, CT
Vision, Berkeley, CA
Vista, Chicago, IL
Vocations for Social Change, Canyon, CA
Voice from the Mother Country, Washington, DC*
Voice of Black Community, The, Decatur, IL
Voice of the City, Phoenix, AZ
Vortex, Kansas City, MO
    Lawrence, KS
Waco Organizer, San Francisco, CA*
Walrus, Champaign-Urbana, IL
War Bulletin, Berkeley, CA
War Tax Monthly, San Francisco, CA*
Warpath, San Francisco, CA*
Warren Free Press, Warren, OH
Washington Blade, The, Washington, DC
Washington Free Press, Washington, DC
Washington Weekly, Washington, DC
Wassaja, San Francisco, CA
Watcher, The, Winter Park, FL
Water Tunnel, State College, PA
Weakly Citizen Harold, Santa Barbara, CA
Weather Report, San Marcos, TX
Weekly People, Brooklyn, NY*
Weekly People, The, Palo Alto, CA#
Wei Min, San Francisco, CA*
Well, Bethlehem, PA
West Side News, New York, NY
West Side Story, Iowa City, IA
Western Activist, Kalamazoo, MI
Western Prisoners, Venice, CA
Western Star, The, Missoula, MT
Westport Trucker, Kansas City, MO
Whippersnapper, Mc Connellsburg, PA

Whipping Post/Starship, Nelsonville, WI
    Stevens Point, WI
White Lightning, Bronx, NY
White Power, Arlington, VA*
Whole Earth Catalog, Menlo Park, VA*
Wilcox Report, The, Kansas City, MO*
Wild Currents, Duluth, MN
Wild Flowers, Stow, MA
Wildcat, San Francisco, CA*
Willamette Bridge, Portland, OR
Willamette Valley Observer, Eugene, OR
Win, Brooklyn, NY
    New York, NY
    Rifton, NY
Winds, Stanford, CA*
Winter Soldier, Chicago, IL*
Wisconsin Patriot, The, Madison, WI*
Witzend, New York, NY
Women, Baltimore, MD
Women's Liberation, New York, NY
Woodwind, Washington, DC*
Worker's Power, Detroit, MI
    Highland Park, MI
Workers Vanguard, New York, NY*
Workers World, New York, NY*
Workforce, Oakland, CA
World Countdown, Los Angeles, CA
W R L, New York, NY#
Xanadu, St. Louis, MO
XEX Graphix, Memphis, TN
Yarrow Stalks, Philadelphia, PA
Yellow Dog, Berkeley, CA
Yellow Silk, Albany, CA
Yipster, Staten Island, NY
Yipster Times, New York, NY
El Young Lord, Milwaukee, WI*
Young Socialist, New York, NY
Young Spartacus, New York, NY
Youth and Nation, New York, NY
Youth Awareness Press, Tucson, AZ
Der Zeitgeist, Phoenix, AZ
Zig Zag, Montague, MA

*Indicates new title in Hoover Institution supplement.
#indicates new title in Missouri supplement.

Sources: *Underground Press Collection, Listing of Contents, 1963-1985.* Ann Arbor, MI: University Microfilms International, 1986; *Underground Newspaper Collection: UM* [University of Missouri-Columbia] *Libraries* (n.d.); *Underground Press Collection: A Guide to the Microfilm Collection, Hoover Institution Supplement.* Ann Arbor, MI: University Microfilms International, 1988.

Appendix C: Herstory Microfilm Collection: 1960s-1970s U.S. Titles

Abogada Internacional, New York, NY*

Abogada Newsletter, New York, NY*

ACDS (Assn. for Children Deprived of Support), Northridge, CA

Action for Children, Los Angeles, CA*

Advocates for Women Newsletter, San Francisco, CA*

Ain't I a Woman?, Iowa City, IA

Akamai Sister (Hawaii Women's Liberation), Honolulu, HI

ALA/SRRT (Status Women in Librarianship), Chapel Hill, NC

Alert: Federation of Organizations for Professional Women, Washington, DC#

Alert: Women's Legislative Review, Middletown, CT*

Amazon, The, Milwaukee, WI*

Amazon - National Newsletter, The, Milwaukee, WI*

American Association of Women in Community and Junior Colleges Newsletter, Phoenix, AZ#

American Education Research Association Women's Caucus Newsletter, San Francisco, CA*

American Friends Service Committee Women's Newsletter, San Francisco, CA*

American Library Association - Social Responsibilities Round Table - Task Force on the Status of Women in Librarianship, Seattle, WA*

American Negro Woman, The, Cleveland, OH#

American Society for Psychoprophylaxis in Obstetrics Bay Area (ASPO News), Berkeley, CA*

American Society for Public Administration - Task Force on the Status of Women and Minorities - Bay Area, Oakland, CA*

And Ain't I a Woman!, Seattle, WA

Another Mother for Peace, Beverly Hills, CA

Antioch College Women's Liberation, Yellow Springs, OH

Aphra, New York, NY

Aradia (Pittsburgh Women's Union), Pittsburgh, PA

Asian Women, U.C. Berkeley, CA

Asian Women's Center Newsletter, Los Angeles, CA*

Association for Women in Mathematics Newsletter, Washington, DC*

Association for Women in Psychology Newsletter, New York, NY*

Association of American Colleges - Project on the Status and Education of Women, Washington, DC*

Association of American Colleges - Project on the Status and Education of Women (on Campus with Women), Washington, DC*

Association of American Law Schools, Washington, DC*

Association of Faculty Women Newsletter, Madison, WI#

Association of Married Women, Arlington, VA*

Association to Repeal Abortion Laws, San Francisco, CA

Atlanta Women's Club Bulletin, Atlanta, GA*

Aurora, Suffern, New York, NY

Awake and Move, Philadelphia, PA

A.W.I.S. (Assn. of Women in Science), New York, NY

AWP (Assn. for Women in Psychology), St. Louis, MI

Battle Acts, New York, NY

Bay Area Women's Liberation, San Francisco, CA

Bella Abzug Reports, Washington, DC*

Berkeley Women's Liberation, Berkeley, CA

Berkeley/Oakland Women's Union: A Socialist/Feminist Organization, Berkeley, CA#

Best Friends, Albuquerque, NM

Big Mama Rag, Denver, CO*

Birthright, Tampa, FL*

Bitch, Milwaukee, WI

Black Maria, River Forest, IL*

Bloomington Women's Liberation, Bloomington, IN

Born a Woman, Los Angeles, CA*

Bread and Roses, Boston, MA

Bread and Roses Newsletter, Cambridge, MA*

Breakthrough, Lawrence, KS*

Bridge, The, Boston, MA

Broadside, Berkeley, CA*

Broadside, New York, NY

Calafia Clarion, Santa Monica, CA#

California Division - American Association of University Women, San Jose, CA*

California Personnel and Guidance Association Women's Caucus Newsletter, Fullerton, CA#

California Service Worker, Sacramento, CA#

Cape Cod Women's Liberation Newsletter, East Sandwich, MA*

Capitol Alert (Legislative Committee of NOW Sacramento), Sacramento, CA

Capitol: Woman, Lansing, MI*

Career Newsletter, Lawrence, KS#

Cassandra, Chicago, IL

Caucus for Women in Statistics, Washington, DC*

Caucus of Women in History, Chapel Hill, NC*

Caucus of Women in History of the S.H.A., Atlanta, GA

CCWHP (Coordinating Committee on Women in the Historical Profession), Chicago, IL

Center for Continuing Education of Women, Ann Arbor, MI

Change Is Gonna Come, A, San Francisco, CA

Changing Woman, Portland, OR*

Chicana Service Action Center News, Los Angeles, CA#

Chisholm Trail, The, San Francisco, CA*

Church Women United State News, Whittier, CA*

City Wide Women's Liberation Newsletter, New York, NY*

Cleveland Feminist, The, Cleveland, OH#

Cold Day in August, A, Baltimore, MD*

College Park: Women's Studies Newsletter, College Park, MD#

Coming Out, Oberlin, OH*

Comisión Femenil Mexicana Report, Los Angeles, CA*

Comment, Cambridge, MA*

Commission on the Status of Women - California, Sacramento, CA#

Commission on the Status of Women - District of Columbia, Washington, DC#

Commission on the Status of Women News - Pennsylvania, Harrisburg, PA*

Commission on the Status of Women Report - Pennsylvania, Harrisburg, PA*

Common Sense, Portland, OR*

Common Woman, Berkeley, CA*

Common Woman Is the Revolution, The, Berkeley, CA

Concern for Health Options: Information Care and Education Resource and News Bulletin, Philadelphia, PA#

Concerns (Women's Caucus for the Modern Languages), Charleston, IL

Congress to Unite Women, New York, NY

Connecticut Woman, Bristol, CT#

Connections, San Francisco, CA

Consciousness Up, Smithtown, NY#

Continuing Currents, Honolulu, HI*

Continuing Education for Women - Temple University, Philadelphia, PA*

Continuing Education for Women - University of Delaware, Newark, DE*

Continuing Education for Women - Newsletter - Minnesota, Minneapolis, MN#

Coordinating Committee on Women in the Historical Profession, Woodside, CA*

Council for Women's Equality, Portland, OR

Country Women, Albion, CA*

Cowrie, New York, NY*

Coyote, San Francisco, CA*

Cries from Cassandra, Chicago, IL*

Cry Out, Roanoke, VA*

CWSS (Center for Women's Studies and Services), San Diego, CA

Daughters of Bilitis - Boston, Boston, MA*

Daughters of Bilitis - Dallas (The Monthly DOB'R), Dallas, TX#

Daughters of Bilitis - Detroit (Reach Out), Detroit, MI*

Daughters of Bilitis, New York, NY

Daughters of Bilitis - San Francisco (Sisters) San Francisco, CA*

Dayton Women's Liberation Newsletter, Dayton, OH*

Definitely Biased, Santa Cruz, CA*

Denver Women's Newsletter, Denver, CO*

Distaff, New Orleans, LA*

Earth's Daughters, Buffalo, NY

East Bay Feminists, Berkeley, CA

East Bay Women for Peace, Berkeley, CA

Echo of Sappho, Brooklyn, NY*

Ecumenical Women's Centers, Chicago, IL#

Electra, Rochester, NY

Elizabeth Blackwell's Women's Health Center Newsletter, Minneapolis, MN#

Employee Press, Berkeley, CA

Equal Times Newsletter, Washington, DC#

Eve, Playa Del Rey, CA*

Eve News, The, Union, NJ

Everywoman, Los Angeles, CA

Everywoman, Omaha, NE*

Everywoman's Center Newsletter, Amherst, MA*

Executive Woman, New York, NY#

Fair Employment Practice Commission News, San Francisco, CA*

Familia, Kingston, NY#

Family in Historical Perspective, The, Cambridge, MA*

Federally Employed Women's News and Views, Washington, DC*

Feelings, Brooklyn, NY

Female Liberation, Berkeley, CA

Female Liberation, Boston, MA

Female Liberation, Minneapolis, MN

Feminine Focus, Lansing, MI

Feminist, Wallingford, PA*

Feminist Art Journal, Brooklyn, NY*

Feminist Bulletin, The, Scarborough, NY#

Feminist Coalition Newsletter, New Brunswick, NJ#

Feminist Forum, Tacoma, WA*

Feminist Journal, The, Minneapolis, MN

Feminist Media Project Newsletter, Washington, DC#

Feminist News, Sacramento, CA*

Feminist Party, San Francisco, CA#

Feminist Party News, New York, NY*

Feminist Studies, New York, NY*

Feminist Voice, Chicago, IL

Feminist Women's Health Center - Oakland, Oakland, CA#

Feminist Women's Health Center Report - Los Angeles, CA#

F.E.W.'s (Federally Employed Women), Washington, DC

FEW'S News and Views, Washington, DC*

51%: A Paper of Joyful Noise, Lomita, CA*

Focus, Boston, MA
Focus on Women, Orange, NJ*
Foote and Schoe, Norwalk, CT*
Fourth World, Oakland, CA
Frankly Female, Knoxville, TN*
Free and Proud, Tallahassee, FL
From the Bench, San Jose, CA*
Front Page, Bloomington, IN*
Full Moon, Northampton, MA*
Furies, The, Washington, DC*
Gay Blade, The, Washington, DC*
Gay People and Mental Health; a Monthly Bulletin, Minneapolis, MN*
Gay Teacher's News, Chicago, IL#
Gay Women's Newsletter, Champaign, IL*
Gayly Forward, Seattle, WA*
Genesis III (Philadelphia Task Force on Women in Religion), Philadelphia, PA
Geographers for Women's Achievement Newsletter, Syracuse, NY*
Getting on Women Collective, East Lansing, MI
Give a Sister a Lift, Santa Cruz, CA*
Gold Flower, Minneapolis, MN*
Goodbye to All That, San Diego, CA
Grail, The, Grailville, OH*
Half of Brooklyn Newsletter, Brooklyn, NY*
Hand That Rocks the Rock, The (formerly Lysistrata), Slippery Rock, PA
Harrisburg's Women's Rights Movement Newsletter, Harrisburg, PA*
Her Own Right, New Orleans, LA
Her-self: Community Women's Newsletter, Ann Arbor, MI*
Highschool Women's Newsletter, Mill Valley, CA*
Hijas de Cuahtemoc, Long Beach, CA*
Human Equality, Honolulu, HI*
Human Rights for Women, Washington, DC
Hysteria, Boston, MA
IAWS (Intercollegiate Assn. of Women Students), East Lansing, MI
In Touch, Trenton, NJ#
Indiana Abortion Law Repeal Coalition, Bloomington, IN
Indianapolis Women's Liberation, Indianapolis, IN
Inter-Studio Feminist Alliance Newsletter (Ms. on Scene), Hollywood, CA*
It Ain't Me Babe, Berkeley, CA
Jeanette Rankin Brigade, San Francisco, CA
Joint Strategy and Action Committee (JSAC Grapevine), New York, NY*
Journey, The, Des Moines, IA,*
Joyous Struggle, Albuquerque, New Mexico*
Junior League Fogcutter, San Francisco, CA
Just Like a Woman, Atlanta, GA
Kaliflower, San Francisco, CA

Killer Dyke, Chicago, IL
Know, Inc., Pittsburgh, PA*
Know News, Pittsburgh, PA
Labor Pains Newsletter, The, Cambridge, MA
Ladder, The, Kansas City, MO
Ladder, The, San Francisco, CA
Lancaster Women's Liberation, Lancaster, PA*
Lavender Vision, Cambridge, MO
Lavender Woman: A Lesbian Newspaper, Chicago, IL*
L.A. Women's Liberation, Los Angeles, CA
League of Associated Women, Berkeley, CA*
Lesbian Feminist, New York, NY#
Lesbian Tide (D.O.B.), Los Angeles, CA
Lesbians Fight Back, Philadelphia, PA*
Libera, Berkeley, CA*
Liberated Space for the Women of the Haight, San Francisco, CA
Liberator, Fort Worth, TX*
Lilith, Fresno, CA*
Lilith, Seattle, WA
Lilith's Rib, Chicago, IL#
Link, The, Chicago, IL#
Lobbyist, The, Los Angeles, CA
Maine Freewoman's Herald, Brunswick, ME#
Majority Report, New York, NY
Marin Women's News Journal, San Rafael, CA*
Matrix, Los Angeles, CA*
Matrix, Washington, DC
Media Report to Women, Washington, DC*
Media Women's Monthly, New York, NY
Memo, Washington, DC, and New York, NY
Midwest Women's Legal Group Newsletter, Chicago, IL*
Modern Language Assn. Commission on the Status of Women, New York, NY
Modern Language Association - Commission on the Status of Women in the Profession/Women's Caucus for the Modern Languages (Convention Publication), Slippery Rock, PA*
Modern Language Association - Women's Caucus for the Modern Languages (Concerns), West Lafayette, IN*
Modern Language Association - Women's Caucus for the Modern Languages (Research in Progress), Pittsburgh, PA*
Momma: The Newspaper Magazine for Single Mothers, Venice, CA*
Momma - The Organization for Single Mothers, Venice, CA*
Monthly Extract: An Irregular Periodical, The, Stamfort, CT*
Moonshadow, Miami Beach, FL#
Mother, Stanford, CA
Mother Jones Gazette, Knoxville, TN*

Mother Lode, San Francisco, CA
Mothers for Fair Child Support, Forestville, NY*
Mountain Moving Day, Carbondale, IL*
Moving Out, Detroit, MI
Ms., New York, NY*
Ms. Archivist, Columbus, OH
Muthah, Sacramento, CA
Napa Valley Women's Center Newsletter, Napa, CA*
N.A.R.A.L. (National Assn. for the Repeal of Abortion Laws), New York, NY
Nassau Herald's Sisterhood Week, Far Rockaway, NY*
National Ad Hoc Committee for ERA (Equal Rights Amendment), Falls Church, Virginia
National Association for Women Deans, Administrators and Counselors, Washington, DC#
National Council of Administrative Women in Education (NCAWE News), Washington, DC*
National Lesbian Information Service, San Francisco, CA*
N.C.H.E. (National Committee on Household Employment) News, Washington, DC
NOW (National Organization for Women) Acts, Los Angeles, CA
NOW Albuquerque, Albuquerque, NM*
NOW Ann Arbor, Ann Arbor, MI#
NOW Annapolis, Annapolis, MD#
NOW Anne Arundel County, Annapolis, MD*
NOW Atlanta, Atlanta, GA*
NOW Bakersfield, Bakersfield, CA*
NOW Baton Rouge, Baton Rouge, LA
NOW Beach Cities, Manhattan Beach, CA#
NOW Berkeley, Berkeley, CA
NOW Berks County, Reading, PA#
NOW Boston (News about NOW), Boston, MA*
NOW Boulder, Boulder, CO*
NOW Bronx, Bronx, NY*
NOW Brooklyn, Brooklyn, NY
NOW Buffalo, Buffalo, NY
NOW Butler County (Up to NOW), Fairfield, OH#
NOW Caddo-Bossier City (Press On), Shreveport, LA*
NOW California, San Diego, CA*
NOW Central Connecticut, West Hartford, CT*
NOW Central New Jersey, Princeton, NJ
NOW Central New York (NOW News and Notes), Syracuse, NY*
NOW Central Savannah River Area (Applecart), Augusta, GA*
NOW Chicago, Chicago, IL
NOW Cincinnati (NOW News), Cincinnati, OH*
NOW Clark Campus, Worcester, MA
NOW Cleveland, Cleveland, OH
NOW Columbus, Columbus, OH*
NOW Committee to Promote Women's Studies (The News Sheet), Cherry Hill, NJ#
NOW Conejo Valley, Thousand Oaks, CA*

NOW Connecticut, Elmwood, CT
NOW Contra Costa County, Walnut Creek, CA*
NOW Dade County, Coconut Grove, FL
NOW Dallas County (Now Hear This), Dallas, TX#
NOW Denver, Denver, CO
NOW Des Moines, Des Moines, IA
NOW Detroit (As We See It NOW), Detroit, MI*
NOW Dupage (The Torch), Glen Ellyn, IL*
NOW Durham, Durham, NC*
NOW Eastern Massachusetts, Boston, MA
NOW El Paso County, Colorado Springs, CO*
NOW Erie County, Hiler, NY#
NOW Essex County, Maplewood, NJ*
NOW Fort Worth, Fort Worth, TX
NOW Fox Valley/Elgin, Elgin, IL#
NOW Fresno, Fresno, CA*
NOW Fullerton, Fullerton, CA*
NOW Genesee Valley (The Forum), Rochester, NY*
NOW Great Falls and Missoula (Around and about NOW), Great Falls, MT#
NOW Greater Kansas City (Here and NOW) Kansas City, MO*
NOW Greater Pittsburgh, Pittsburgh, PA
NOW Green Bay, Green Bay, WI*
NOW Harbor-South Bay, San Pedro, CA*
NOW Houston, Houston, TX
NOW Indianapolis, Indianapolis, IN*
NOW Jacksonville, Jacksonville, FL*
NOW Kansas City, Kansas City, MO
NOW Kitsap County, Bremerton, WA*
NOW Laguna Beach, Newport Beach, CA*
NOW Las Vegas, Las Vegas, NV*
NOW Lehigh Valley, Bethlehem, PA*
NOW Lincoln (Lincoln NOWsletter), Lincoln, NE*
NOW Long Beach, Long Beach, CA#
NOW Long Island, Great Neck, NY
NOW Los Angeles, Los Angeles, CA
NOW Madison (Equality NOW), Madison, WI*
NOW Maine (Mainely NOW), Portland, ME#
NOW Marin, San Rafael, CA
NOW Martha's Vineyard Task Force in the Image of Women, Martha's Vineyard, MA
NOW Michigan, Detroit, MI
NOW Middlesex County, Iselin, NJ#
NOW Midland, (AnNOWncements), Midland, MI*
NOW Milwaukee, Milwaukee, WI
NOW Monmouth County, Red Bank, NJ*
NOW Monterey, Monterey, CA
NOW Montgomery (From NOW On), Montgomery, AL#
NOW Montgomery County (From NOW On), Rockville, MD*
NOW Muncie, Muncie, IN
NOW National Federal Communications Commission Task Force, Chicago, IL*

NOW National Headquarters (NOW Acts), Chicago, IL*

NOW National Task Force: Marriage, Divorce, and Family Relations, New York, NY*

NOW New Jersey (Newsletter NOW New Jersey), Tenafly, NJ#

NOW New Mexico, Albuquerque, NM

NOW New Orleans (Here and NOW), New Orleans, LA*

NOW New York (The NOW York Woman), New York, NY*

NOW New York City, New York, NY

NOW New York State, Skaneateles, NY

NOW Norfolk, Norfolk, VA#

NOW North Palm County (The Liberator), Lake Worth, FL*

NOW North Shore Massachusetts, Beverly, MA

NOW North Suburban Chicago (NOW North), Northbrook, IL*

NOW Northeast Bucks, Penndel, PA*

NOW Northern California, San Francisco, CA*

NOW Northern Chautauqua County (NOW NEWS), Fredonia, NY#

NOW Northern Nevada (Androgyny), Sparks, NV#

NOW Northern New Jersey, Westwood, NJ

NOW Northern Prince George's County (Shakti), Greenbelt, MD#

NOW Northern Virginia, Falls Church, VA

NOW Notes, Atlanta, GA

NOW Orange County, Fullerton, CA

NOW Orlando (News for NOW), Orlando, FL#

NOW Palo Alto, Palo Alto, CA*

NOW Passaic County (NOW News), Passaic, NJ*

NOW Peninsula Women's Coalition, Rolling Hills Estates, CA*

NOW Peoria, Peoria, IL#

NOW Philadelphia, Philadelphia, PA

NOW Phoenix, Phoenix, AZ

NOW Pomona Valley (Pomona Valley Newsletter), Claremont, CA*

NOW Portland, Portland, OR

NOW Princeton, Princeton, NJ*

NOW Quad Cities, Moline, IL*

NOW Regional News West, Costa Mesa, CA

NOW Rhode Island, Providence, RI*

NOW Riverside, Riverside, CA

NOW Roanoke Valley (Moving), Salem, VA#

NOW Rochester (The Freedom Press), Rochester, MN#

NOW Rockford (Muliebrity Majority), Rockford, IL*

NOW Rockport (Essecondsex), Rockport, MA*

NOW Sacramento, Sacramento, CA

NOW St. John's County, St. Augustine, FL*

NOW St. Louis, St. Louis, MO

NOW Salem, Salem, OR

NOW San Antonio, San Antonio, TX*

NOW San Diego, San Diego, CA

NOW San Fernando Valley, Sherman Oaks, CA

NOW San Francisco, San Francisco, CA

NOW San Gabriel Valley, La Crescenta, CA#

NOW San Joaquin, Stockton, CA*

NOW San Jose (NOW News), San Jose, CA#

NOW San Mateo County, San Mateo, CA

NOW Santa Barbara (NOW Newsletter), Santa Barbara, CA*

NOW Santa Cruz (Here and NOW), Soquel, CA*

NOW Schoolcraft/Livonia Chapter, Farmington, MI#

NOW Seattle, Seattle, WA

NOW Snohomish County, Montlake Terrace, WA

NOW Solano County (Lysistrada), Fairfield, CA*

NOW Somerset County, Martinsville, NJ#

NOW South Bay, Sunnyvale, CA

NOW Southeastern Connecticut, Stonington, CT*

NOW Southern Prince George's County (Nowletter), Temple Hills, MD#

NOW Southwest Cook County (NOW or Never), Worth, IL*

NOW Springfield, Springfield, IL#

NOW Staten Island, Staten Island, NY*

NOW Suffolk County, Stony Brook, NY*

NOW Sunnyvale-South Bay, Sunnyvale, CA*

NOW Tacoma (NOW Notes), Tacoma, WA*

NOW Task Force: Education, La Mesa, CA#

NOW Task Force: Women and Arts, Rowayton, CT#

NOW Texas (Broadside), Bellaire, TX*

NOW Thurston (NOW Is the Time), Olympia, WA*

NOW Tippecanoe, West Lafayette, IN#

NOW Trenton, Trenton, NJ#

NOW Tri-Cities, Richland, WA#

NOW Tri-State, Evansville, IN#

NOW Tucson, Tucson, AZ*

NOW Twin Cities (NOW Newsletter), Minneapolis, MN*

NOW Union County, Mountainside, NJ*

NOW Ventura, Ventura, CA*

NOW Virginia Beach Chapter (Right NOW), Virginia, Beach, VA*

NOW Washington County (Washington County Woman), Hagerstown, MD#

NOW Washington DC, Washington, DC

NOW Western Connecticut, Stratford, CT

NOW Western Region, Seattle, WA*

NOW Wichita, Wichita, KS

NOW Willamette Valley, Oregon (News and Views), Salem, OR*

National Women's Political Caucus, Alameda County, Berkeley, CA*

National Women's Political Caucus, Arizona, Phoenix, AZ*

National Women's Political Caucus, Contra Costa County, Walnut Creek, CA#

National Women's Political Caucus, Los Angeles Metro, Los Angeles, CA*

National Women's Political Caucus, Orange County, Irvine, CA#

National Women's Political Caucus, Philadelphia, Philadelphia, PA*

National Women's Political Caucus, San Diego, La Jolla, CA*

National Women's Political Caucus, San Fernando Valley, North Hollywood, CA*

National Women's Political Caucus, Santa Clara County, San Jose, CA*

National Women's Political Caucus, Texas, Austin, TX#

National Women's Political Caucus, Washington, DC - National Headquarters, Washington, DC*

National Women's Political Caucus, Wichita, Wichita, KS*

New American Movement: Women's Newsletter on Socialist Feminism, Durham, NC*

New Broom, The, Boston, MA

New Carolina Woman, Knightdale, NC

New Directions for Women in Delaware, Newark, DE#

New Directions for Women in New Jersey, Dover, NJ*

New Womankind, Louisville, KY#

New York Radical Feminists Newsletter, New York, NY*

New York Women Strike for Peace Peaceletter, New York, NY

New York Women's Liberation, New York, NY

New Yorkers for Abortion Law Repeal, New York, NY

Newsletter: Center for Continuing Education of Women - University of Michigan, Ann Arbor, MI*

Newsletter of the Association of Women in Science, Bronx, NY*

Newsletter of the Women's Liberation Center of Nassau County, The, Hempstead, NY*

9 to 5: Newsletter for Boston Area Office Workers, Boston, MA

No More Fun and Games, Cambridge, MA

North Dakota Women's Liberation, Minot, ND

Notes from the First Year, New York, NY

Notes from the Second Year, New York, NY

Notes from the Third Year, New York, NY

Notes to Sisters in Social Work, Urbana, IL*

Now York Times, New York, NY

Now York Woman, New York, NY

Oakes Newsletter, The, Philadelphia, PA*

Oakland Women's Liberation, Oakland, CA*

off our backs, Washington, DC

Ohio Woman, Columbus, OH*

Ombudswoman, Tucson, AZ#

On Our Way, Cambridge, MA*

On Our Way, Waterbury, CT#

On the Way, Anchorage, AK

One to One: A Lesbian Feminist Journal, New York, NY*

Opening, The, Pittsburgh, PA

Orange County Women's Coalition, Costa Mesa, CA

Oregon Council for Women's Equality, Portland, OR*

O.S.U. Women's Liberation, Columbus, OH

Our Country Newsletter, San Francisco, CA#

Our Sisters, Ourselves, Palo Alto, CA*

Page One, Atlanta, GA*

Paid My Dues, Milwaukee, WI#

Pandora, Seattle, WA

Pandoras Box, San Diego, CA

Panorama Preview, New York, NY*

Paraclete, The, San Francisco, CA#

Penn Women's News, Philadelphia, PA#

Pennsylvanians for Women's Rights, Lancaster, PA*

Philadelphia Women's Center, Philadelphia, PA*

Pioneer Woman, New York, NY#

Pittsburgh Women's Center, Pittsburgh, PA*

Plainfield Organization for Women's Equal Rights, Plainfield, NJ*

Planned Parenthood - World Population Washington Memo, Washington, DC#

Planner, The, Minneapolis, MN

Plexus, Berkeley, CA#

Portcullis, Los Angeles, CA*

Poughkeepsie Women's Center Newsletter, Poughkeepsie, NY#

Prime Time, Piermont, NY*

Pro Se: National Law Women's Newsletter, Boston, MA*

Professional Women's Caucus, New York, NY*

Progressive Woman, Middlebury, IN

Proud Woman, Stanford, CA*

Purple Rage, New York, NY*

Purple Star, Ann Arbor, MI

Raising Cain, Washington, DC*

Rapport, Evanston, IL#

Rat Women's Liberation, New York, NY

La Razón Mestiza, San Francisco, CA#

Reach Out (D.O.B.), Dearborn, MI

Real Women, St. Louis, MO

Red Star, New York, NY

Remember Our Fire, Berkeley, CA

Research Committee on Sex Roles in Society, Boulder, CO*

Research in Progress (Women's Caucus for Modern Languages), Slippery Rock, PA

Restless Eagle, The, Goleta, CA

Revolution within the Revolution, Cambridge, MA*

Rock, The, Rockwell City, IA

Room of Our Own, Baltimore, MD#

Rutgers Women's Caucus Newsletter, New Brunswick, NJ*

Sabot, Seattle, WA*
Sacramento Women for Peace, Sacramento, CA
Sacramento Women's Center and Bookstore, Sacramento, CA*
Saint Joan's Alliance Newsletter, Milwaukee, WI
Saint Joan's International Alliance, Milwaukee, WI*
St. Louis Organization for Women's Rights, St. Louis, MO*
San Francisco Bay Area Women in the Technical Trades, Berkeley, CA
San Francisco Women for Peace, San Francisco, CA
San Francisco Women's Centers, San Francisco, CA
San Francisco Women's Liberation, San Francisco, CA
Santa Fe Women's Community Magazine, Santa Fe, NM#
Sapphire, San Francisco, CA
Scarlet Letter, Madison, WI
Seattle Women Act for Peace, Seattle, WA*
Second Coming, Austin, TX
Second Page, San Francisco, CA*
Second Revolution, The, San Diego, CA
Second Wave, Boston, MA*
Second Wave, The, Ann Arbor, MI
Sheryns Nufty Newsletter, Berkeley, CA
Siren, Chicago, IL
Sister: Los Angeles Feminist Newspaper, Venice, CA*
Sister News, Storrs, CT*
Sister Switchboard, Denver, CO#
Sisterhood, New York, NY
Sisterlife, Columbus, OH*
Sisters, Tallahassee, FL
Sisters in Poverty (Now New Mexico) Albuquerque, NM
Sisters in Solidarity, Denver, CO
Sisters in Struggle, Oakland, CA*
Sisters Stand, Salt Lake City, UT*
Sisters Unite, Houston, TX
Skirting the Capitol, Sacramento, CA
Smogbelly, Riverside, CA#
Society for Humane Abortion, San Francisco, CA
Society for the Study of Social Problems, El Cajon, CA*
Society for Women in Philosophy, Malcomb, IL*
Society of Women Engineers, New York, NY*
Sociologists for Women in Society, San Francisco, CA
So's Your Old Lady, Minneapolis, MN*
Source: A Feminist Newsletter, The, Newtown, PA*
Spare Rib, The, Chicago, IL
Spazm, Berkeley, CA
Speak Out Sisters, Philadelphia, PA*
Speakout: A Feminist Journal, Albany, NY*
Speakout: News Views, Boston, MA*
Spectre, Ann Arbor, MI
Speculator, Honolulu, HI#
Spokeswoman, The, Chicago, IL

Sportswoman, Culver City, CA*
Statutes of Liberty, Rochester, NY
Stephanies Office Service, Syracuse, NY
Stewardesses for Women's Rights, New York, NY*
Street Paper, Salt Lake City, UT*
Sunbury, New York, NY#
Switchboard, New York, NY
Tell-A-Woman, Philadelphia, PA*
Texan Woman, The, Austin, TX#
Through the Looking Glass, Philadelphia, PA
Tide, The, Los Angeles, CA*
Title VIII Report, New York, NY
To, for, by and about Women, Charlotte, NC
Together, Los Angeles, CA*
Tooth and Nail Journal, Palo Alto, CA
Traffic Jam, Seattle, WA
Trans Sister, Chicago, IL
Trial, Chicago, IL
Triple Jeopardy, New York, NY
Turn of the Screwed, Dallas, TX
Twin Cities Women's Union, Minneapolis, MN*
Udder Side, New York, NY*
Underground Woman, St. Louis, MO
Union W.A.G.E. (Women's Alliance to Gaine Equality), Berkeley, CA
Unitarian Universalist Women's Federation, Boston, MA
United Auto Workers Women's Department Special Bulletin, Detroit, MI*
United Women's Contingent, Washington, DC
University Women's Association, Chicago, IL
Up from the Basement, San Jose, CA#
Up from Under, New York, NY
"U.S." (United Sisters), Tampa, FL*
Valley Women's Center, The, Northampton, MA*
Vassar Newsletter, San Francisco, CA
Velvet Glove, Livermore, CA
Vocational Center for Women, Carle Place, NY*
Voice of Women, New England, Newtonville, MA
Voice of the Women's Liberation Movement, Chicago, IL
Washington Newsletter for Women, Washington, DC
Washington State Women's Political Caucus, Tacoma, WA#
Way We See It, The, Springfield, MA
WEAL (Women's Equity Action League), Silver Springs, MD
West Coast Association of Women Historians Newsletter, Sacramento, CA*
West East Bag, Washington, DC#
West East Coast Bag, Oakland, CA*
West-East Bag, Los Angeles, CA, and New York, NY
What She Wants, Cleveland Heights, OH*
Whirlwind, Chicago, IL#
Whole Woman, Madison, WI*

Whole Woman Catalog, The, Portsmouth, NH*
WICCE - A Lesbian/Feminist Newspaper, Philadelphia, PA#
Wildcat Women, Baltimore, MD#
Wildflowers, Isla Vista, CA
W.I.L.P.F. (Women's International League for Peace and Freedom) - Baltimore, Baltimore, MD
W.I.L.P.F. - Berkeley East Bay, Berkeley, CA
W.I.L.P.F. - Fresno, Fresno, CA
W.I.L.P.F. - Livermore, Livermore, CA
W.I.L.P.F. - Marin, Corte Madera, CA
W.I.L.P.F. - Monterey, Seaside, CA
W.I.L.P.F. - National, Philadelphia, PA
W.I.L.P.F. - New England, Boston, MA
W.I.L.P.F. - Northern California, Monterey, CA
W.I.L.P.F. - Palo Alto, Palo Alto, CA
W.I.L.P.F. - Paterson/Wayne, Paterson, NJ#
W.I.L.P.F. - Philadelphia, Philadelphia, PA#
W.I.L.P.F. - San Francisco, San Francisco, CA
W.I.L.P.F. - San Gabriel Valley, Monterey Park, CA
W.I.L.P.F. - San Jose, San Jose, CA
W.I.L.P.F. - San Mateo, Millbrae, CA
W.I.L.P.F. - Seattle, Montlake Terrace, WA
W.I.L.P.F. - Union County Newsletter, Fanwood, NJ#
W.I.L.P.F. - Washington, Washington, DC
Wisconsin Women's Newsletter, Madison, WI
Wise (Women for the Inclusion of Sexual Expression), New York, NY
Wisp, La, Los Angeles, CA
Woman Activist, The, Falls Church, VA
Woman Becoming, Pittsburgh, PA*
Woman - Berkeley, Berkeley, CA*
Woman Constitutionalist, The, Summit, MS
Woman - Davis, Davis, CA*
Woman - Kalamazoo, Kalamazoo, MI*
Woman - Los Angeles, Los Angeles, CA*
Woman Worker, Los Angeles, CA*
Womankind, Chicago, IL
Womankind, Detroit, MI
Womankind, Louisville, KY
Womanpower, Brookline, MA
Woman's Journal, The, Northampton, MA
Woman's Voice, Boston, MA*
Woman's Way, San Anselmo, CA*
Woman's World, New York, NY
Womanspace Journal, Los Angeles, CA*
Women, Philadelphia, PA
Women - A Berkshire Feminist News Journal, Lenox, MA*
Women - A Journal of Liberation, Baltimore, MD
Women and Art, New York, NY*
Women and Film, Santa Monica, CA*
Women and Revolution, San Francisco, CA
Women and Work, Washington, DC*
Women Are Human, Columbus, OH*

Women As Women As Women, Kansas City, MO*
Women for Change Center, Dallas, TX*
Women for Legislative Action Bulletin, Los Angeles, CA*
Women Historians of the Midwest Newsletter (WHOM), St. Paul, MN*
Women in Action, Washington, DC*
Women in Cell Biology, New Haven, CT#
Women in City Government United, New York, NY
Women in Geography, Syracuse, NY#
Women in Struggle, Winneconne, WI
Women in the Arts Newsletter, New York, NY*
Women in the Church, Los Angeles, CA*
Women in the World, Washington, DC#
Women Lawyers Journal, San Francisco, CA*
Women Mobilized for a Change, Chicago, IL
Women on Top, Richmond, IN#
Women Organized Against Rape Newsletter, Philadelphia, PA#
Women Strike for Peace - National Headquarters (Memo), New York, NY*
Women Strike for Peace - New York (Peaceletter), New York, NY*
Women Studies Abstracts, Rush, NY*
Women (To, by, of, for, and About), Stamford, CT
Women Today, Washington, DC
Women United, Washington, DC*
Women United for Action, New York, NY*
Women United for November 6, San Francisco, CA*
Women West, El Monte, CA
Women's Abortion Coalition Newsletter - Western Branch of WONAAC, San Francisco, CA*
Women's Ad-Hoc Abortion Coalition, San Francisco, CA
Women's Almanac, Cambridge, MA#
Women's Caucus for Modern Languages - Midwest Newsletter, Whitewater, WI#
Women's Caucus for Political Science, Gainesville, FL
Women's Caucus for Political Science Newsletter, Ithaca, NY*
Women's Caucus Newsletter, Wellesley, MA#
Women's Caucus of the New University Conference, Chicago, IL
Women's Caucus Religious Studies Newsletter, Berkeley, CA*
Women's Center - Baltimore, Baltimore, MD#
Women's Center Bulletin - Tampa, Tampa, FL*
Women's Center Bulletin - Honolulu, HI*
Women's Center Newsletter - New York City, New York, NY*
Women's Center Newsletter - Poughkeepsie, Poughkeepsie, NY*
Women's Center Newsletter - Stanford, Stanford, CA*

Women's Center Newsletter - University of Idaho, Moscow, ID*
Women's Communication Network, Madison, WI#
Women's Equity Action League - National Newsletter, Washington, DC#
Women's Equity Action League - New Jersey, Wrightstown, NJ*
Women's Equity Action League - Pennsylvania, State College, PA*
Women's Equity Action League - Texas, Dallas, TX*
Women's Equity Action League - Washington Report, Washington, DC*
Women's Forum, Bloomington, IN#
Women's Forum, Davis, CA
Women's Free Express, Nashville, TN#
Women's Information Center Newsletter, De Witt, NY*
Women's Information Network Bulletin, Ann Arbor, MI*
Women's Institute, The, Paramus, NJ#
Women's Interart Center Newsletter, New York, NY*
Women's International Network (WIN), Lexington, MA*
Women's Law Center, New York, NY#
Women's Liberation, Cambridge, MA
Women's Liberation Center, New York, NY
Women's Liberation Coalition, Detroit, MI
Women's Liberation News, Dayton, OH
Women's Liberation News, Providence, RI
Women's Liberation Newsletter, Kansas City, MO
Women's Liberation Newsletter - San Francisco, San Francisco, CA*
Women's Liberation of Michigan, Detroit, MI*
Women's Liberation Union of Rhode Island, Providence, RI*
Women's Media Project, Memphis, TN*
Women's National Abortion Action Coalition Newsletter, New York, NY*
Women's News Exchange, Boca Raton, FL*
Women's Newsletter, Berkeley, CA
Women's Newsletter for, by, and about Woman, North Dartmouth, MA*
Women's Opportunities Center Newsletter, Irvine, CA*

Women's Page, San Francisco, CA
Women's Pages, Richmond, VA#
Women's Press, Eugene, OR
Women's Rights, Los Angeles, CA
Women's Rights Law Reporter, New York, NY
Women's Rights Law Reporter, Newark, NJ*
Women's Studies, an Interdisciplinary Journal, Flushing, NY*
Women's Studies Newsletter, Old Westbury, NY*
Women's Universal Movement, Inc., New York, NY*
Women's Voices, Buffalo, NY*
WONAAC (Women's National Abortion Action Coalition), Washington, DC
Worcester Women's Press, Worcester, MA#
Working Mother, The, New York, NY
W.S.P. at the United Nations, New York, NY
W.S.P. National, New York, NY
W.S.P. National, Washington, DC
W.S.P. Philadelphia, Philadelphia, PA
Yale Break, New Haven, CT
Yellow Ribbon, The, Evanston, IL*
Young Women's Christian Association - Atlanta, Atlanta, GA#
Young Women's Christian Association - Berkeley, Berkeley, CA#
Young Women's Christian Association in Motion, San Francisco, CA*
Young Women's Christian Association - Women's Resource Center - Natick, Natick, MA*
Your Cue from CCEW (Council for the Continuing Education of Women) - Miami Dade Community College, Miami, FL*

* New title in supplement I
# New title in supplement II

Sources: *Herstory Microfilm Collection: Table of Contents*. Berkeley, CA: Women's History Library, n.d.; *Reel Guide to Herstory Supplementary Set I....* Berkeley, CA: Women's History Research Center, 1976; *Reel Guide to Herstory Supplementary Set II....* Berkeley, CA: Women's History Research Center, 1976.

Appendix D: Native American Press from the 1960s-1970s:
Selected Titles from the North American Indian Periodicals Collection
(Microfilm Corporation of America—now distributed by UPA)

Agenutemagen, 1971-1975
Albuquerque Area Education Profile, 1971-1975
American Indian Culture Research Newsletter, 1969-1970
American Indian Education, 1961-1972

American Indian Law Newsletter, 1968-1975
Announcements (Native American Rights Fund), 1972-1975
Argus, 1967-1975
Arizoniana, 1960

Arizoniana, the Journal of Arizona History, 1961-1964
Attan-Akamik, 1970-1972
Bear Facts Newsletter, 1973-1975
Birney Arrow, 1959-1962, 1965, 1968-1970
Blue Cloud News, 1971-1973
Calumet, 1973
Camsell Arrow, 1947-1969
Chahta Anumpa, 1968-1969, 1971
Cherokee Boys Club Newsletter, 1970-1975
Cherokee One Feather, 1969-1975
Choctaw Community News, 1969-1975
Crow Agency Flashes, 1968-1972
Dee-Ha-Nee, 1972
D.N.A. in Action, 1968-1973
Drum Beat, 1971-1972
Elbow Drums, 1971-1975
E.R.I.C. / C.R.E.S.S. Newsletter, 1966-1973
Eskimo, 1946-1975
F.I.S. Newsletter, 1967-1974
Flandreau Spirit, 1971-1975
Haa Kusteeyef Aya, 1973
Halne'ii of the San Juan Mission, 1966-1967, 1969-
    1973
Indian Education Club, 1969-1973
Indian Forerunner, 1971-1973
Indian Highways, 1945-1975
Indian Historian, 1967-1975
Indian Life and Ceremonial Magazine, 1954-1961
Indian Magazine, 1970
Indian Record, 1954-1972, 1974-1975
Indian Trader, 1970-1975
Indian Travel Newsletter, 1972-1975
Indian Voice, 1971-1973, 1975
Inuttituut, 1959-1975
Journal of Arizona History, 1965-1975
Little Bronzed Angel, 1924-1932, 1937-1943, 1959-
    1973, 1975
Little Sioux, 1975
Lummi Indian Progress, 1970
Lummi Indian Review, 1972
Lummi Squol Quol, 1973
Many Smokes, 1966-1975
Messenger (Tasautit), 1966-1970
Midnight Sun, 1973-1974
Mission, 1974-1975
Mission Fields at Home, 1928-1934, 1940-1973
Morning Star People, 1954-1975
Native News and B.I.A. Bulletin, 1973, 1975
Native People, 1973-1975
Navajo Area Progress Report, 1975
Navajo Community College Newsletter, 1969-1973
Navajo Education Newsletter, 1974-1975

N.C.A.I. Bulletin, 1945-1974
N.C.A.I. Sentinel Bulletin, 1975
N.C.I.O. News, 1970-1972
New Breed News, 1975
New Mexico, 1931-1936, 1941-1975
Niagi News, 1969-1974
Nishnawbe News, 1971-1975
Northern Lights, 1932-1952, 1954-1972
Northian, 1972-1975
Northian Newsletter, 1971-1975
Northwest Indian News, 1971-1975
Northwest Indian Times, 1969-1972
Office of Navajo Economic Opportunity Dee-Ha-Ne',
    1973-1975
Our Native Land, 1970-1974
Padres' Trail, 1945-1976
Pioneer News-Observer, 1970-1974
Powwow Trails, 1946-1970
Race of Sorrows, 1956-1971
Raven Speaks, 1968-1972
Rawhide Press, 1958-1975
Red Cloud Country, 1963-1975
Renegade, 1969-1972
Rough Rock News, 1966-1975
Science of Man, 1960-1962
Si Wong Geh, 1973-1975
Smithsonian Contributions to Anthropology, 1965-1975
Southern Indian Studies, 1949-1971
State University of South Dakota / News Report, 1955-
    1960
State University of South Dakota Bulletin / News
    Report, 1961-1963
Taiga Times, 1971-1974
Tekawennake, 1973-1975
Three Tribes Herald, 1975
Thunderbird Quill Newsletter, 1969-1971
Tosan, 1971-1975
U.I.D.A. Reporter, 1972-1975
University of South Dakota Bulletin (Institute of Indian
    Studies), 1973-1975
University of South Dakota / News Report, 1964-1972
Viltis, 1965-1975
Voice of Brotherhood, 1972-1973
Warpath, 1968-1972
Whispering Wind Magazine, 1971-1975
Wopeedah, 1937-1975
Zuni Tribal Newsletter, 1974-1975

Source: "Native American Periodicals." In *Journals of Dissent and Social Change*, comp. by John Liberty, 211-36. Sacramento: California State University Library, 1986.

Appendix E: U.S. Underground and Alternative Press from the 1960s-1970s:
Selected Titles on Microform Filmed by the State Historical Society of Wisconsin

Alternatives

Bay Guardian, San Francisco, CA
Bayou La Rose, New Orleans, LA
Come Unity, Saint Petersburg, FL
Communities, Louisa, VA
Fifth Estate, Detroit, MI
Free Venice Beachhead, Venice, CA
Grassroots, Berkeley, CA
Green Revolution, Freeland, MD
Hardrain, Eau Claire, WI
Issues in Radical Therapy, Springfield, IL
Lancaster Independent Press, Lancaster, PA
Michigan Voice, Burton, MI
Newsreal, Tucson, AZ
North Country Anvil, Millville, MN
Northwest Passage, Seattle, WA
Overthrow, New York, NY
Post Amerikan, Bloomington, IL
Santa Barbara News & Review, Santa Barbara, CA
Shift in the Wind, San Francisco, CA
Sipapu, Winters, CA
Spectrum, Tallahassee, FL
Sun: A Magazine of Ideas, Chapel Hill, NC
Utopian Classroom: Journal of Do-It-Yourself..., San
    Francisco, CA
Weekly Newsmagazine, The, Seattle, WA
Willamette Week, Portland, OR
World Citizen, San Francisco, CA

Minorities

A & T Register, Greensboro, NC
Ahead of the Herd, New Town, ND
Akwesasne Notes, Middletown, CT
American Indian Baptist Voice, Okmulgee, OK
American Indian Culture and Research Journal, Los
    Angeles, CA
Ang Katipunan, Oakland, CA
Arizona Informant, Phoenix, AZ
Atlanta Inquirer, The, Atlanta, GA
Bishinik, Durant, OK
Black News, Brooklyn, NY
Buckeye Review, Youngstown, OH
Camagueyano, El, Miami, FL
Carolina Indian Voice, The, Pembroke, NC
Carolinian, Raleigh, NC
Cherokee Advocate, Tahlequah, OK
Chicago Independent Bulletin, Chicago, IL
Chicago Metro News, Chicago, IL
Chickasaw Times, The, Norman, OK
Choctaw Community News, Philadelphia, MI

Circle (Boston Indian Council), Boston, MA
Claridad (Edicion De Estados Unidos), New York, NY
Columbus Times, The, Columbus, GA
Commission on Indian Services Newsletter, Salem, OR
Dakota Sun, The, Fort Yates, ND
Dat Moi/New Land, Seattle, WA
Daybreak Star, Seattle, WA
De-Bah-Ji-Mon, Cass Lake, MN
Delta, Washington, DC
Dxwhiide, Seattle, WA
Eagle's Eye, Provo, UT
Early American, Modesto, CA
East West: The Chinese-American Journal, San
    Francisco, CA
Echo (Ute Mountain Tribe), Towoac, CO
Fort Apache Scout, White River, AZ
Fort Lauderdale Westside Gazette, Fort Lauderdale,
    FL
Frente A Frente, Notre Dame, IN
Gary Crusader, Gary, IN
Genesee Valley Indian Association Grapevine, Flint,
    MI
Herald Dispatch, Los Angeles, CA
Hispano, El, Sacramento, CA
Indian Affairs Newsletter, New York, NY
Indian Center of San Jose Newsletter, San Jose, CA
Indian Crusader, The, Inglewood, CA
Indian Leader, Lawrence, KS
Indian Life, Rapid City, SD
Indian Progress, Noblesville, IN
Indian Times, Denver, CO
Indian Truth, Philadelphia, PA
Inter-Com (Indian Community Inter-Agency Communi-
    cation), Chicago, IL
Inter-Tribal Tribune, Kansas City, MO
Iowa Orienting Express, The, Des Moines, IA
Jade: The Asian-American Identity, Los Angeles, CA
Jicarilla Chieftain, Dulce, NM
Ka Ri Wen Ha Wi, Hogansville, NY
Lac Courte Oreilles Journal, Hayward, WI
Letan Wankatakiya, Vermilion, SD
MALDEF: Mexican American Legal Defense & Educa-
    tional Fund, San Francisco, CA
Management Memo (California Urban Indian Health
    Council), Oakland, CA
Menominee Tribal News, Keshena, WI
Miccosukee Everglades News, Miami, FL
Missionary Magazine of the Woman's Missionary
    Society, Birmingham, AL
Missionary Seer, The, New York, NY
Mobile Beacon & Alabama Citizen, Mobile, AL
Morning Star People, Ashland, MT

Mukluks Hemcunga/Indian Talk, Klamath Falls, OR
Muscogee Nation News, Okmulgee, OK
National Insurance Association, Chicago, IL
National Technical Association Newsletter, Washington, DC
Native Sun, Detroit, MI
Navajo Times, Window Rock, AZ
New Crusader, The, Chicago, IL
New River Times (Fairbanks Native Association), Fairbanks, AK
New York Recorder, Brooklyn, NY
Northwest Indian Fisheries Commission News, Olympia, WA
Now, Detroit, MI
Nuestra Lucha: Hasta La Victoria, Toledo, OH
O He Yoh Noh: Allegheny Indian Reservation Newsletter, Salamanca, NY
Oakland Post, Berkeley, CA
Obreros En Marcha, New York, NY
OKC Camp Crier, The, Oklahoma City, OK
Orange County Indian Center Telegraph, Garden Grove, CA
Paha Sapa Report, Rapid City, SD
Papago Runner, Sells, AZ
Popo Feminil, El, Northridge, CA
Portland Observer, Portland, OR
Puerto Rico Libre!, New York, NY
Qua Toqti, The Eagle's Cry, Oraibi, AZ
Red Cliff Newsletter, Bayfield, WI
Red Cloud Country, Pine Ridge, SD
Renacimiento, El, Lansing, MI
Reporter (United Indian Development Association), Los Angeles, CA
San Francisco Journal, San Francisco, CA
SCLC: Southern Christian Leadership Conference Magazine, Atlanta, GA
Sinta Gleska College News, Mission, SD
Smoke Signals from Bacone College, Muskogee, OK
Smoke Signals News Letter, Baltimore, MD
Snee-Nee-Chum, Deming, WA
Sota Eya Ye Yapi, Sisseton, SD
Source, The, Santa Fe, NM
Southern Ute Drum, Ignacio, CO
Spanish Journal, Milwaukee, WI
Speaking of Ourselves/Ni-Mah-Mi-Kwa-Zoo-Min, Cass Lake, MN
Spilyay Tymoo: Coyote News, Warm Springs, OR
Sun Reporter, San Francisco, CA
Talking Leaf, Los Angeles, CA
Three Tribes Herald, The, New Town, ND
Treaty Council News, San Francisco, CA
Tri-State Defender, Memphis, TN
Tsa'Aszi, Pine Hill, NM
Tulalip See-Yaht-Sub, Tulalip, WA
Turtle, Niagara, NY

Twin Cities Courier, Minneapolis, MN
United Indian Association of Central Washington Newsletter, Yakima, WA
United Methodist Reporter Advocate, The, Dallas, TX
United National Indian Tribal Youth, Oklahoma City, OK
Utah Navajo Baa Hane, Blanding, UT
Ute Bulletin, Fort Duchesne, UT
Vision on the Wind, Minneapolis, MN
Visiones De La Raza, Minneapolis, MN
Voz De Colorado, Denver, CO
Voz Fronteriza, La Jolla, CA
Washington Informer, The, Washington, DC
Watts Star Review, Los Angeles, CA
Wind River Journal, Fort Washakie, WY
Wind River Rendezvous, Saint Stephens, WY
Wotanin Wowapi, Poplar, MT

Politics

American, Lexington, KY
American Foreign Policy Newsletter, New York, NY
American Independent, The, Lemon Grove, CA
American Sentinel, Washington, DC
Anarcho-Syndicalist Ideas and Action, San Francisco, CA
Ann Watson Report, The, San Diego, CA
Answers to Economic Problems, Houston, TX
Appeal to Reason, The, Birmingham, AL
Armed Citizen News, Seattle, WA
Blind Justice, New York, NY
Bulletin (Committee to Restore the Constitution), Fort Collins, CO
California Socialist, Los Angeles, CA
California Statesman, Lemon Grove, CA
Capitol Community Citizens Newsletter, Madison, WI
Catholic Worker, New York, NY
CC: Wisconsin Common Cause News, Madison, WI
CCCO News Notes, Philadelphia, PA
Challenge/Desafio, New York, NY
Citizens for the Republic Newsletter, Santa Monica, CA
Citizens' Governmental Research Bureau Bulletin, Milwaukee, WI
Citizens Informer, Kirkwood, MO
Citizens Party of Minnesota Newsletter, Minneapolis, MN
Citizens' Report, Metairie, LA
Civil Liberties, New York, NY
Civil Liberties Alert: A Legislative Newsletter, Washington, DC
Civil Liberties News, Milwaukee, WI
Clarion Call, The, National City, CA
Clearwater Navigator, Poughkeepsie, NY
Common Cause: Washington, DC

Common Sense: Newsletter for Libertarians & Other Friends, Miami, FL
Conspiracy, San Francisco, CA
Controversy, Norbone, MO
CovertAction Information Bulletin, Washington, DC
Cultural Correspondence, New York, NY
Cultural Correspondence, Providence, RI
Dandelion (Movement for a New Society), Philadelphia, PA
DCLP News (Dallas County Libertarian Party), Dallas, TX
Democratic Left, New York, NY
Dialogue on Liberty, Washington, DC
Eagle Forum-Wisconsin, Milwaukee, WI
Energy News Digest, Allendale, NJ
Facts for Action, Eureka Springs, AR
First Principles, Washington, DC
Focus (Joint Center for Political Studies), Washington, DC
Forewarned!, Vienna, VA
Freedom Alert, Springfield, VA
Freedom Socialist, Seattle, WA
Friendly Agitator, The, Media, PA
Gray Panther Network, Philadelphia, PA
Griffiss Plowshares Update, Syracuse, NY
Guild Notes, New York, NY
Hammer and Tongs, Austin, TX
Illinois Libertarian, Chicago, IL
Impact Journal, Washington, DC
Imprimis, Hillsdale, MI
In the Public Interest, Washington, DC
Independent American, New Orleans, LA
Individual Liberty, Warminster, PA
Industrial Worker, Chicago, IL
Internationalist Worker, New York, NY
John Birch Society Bulletin, The, Belmont, MA
John Herling's Labor Letter, Washington, DC
Klansman, The, Denham Springs, LA
Land Leaf, Stevens Point, WI
Leaflet (National Organization for the Reform of Marijuana), Washington, DC
League of Women Voters of Madison Bulletin, Madison, WI
Legislative Bulletin (Women's International League for Peace & Freedom), Washington, DC
Libertarian Connection, Los Angeles, CA
Libertas, Sterling, VA
Massachusetts Liberty: Bimonthly News and Comment, Boston, MA
Match!, The, Tucson, AZ
McAlvany Intelligence Advisor, The, Phoenix, AZ
Midnight Notes, Jamaica Plain, MA
Midwest Peace and Freedom, Minneapolis, MN
Militant, New York, NY
Mobilizer, The, Philadelphia, PA

National Chronicle, Hayden Lake, ID
National Educator, Fullerton, CA
National Fluoridation News, Gravette, AR
National Pro-Life Journal, The, Fairfax, VA
National Socialist Mobilizer, Los Angeles, CA
National Statesman, Kalamazoo, MI
National Vanguard, Washington, DC
Nature Conservancy Newsletter, Madison, WI
New America, New York, NY
New Indicator, La Jolla, CA
New Jersey Libertarian Party Newsletter, Far Hills, NJ
New Order, The, Lincoln, NE
New Solidarity, New York, NY
News & Letters, Detroit, MI
News behind the News, Tulsa, OK
Northern Lights Glimmer, The, Anchorage, AK
Northern Sun News, Minneapolis, MN
NRC Perspective, Madison, WI
Nuclear Resister, Madison, WI
Objector, The, San Francisco, CA
Organizer (National Alliance Against Racist and Political Repression), New York, NY
Orthodox Marxist, The, New York, NY
Peace Newsletter, Syracuse, NY
Peace Times (American Friends Service Committee), Austin, TX
Peace Work: New England Peace Movement Newsletter, Cambridge, MA
Peacemaker (Peacemaker Movement), Garberville, CA
People, Food, & Land, Fresno, CA
People's Tribune, Chicago, IL
Plain Truth, Pasadena, CA
Point Blank, Bellevue, WA
Political Stethoscope, Washington, DC
Public Expenditure Survey of Wisconsin Newsletter, Madison, WI
Public Eye (Center for Public Representation), Madison, WI
Public Justice Report, Washington, DC
Quash: Newsletter of the Grand Jury Project, New York, NY
RECON, Philadelphia, PA
Red Line, The, Saint Louis, MO
Report from Valley Forge, Valley Forge, VA
Resist: A Call to Resist Illegitimate Authority, Somerville, MA
Revolution, Chicago, IL
Revolutionary Worker (Seattle, WA), Seattle, WA
Rights, New York, NY
Shelterforce, East Orange, NJ
Socialist for Ohioans, Ashtabula, OH
Socialist Republic, The, New York, NY
Socialist Tribune, Miami Beach, FL

Socialist Worker: Paper of the International Socialist, Cleveland, OH
Soil of Liberty, Minneapolis, MN
Sojourner (National Sojourners), Alexandria, VA
Sojourners, Washington, DC
Sounds of Truth and Tradition, New York, NY
Southern Changes, Atlanta, GA
Southern Libertarian Messenger, The, Florence, SC
Sparticist 4 (English Edition), New York, NY
Sparticist 4 (Spanish Edition), New York, NY
Spotlight (American Friends Service Committee), Pasadena, CA
SRA (Social-Revolutionary Anarchist) Federation Bulletin for Anarchist Agitators, Mountain View, CA
Statewatch, Minneapolis, MN
Straight Talk, Gatlinburg, TN
Strike!, Farmingdale, NY
Synthesis: Anti-Authoritarian Newsletter for, San Pedro, CA
TAP (Technological American Party), New York, NY
Texas Tribune, Houston, TX
Thunderbolt (Savannah, GA), Savannah, GA
Torch (Revolutionary Socialist League), Highland Park, MI
TRIM (Tax Reform Immediately) Bulletin, Hales Corners, WI
Trumpet (Clearinghouse on Georgia Prisons & Jails), Atlanta, GA
U.N. Reform Campaigner, Wayne, NJ
Unity (San Francisco, CA), San Francisco, CA
Update on the Libertarian Movement, Washington, DC
Uus Ilm/New World, Monroe, NY
Veteran, Chicago, IL
Vets Grapevine, Madison, WI
Virginia Association of Pro-Life Nurses Newsletter, Fairfax, VA
Voice of Freedom, Dallas, TX
Voice of Liberty, Decatur, GA
Volunteer (Veterans of the Abraham Lincoln Brigade), New York, NY
Washington Report (American Security Council), Boston, VA
Ways and Means, Washington, DC
WEHA News, Middleton, WI
Western Goals Report, Alexandria, VA
Wisp, La, Los Angeles, CA
Women for Peace Bulletin, Chicago, IL
Workbook, Albuquerque, NM
Workers' Advocate, Chicago, IL
Workers Vanguard, New York, NY
Workers World, New York, NY
Workman's Circle Call, New York, NY
Workplace Democracy, Amherst, MA
World Order, Wilmette, IL

WRL (War Resisters League), New York, NY
Young Socialist, New York, NY
Young Spartacus, New York, NY
Young Worker, New York, NY

Women

Advocate (United Society of Friends Women), Columbus, OH
ARC (Abortion Rights Council), Minneapolis, MN
Association of Libertarian Feminists News, New York, NY
Broomstick, San Francisco, CA
CCWHP (Coordinating Committee/Women in History) Newsletter, Woodside, CA
CLUW (Coalition of Labor Union Women) News, New York, NY
Common Ground: The Women's Coalition Monthly News, Milwaukee, WI
Comparable Worth Project Newsletter, Oakland, CA
Equality Now!, Madison, WI
Exponent II, Arlington, MA
Feminist Bookstore News, San Francisco, CA
Force, The, Albany, NY
Forward (League of Women Voters of Madison), Madison, WI
Friendly Woman, Seattle, WA
GFWC (General Federation of Women's Clubs) Clubwoman, Washington, DC
Media Report to Women, Washington, DC
Michigan Women, Lansing, MI
Minnesota Working Women Memo, Minneapolis, MN
Moteru Dirva (Women's Field), Brookfield, WI
Motor, Ripon, WI
NCJW (National Council of Jewish Women) Journal, New York, NY
New D.A.W.N., Ypsilanti, MI
NOW Newsletter, Eau Claire, WI
off our backs, Washington, DC
Our OWN (Older Women's Network), Santa Barbara, CA
Pioneer Woman, New York, NY
Plainswoman, Grand Forks, ND
Plexus, Berkeley, CA
Polka (Polish Woman), Scranton, PA
Reproductive Rights News, Madison, WI
SAA Women's Caucus Newsletter, Cambridge, MA
Soundings (Girl Scouts of the Milwaukee Area Inc.), Milwaukee, WI
Thesmophoria, Los Angeles, CA
Transit Home Companion, Madison, WI
WEAL (Women's Equality Action League) Washington Report, Washington, DC
What NOW (National Organization for Women), Milwaukee, WI

WHOM (Women Historians of the Midwest) Newsletter, Saint Paul, MN
WIC Status Report, Columbus, OH
Wisconsin Clubwoman, Sheboygan, WI
Womankind, Indianapolis, IN
Women and Revolution, New York, NY
Women Today, Washington, DC
Womenews (Pennsylvania Commission for Women), Harrisburg, PA
Women's Press, Eugene, OR
Women's International League for Peace & Freedom Newsletter, Madison, WI

WomenWise: The N.H. Feminist Health Center Quarter, Concord, NH

Note: For exact coverage and prices of individual rolls of 35-mm microfilm, contact The Society. See also Appendix H.

Source: *Periodicals and Newspapers Acquired by the State Historical Society of Wisconsin Library*. Edited by James P. Danky and Clifford W. Bass. Madison, WI: The Society, 1986.

Appendix F: Chicano Press from the 1960s-1970s on Microform:
Selected Titles from the Chicano Studies Library, University of California, Berkeley

Actualidad, La, Huntington Park, CA, 1971
Adelante, Riverside, CA, 1969 complete
Adelante, San Jose, CA, 1968
Adelante, Topeka, KS, 1972-1977 complete
Adobe, San Luis, CO, 1974-1977 complete
Agenda, Washington, DC, 1971-1976 complete
Agenda, Washington, DC, 1976-1980
Aguila, El, Santa Monica, CA, 1971-1972 complete
Aguila, El, Susanville, CA, 1971-1974
Alacran, El, Long Beach, CA, 1970-71
Alambtes de N.E.L., Oakland, CA, 1975-1978 complete
America, San Francisco, CA, 1968-1970
Amigos, Tucson, AZ, 1975-1977 complete
Atisbos, Stanford, CA, 1975-1978 complete
Aztlan, Leavenworth, KS, 1971
Barrio, Corpus Christi, TX, 1972
Basta Ya, San Francisco, CA, 1969-1971
Bautista Mexicano, El, San Antonio, TX, 1939-1978 complete
Bilingual Journal, Cambridge, MA, 1979-1984 complete
Bilingual Review, The/La Revista Bilingue, Binghamton, NY, 1974-1984
Books for Children, Latin Times, East Chicago, IN, 1956-1975
Borderlands, Brownsville, TX, 1978-1983 complete
Bronce, Oakland, CA, 1969 complete
Bronze, Oakland, CA, 1968-1969 complete
Camino, El, Cutler, CA, 1971
Campesino, El, San Juan, TX, 1973-1974
Caracol, San Antonio, TX, 1974-1977
Caracol, San Antonio, TX, 1977-1979
Carta Abierta, Seattle, WA, 1975-1978 complete
Cartel, Austin, TX, 1973-1976
Catolicos por la Raza, Los Angeles, CA, 1970
Causa, La, Los Angeles, CA, 1969-1972
Centro, Santa Barbara, CA, 1973-1974

Centro Chicano Cultural, El, Woodburn, OR, 1973-1974
Centro Tiburcio Vasquez Noticias/Newsletter, Santa Barbara, CA, 1972
C.F.M. Report, Los Angeles, CA, 1973
Chicana Service Center, Los Angeles, CA, 1973
Chicano, El, Colton, CA, 1968-1975
Chicano, El, San Diego, CA, 1973
Chicano de Riverside, El, Riverside, CA, 1975
Chicano Federation Newsletter, San Diego, CA, 1970-1977
Chicano Law Review, Los Angeles, CA, 1972-1977 complete
Chicano-Pomona Edition, El, Colton, CA, 1974
Chicano Student, Los Angeles, CA, 1968 complete
Chicano Student Movement, Los Angeles, CA, 1968-1969 complete
Chicano Student News, Los Angeles, CA, 1968 complete
Chismearte, Los Angeles, CA, 1976-1984
CHPAOC, Santa Barbara, CA, 1972-1973
Clamor del Pueblo, El, Santa Barbara, CA, 1972 complete
Clarin Chicano (el), Chicago, IL, 1974-1975
Clarin Chicano/Clarin, Chicago, IL, 1974-1975
Columnas Newsletter, Davenport, IA, 1971-1972
Compass, Houston, TX, 1968-1972
Con Safos, Los Angeles, CA, 1968-1972 complete
Confluencia, La, Santa Fe, NM, 1976-1978
Coraje, Tucson, AZ, 1969
Cry of Color, San Jose, CA, 1970 complete
Cuaderno, El, Dixon, NM, 1971-1976 complete
Cuadernos de Actividades, El Paso, NM, 1961-1976
Deadline, New York, NY and Berkeley, CA, 1974-1977 complete
Deganawidah Quetzacoatl, Davis, CA, 1971
Despertador de Tejas, El, Austin, TX, 1971

Despierten-Pueblo y Campo, Hayward, CA,
    1970 complete
Diario de La Gente, Boulder, CO, 1972-1977
D.Q.U. Report, Davis, CA, 1971
Echo, Austin, TX, 1970-1974 complete
Editorial, El Paso, TX, 1973
Encuentro Feminil, San Fernando, CA, 1973-1974
Enterado, The, Richmond, CA, 1970-1973
Es Tiempo, Los Altos Hills, CA, 1971-1973
Excentrico, San Jose, CA, 1949-1977,
Familia Center Newsletter, San Ralael, CA, 1974-1977
    complete
Farm Labor, Berkeley, CA, 1966
Farm Labor: Equal Rights for Agricultural Workers,
    Berkeley, CA, 1963-1967
Fuego de Aztlan, El, Berkeley, CA, 1970-1977
    complete
Gente de Aztlan, La, Los Angeles, CA, 1971-1986
Golpe Avisa, El, Waco, TX, 1970-1971
Grafica, Hollywood, CA, 1949-1977 complete
Grito, El, (bilingual), Berkeley, CA, 1967-1974
Grito de Aztlan, San Diego, CA, 1970 complete
Grito del Norte, Las Vegas, NM, 1968-1973 complete
Grito del Sol, Berkeley, CA, Jan. 1976-1979
Griton de M.E.C.H.A., El, Porterville, CA, 1972
    complete
Guardia, La, Milwaukee, WI, 1969-1977
Guia Para Maestros de Ninos, El Paso, TX, 1957-1972
H.A.B.L.E., New York, NY, 1972
Hijas de Cuauhtemoc, Long Beach, CA, 1971 complete
Hispanic Business, Santa Barbara, CA, 1979-1986
Hispanic Journal of Behavioral Sciences, Los Angeles,
    CA, 1979-1985
Hispano, El, Sacramento, CA, 1968-1976
Hormiga, La, Oakland, CA, 1968 complete
Hoy, San Juan, CA, 1969 complete
Ideal, Coachella, CA, 1969-1977
Impacto, San Francisco, CA, 1970 complete
Independent-El Exito, Beeville, TX, 1973
Indigena, El, Berkeley, CA, 1974-1977 complete
Informador, Fresno, CA, 1969-1976
Informador-Post, El, Berkeley, CA, 1967
Inmigrante Militante, El, San Jose, CA, 1974 complete
Inside Eastside, Los Angeles, CA, 1968-1969
Inside the Beast, San Diego, CA, 1972-1974
Interracial Digest; Interracial, New York, NY,
    1976-1977
Jalamate, San Francisco, CA, 1971-1977 complete
Joaquin, Fort Wayne, CA, 1972
Journal of Mexican American Studies, Anaheim, CA,
    1970-1972
Juntos (Annuals of the Presbyterian Pan American
    School), Kingsville, TX, 1958-1978
Justicia 0. . . ?, Los Angeles, CA, 1970-1975
L.A.D.O., Chicago, IL, 1967-1971

L.A.D.O.-Voz de Nuestro Pueblo, Chicago, IL, 1967-
    1971
Latin America & Empire Report, New York, NY,
    1971-1976 complete
Leno, El, San Diego, CA, 1968 complete
Luz, La, Denver, CO, 1972-1978
Machete, El, San Jose, CA, 1968
Maize, San Diego, CA, 1977-1983 complete
Malcriada de Santa Clara, La, Santa Clara, CA, 1973
    complete
Malcriado, El, McAllen, TX, 1967
Malcriado-English Edition, El, Delano & Keene, CA,
    1969-1976, 10 years complete
Malcriado-Spanish Edition, El, Delano & Keene, CA,
    1969-1975, 10 years complete
Mano a Mano, Houston, TX, 1972-1977 complete
Mayo Newsletter, San Antonio, TX, 1971 complete
M.E.Ch.A., Los Angeles, CA, 1971-1972 complete
Melus, Houston, TX, 1976-1985
Mestizo, El Paso, TX, 1973-1976 complete
Metamorfosis, Seattle, WA, 1977-1983 complete
Mexican-American, National City, CA, 1964
Mexican-American, The, Odessa, TX, 1972
Mexicanista, El, San Diego, CA, 1973
Mexicoameicano De Colores, Albuquerque, NM,
    1973-1980 complete
Minority Voices, University Park, PA, 1977-1981
Mision del Valle, La, Northridge, CA, 1971 complete
Mundo, El (includes, El Informador 1967, La Prensa
    Libre 1967 Mundo Hispano 1967-1970 as prede-
    cessor titles), Oakland, CA, 1967-1976
Mundo Hispano, Berkeley, CA, 1970
N.A.C.L.A. Newsletter, New York, NY, 1967-1970
Nosotros, Detroit, MI, 1971-1972
Noticias de la Semana, Washington, DC, 1972-1977
Nuestra Cosa, Riverside, CA, 1973-1975
Nuestra Lucha, Naco, AZ, 1973 complete
Nuestras Palabras, Seattle, WA, 1971 complete
Nuestros: The Magazine for Latinos (Bilingual), New
    York, NY, 1977-1980
Nueva Mission, San Francisco, CA, 1968-1969
Obrero, El, Los Angeles, CA, 1973
Palabra, La, Phoenix, AZ, 1979-1981 complete
Papel, El, Albuquerque, NM, 1969
Papel Chicano, Houston, TX, 1971-1973
Papel-San Diego Times, El, San Diego, CA, 1973
Pastor Evangelico, El, El Paso, TX, 1959-1972
Pensamientos de Aztlan, Los, Visalia, CA, 1971
Periodico Bilingue, Garden City, KS, 1974-1976
Prensa, La, Berkeley, CA, 1970
Prensa, La, San Antonio, TX, 1959-1963
Prensa de Bronce, Los Angeles, CA, 1969 complete
Prensa Grafica, Hartford, CT, 1975
Prensa Libre, La, Berkeley, CA, 1969
Prensa Popular, La Jolla, CA, 1973-1975

Presbyterian Panamericana, Kingsville, TX, 1956-1978
Que Tal, San Jose, CA, 1970-1976
Raices, Fresno, CA, 1970-1971
Rayas, Albuquerque, NM, 1978-1979
Raza, La, Los Angeles, CA, 1967-1970
Raza, La, Los Angeles, CA, 1968-1974
Raza Cosmica, La, Azusa, CA, 1972
Raza de Bronce, San Diego, CA, 1973 complete
Raza de Bronce, La, Ontario, CA, 1972-1973
Raza Habla, La, Las Cruces, NM, 1976-1986
Raza Newsletter, La, U.C. San Francisco, CA, 1972
    complete
Recent Additions to Chicano Studies Library, U.C.
    Berkeley, CA, 1973-1977
Regeneracion, Los Angeles, CA, 1970-1975
Relampago, El, Woodburn, OR, 1970-1971 complete
Renacimiento, El, Lansing, MI, 1970-1973
Renacimiento, El, Lansing, MI, 1970-1975
Reportero, El, Morgan Hill, CA, 1973
Revista Chicano Riquena, Gary, IN, 1973-1980
Rural Tribune, Hillsboro, OR, 1972-1976 complete
Ruta de Libertad, Los Angeles, CA, 1969
Sal Si Puedes, Santa Barbara, CA, 1970-1971
San Francisco Mission News, San Francisco, CA, 1970
    complete
Sangre de la Raza, Cal State Hayward, Hayward, CA,
    1970 complete
Si Se Puede, Santa Barbara, CA, 1973-1980
Simon Ese, Oakland, CA, 1972 complete
Sol, El, Salinas, CA, 1968-1976
Somos, San Bernardino, CA, 1978-1980
Somos Aztlan, Boulder, CO, 1972 complete
Spanish American News, San Francisco, CA, 1970
Speak up Chicanos, Oakland, CA, 1970 complete
Sueno, El, Sacramento, CA, 1971 complete
Teatro, El, Fresno, CA, 1970-1971

Tejidos, Austin, TX, 1973-1975
Tejidos, Austin, TX, 1976-1977 complete
Telpuchcalli y Calpulli, Berkeley, CA, 1970 complete
Tenaz, El, San Juan Bautista, CA, 1971-1972
Tezcatlipoca, Madison, WI, 1975
Tiempo, El, Oakland, CA, 1972
Trabajadores de la Raza, Los Angeles, CA, 1969-1978
    complete
Ultreya, Dallas, TX, 1972-1977
Venceremos, Redwood City, CA, 1970-1971
Verdad, La, Crystal City, TX, 1972-1974
Verdad, La, San Diego, CA, 1969-1971
Vida Nueva, La, Los Angeles, CA, 1969-1970
Visitante Dominical, Huntington, IN, 1974-1979
Vocero Informativo, San Ysidro, CA, 1974
Voz, La, Minneapolis, MN, 1972-1977
Voz Catolica, La, Oakland, CA, 1973 complete
Voz Chicana, La, San Juan, TX, 1972
Voz de Alianza, La, Albuquerque, NM, 1970-1971
Voz de Joaquin, La, Albuquerque, NM, 1970 complete
Voz de La Raza, La, Stockton, CA, 1970-1973
Voz de La Tierra, La, Fresno, CA, 1972
Voz de Los Llanos, La, Lubbock, TX, 1970
Voz del Consejo, San Antonio, TX, 1972
Voz del Pueblo, Hayward, CA, 1970-1972 complete
Voz Latina, La, Newark, CA, 1973-1974
Ya Mero, Pharr, TX, 1969-1972 complete
Yaqui/Compass, Houston, TX, 1968-1970
Zapatista, El, Pueblo, CO, 1968 complete

Source: "Chicano Studies Library Serial Collection."
In *Library Microfilms Annual 1989-1990*, 194-202.
Sunnyvale, CA: Library Microfilms, n.d. These titles
are available on 35-mm roll microfilm from Library
Microfilms (Sunnyvale, CA).

Appendix G: Underground and Alternative Press of the 1960s-1970s:
Selected Titles in Microform from the Contemporary Culture Collection, Temple University

Jesus People, Religious Groups, the Occult, the Extraterrestrial

Acorn, 1971
Ahimsa, 1972-1974
And It Is Divine, 1974
Awake, 1974
Back to Godhead, 1969-1971
The Catacomb Press, 1972
Centerline, 1971-1973
Continuum, 1972
The Cosmic Echo, 1973
Crystal Well (was Waxing Moon), 1970-1974
Diaspora, 1971-1973
The East West Journal, 1972-1975

ECK World News, 1972-1975
ESP Orbit, 1971-1972
Feraferia, 1967
Flying Saucer Review, 1960-1962, 1964, 1966-1974
Flying Saucer Review: Case Histories, 1970-1973
Gandalf's Garden, 1968-1969
Genesis - 3, 1971, 1974
Gnostica News, 1971-1975
Grapevine, 1975
Hashachar, 1972
Hollywood Free Paper, 1971-1972, 1974
Homecoming, 1971

The Ichthus, 1971-1972
Illuminator, one issue
Insight, 1972-1973
Jesus People, 1972-1973
Korythalia, 1970
The Ley Hunter, 1972
New Age Interpreter, 1972-1974
New Age Journal, 1975
New Broom, 1973
Occult Americana, vol. 2, nos. 2 and 3
Occult Oracle, vol. 1, no. 2
Omega (was Nicap Journal), 1970, 1972-1973
Nicap Journal, vol. 1, no. 5
Psychic Register International, 1972
Rejoice, vol. 1, nos. 1 and 2
Rosicrucian Digest, 1968
The Rosicrucian Fellowship Magazine, 1968, 1971
The Word, vol. 1, nos. 1, 2, 3, and 4
Zen Bow, 1967-1969
Zodiac Circle, 1970

Gay Liberation

Agape and Action, 1970-1971
The Body Politic, 1971-1975
California Scene, 1972-1974
Chicago Gay Crusader, 1973
Come Together, vol. 12, no. 15
Come Out!, 1969-1972
The Crusader, 1972
Dignity, 1973
Echo of Sapho, 1972-1973
Ecstasy, 1971
The Effeminist, 1971
Fag Rag, 1971-1975
The Furies, 1972
Gay Activist, 1972-1973
The Gay Alternative, 1972-1973
The Gay Canadian, 1972
The Gay Christian, 1973-1974
Gay Dealer, 1971
Gay Flames, 1970-1971
Gay Liberator (was Detroit Gay Liberator), 1971-1975
Gay Peoples Union News, 1971-1975
Gay Sunshine, 1970
Gayzette Phila., 1974-1975
The Griffin, 1970-1971
Homophile Action League Newsletter, 1968-1970, 1972-1973
The Ladder, 1971-1972
Lavender Woman, 1973-1975
Lesbian Tide, 1971-1973
Lesbians Fight Back, 1972
Mattachine Midwest Newsletter, 1972
MPLS Free, 1970

New York Mattachine Times, 1973
Open Doors, 1972
Radical Caucus Gay Liberation Front Newsletter, 1971
Sisters by and for Gay Women, 1974-1975
Spectre, 1971-1972
Tangents, 1965-1970
Uranian Mirror, n.d.
Vector, 1972-1973
WICCE, 1974

Military Underground

About Face (Germany), 1970
About Face (New York), 1971-1973
About Face: The EM News, 1969
Aboveground, 1969-1970
Act, 1969-1971
Aerospaced, 1969-1970
All Hands Abandon Ship, 1970
All Ready on the Left, 1970-1971
The Ally, 1969-1971
Anchorage Troop, 1970
Anti-Brass, 1970
Antithesis, 1970
As You Were, 1969-1970
Attitude Check, 1969-1970
The Awol Press, 1969
Black Unity, 1970
Bragg Briefs, 1969-1975
Broken Arrow, 1969-1971
Charleston G.I., one issue
Common Sense, 1971
Counter Point, 1969
The Destroyer, 1970-1971
Duck Power, 1969-1971
Dull Brass, 1969
Eat the Apple, 1969-1970
Fall in at Ease, 1972
Fed Up, 1970
Fort Yuma. C.A.P. News, 1971
Forward, 1971-1972
A Four Year Bummer, 1969-1971
Fragging Action, 1972
Fun, Travel, & Adventure, (FTA), 1968-1971
GAF, 1969
GI Organizer, 1969
GI Press Service, 1969-1971
GI Voice, 1969
Gigline, 1972
The Graffitti, 1970
The Green Machine, 1970
Harass the Brass, vol. 1, no. 1
Head On, 1969
Helping Hand, 1971-1974
Korea Free Press, 1971

The Last Incursion, one issue
Lewis-McChord Free Press, 1970-1973
Liberated Barracks, 1972
Marine Blues, 1974
Napalm, 1970
The Obligore, 1969-1970
Offul Times, 1972
Om, 1969-1970
Open Ranks, 1969-1970
The Paper Grenade, 1970-1971
The Pawn, 1969-1970
Potemkin, 1970
Proper Gander, 1970
Rage, 1972
Rap!, 1970-1971
The Raw Truth, 1971
Redline, 1970-1974
Rough Draft, 1969
Shakedown, 1969-1970
Short Time, 1970, 1972
SPD News, 1969
The Star Bungled Beggar, 1972
The Star Spangled Bummer, vol. 10
Top Secret, 1969
Toronto American Deserters' Committee, 1970
The Ultimate Weapon, 1969-1970
Underwood, 1971
Up Against the Bulkhead, 1970-1973
Up Against the Wall (formerly Where It's At), 1970
Up Front, 1969
Venceremos, 1970
Veterans Stars & Stripes, For Peace, 1967-1970
We Got the Brass, 1969
Your Military Left, 1969-1970, 1972

Radical Approaches to Education

Act, 1971
Alternatives for Education Newsletter, 1972-1975
Big Rock Candy Mountain, 1970-1971
Centerpeace, 1971-1973
C.H.O.I.C.E., 1971-1975
Free School Press, 1970-1971
Inequality in Education, 1975
The Innovative Education Newsletter, 1972-1974
Intercom, 1972
Journal of Educational Change, 1969-1972
Journal of the Experimental College, 1972
Journal of World Education, 1972
Media Mix, 1972-1975
New School Movement Newsletter, 1971-1973
New School of Education Journal, 1970-1973
New Schools Exchange Newsletter, 1969-1974
New Ways in Education, 1972-1975
No More Teacher's Dirty Looks, 1970-1973

Outside the Net, 1970-1973
The Red Pencil, 1969-1972
The Red Pencil Bulletin, 1970-1972
Rio Grande Education Association News, 1971-1974
The Summerhill Society of California, 1972
The Teacher Paper, 1971-1973
Teachers and Writers Collaborative Newsletter, 1970-1972
This Magazine Is about Schools, 1971-1973
Zephyros, vol. 4, no. 9

High School Publications

The Alternative, 1971
The Beverly Stash, 1971
Bird, 1971
Brass Tacks, 1970
Brook, 1972
Changes, 1972
Chelmsford Free Press, 1972
Desiderata, 1971
Do It, 1972
The Dungeon, 1972
Family, 1972
First Amendment, 1972
The Fist, 1972
Fly by Night, 1971
FPS, 1970-1975
Free Pest, [n.d.]
Fusion, 1969
Grass High, 1971
Great Society, 1971
Hamilton Gazette, 1972
Happy Trails, 1971
Here and Now, 1971
High School Student Press, 1972
Individual, 1969-1970
Inter-High, 1971
Jailbreak, 1971
Jive Times, 1972
The Liberator, vol. 2 and 3, no. 5
Madison Area H.S. Free Press, 1972
Mark and Charlie Do It Again, 1969
The Midnight Special, 1970-1971
Milestones, 1971
Minor's Lamp, 1968-1969
My Yellow Submarine, 1972
The New Free Press, 1970-1971
New Improved Tide, 1971-1972
New Morning Free Press, 1971
Oracle, 1972
Pack Rat, 1969-1970
El Papel, vol. 2, no. 5
The Paper, 1970
Paper Tiger, 1972-1973

Peach, 1971-1972
The Phantom Press, 1970
Rebel's Voice, 1971-1972
Red Army, 1971
Revelations, 1970
The Running Dog, 1971
A Salty Dog, 1971
The SCS Paper, 1972
Smash, 1970
Stand, 1972
Stand Together, 1970
Star Spangled Revolutionary Press, 1972
Stomp, 1971-1973
Student Independent Press, 1969-1971
Surgery, 1972
Synergy, 1971
The Time Machine, 1972
Twinkle News, 1972
Underneath Metuchen High, 1972
The Unity Paper, 1971-1972
Uprising, 1971
The Vast Minority, 1969
Volunteers, 1970
Voyce, 1972
We Dare Be Free, 1971
W.S.U. Newsletter, 1972

Alternative Lifestyles

Acres, U.S.A., 1971-1975
Alternate Society, 1970-1972
Alternate Sources of Energy, 1971-1974
Alternative to Alienation, 1974
Alternatives, 1971-1975
Alternatives! Foundation Newsletter, 1970
Alternatives Journal, 1971-1973
Alternatives Newsletter, 1971
Amorphia Report, 1973-1974
Arts Labs Newsletter, 1970-1971
Back to the Sticks, 1971
Black Bart Brigade, 1971
The Budget, 1972-1973
The Canadian Whole Almanac, 1970-1972
Clear Creek, 1971-1972
c/o: The Journal of Alternative Human Services, 1974
Co Evolution Quarterly, 1974-1975
Come out to the Good Life, 1974
Communes: Journal of the Commune Movement, 1969-1971
Communication, 1972-1975
Communitarian, 1972
Communitas, 1972
Communities: Journal of the Commune Movement, 1972-1974
Cormallen, 1970-1971

The Country Bizarre, 1971-1972
Country Senses, 1970-1971
Countryside, 1971
Cynthia, 1972
Domebook, 1971
Domeletter, 1971-1973
Earth, 1971-1972
Earth Conscious, 1970
Earth Journal (was Minnesota Earth Journal), 1973-1975
Earth Times, 1970
Ecologist, 1972-1974
Ecology and Politics Newsletter, 1970
Elysium: Journal of the Senses, 1972-1975
Entitas, vol. 2, no. 5
The Environment, 1971
Environmental Action, 1971-1973
Environmental Defense Fund Newsletter, 1970-1974
Family Life, 1971-1974
Family Store, 1971
Flower Patch Magazine, 1971-1972
Greenfeel, 1970
Guyon Society, 1969
Harrad, 1970
The Homesteader, 1970-1971
Homesteaders-Landcrafters Newsletter, 1972
Hunt Saboteurs Association Newsletter 1971
Impact, 1973
Innerspace, one issue
Journal of the New Harbinger, 1971-1973
La Leche League, 1971-1975
The Last Conspiracy, 1971
The Leaflet, 1972-1975
Leaves of Twin Oaks, 1967-1968, 1970-1975
Lifestyle: A Magazine of Alternatives, 1972-1973
Macrobiotic Messenger, vol. 1, no. 2
Minnesota Earth Journal (see Earth Journal), 1971-1972
Monthly News of Co-Op Communities, 1973
Muir and Friends, 1970
Nasha Envelope on Survival, 1971
National Reporter, 1972
Natural Lifestyles, 1971-1972
New Community Projects Communication, 1972-1975
Northwind, 1972-1973
Not Man Apart, 1970-1973
Omen, 1970-1971
Open End, 1972
Organic Gardening and Farming, 1942, 1972-1973
The Ozarks Mountaineer, 1972-1975
The Questers Newsletter, 1970
Radical Software, 1970-1972
Rags, 1970-1971
Sexual Freedom League of Michigan, 1972-1975
Sierra Review, 1971
Sower, 1970

Survival, 1970
Third View, [n.d.]
Toiyabe Trails, 1972-1975
Vegetarian Voice, 1974-1975
Vibrations, 1971
Vibrations: Drug Survival News, 1972
Vision, 1969-1970
Vocations for Social Change (see Workforce), 1969-1973
Well Being, 1972
Whole Earth Catalogue, 1969-1971
The Whole Life Catalog, 1970
The Wildcrafters World, 1971
The Woodheat Quarterly, vol. 1, no. 1
The Woodstock Aquarian, 1971
Workforce (was Vocations for Social Change), 1972-1973

Libertarian

A Is a Newsletter, 1971-1975
The Atlantis News, 1971-1972
The Atlantis Quarterly, 1968-1969
The Ayn Rand Letter, 1971-1974
Commentary on Liberty, 1969, 1971
Efficacy (was Innovator), 1969-1971
Equality, 1965-1976
Ergo, 1972-1973
The Fire Bringer, 1971-1973
The Free Market, 1972-1973
Independent Libertarian Commentary, 1971-1973
Individual Liberty, 1974-1975
Individualist, 1970-1972
Innovator, 1965-1969
Invictus, 1970-1973
Jag, 1971-1975
Liberator, 1970

Libertarian Analysis, 1970-1971
The Libertarian Connection, 1972-1973
Libertarian Option, 1973
The Match, 1970, 1974-1975
The New Banner, 1972-1973
Notes of Fee, 1972-1975
Preform-Inform, 1968-1970
Rampart College Newsletter, 1971-1974
The Shadow, 1973
Society for Individual Liberty News, 1970-1974
Sol III, 1971-1972
Vonu Life (was Preform-Inform), 1973

Radical Health

The Bach Remedy Newsletter, 1957-1958, 1960-1972
Constructive Action for Good Health Magazine, 1970-1972
For the People's Health, 1970
Health/Pac Bulletin, 1970-1971
Health Rights News, 1968-1973
Medical Resistance Union Newsletter, 1968-1970
Occupational Health Project Report, 1972
The Pharmchem Newsletter, 1972-1973
Philadelphia Health News, 1971-1972
Research Network Newsletter, 1972
Rough Times (was The Radical Therapist), 1970-1972
Social Action: Newsletter of Psychologists for Social Action, 1971
Street Medicine, Chicago Style, 1970

Note: 390 titles are preserved on 72 reels of microfilm. All but a few are from the United States. Individual reels are available from Temple University Libraries.

Source: *Alternative Press Periodicals*. Philadelphia: Temple University Libraries, 1976.

Appendix H: U.S. Underground and Alternative Press of the 1960s-1970s:
A Selected List of Microform Masters

Advocate (Los Angeles Advocate), Los Angeles, CA, 1967-, USC; 1967-1970, NYP
ADZ Gayzette, San Francisco, CA, 1970-1972, UCB
Agape and Action, Berkeley, CA, 1970-1971, UCB
Ain't I a Woman?, Iowa City, IA, 1970-1973, UMI
Akwesasne Notes, Mohawk Nation, NY, 1969-, UMI
Alternative Sources of Energy, Milaca, MN, 1971-1988, UMI
Alternatives, Oberlin, OH, 1976-1982, UMI
Amazon Quarterly, Oakland, CA, 1972-1975, UCB
Amerasia Journal, Los Angeles, CA, 1971-, UMI
Amerindian: American Indian Review, Chicago, IL, 1952-1974, UMI

Amicus Journal, New York, NY, 1979-, UMI
Amnesty Action, New York, NY, 1966-, NYP
Ann Arbor Sun (later, Sun), Ann Arbor, MI, 1971-76, UMI
ARC [Association for Responsible Citizenship] News, Sacramento, CA, 1966-1967, UCB
Asian Week, San Francisco, CA, 1979-, LM
Aztlan Chicano Journal, Los Angeles, CA, 1970-1974, LM
Babylon, 1971-1972, New York, NY, NYU
BAR [Bay Area Reporter], San Francisco, CA, 1971-1989, UCB
Bar Rag, San Francisco, CA, 1967, UCB

Berkeley Barb, Berkeley, CA, 1975-1980, NYPL
Berkeley Tribe, Berkeley, CA, 1969-1972, LM
Bill of Rights Journal, New York, NY, 1968- , UMI
Bitalian News, Chicago, IL, 1977-1978, LM
Black Panther, Oakland, CA, 1968-1980, UMI
Black Scholar, San Francisco, CA, 1969- , UMI
Blade, The, Irvine, CA, 1975-1989, CMS
Bridge, New York, NY, 1973-1985, UMI
Bridge, The, San Jose, CA, 1970-1971, UCB
Buffalo Insighter, The, 1967, MSC
Bulletin of Concerned Asian Scholars, Boulder, CO, 1968- , UMI
Call, The, Chicago, IL, 1974-1982, LM
Carta Editoriale, Riverside, CA, 1963-1969, LM
CCCO [Central Committee for Conscientious Objectors] News Notes, Philadelphia, PA, 1949- , UMI
Center for Cuban Studies Newsletter, New York, NY, 1974-1976, LM
CHF [Committee for Homosexual Freedom] Newsletter, San Francisco, CA, 1969, UCB
Chicano, El, San Bernardino, CA, 1968, LM
Chicano Theatre, San Juan Bautista, CA, 1973-1974, LM
Cineaste, New York, NY, 1967- , UMI
Come Out, New York, NY, 1969-1972, NYP
Coming Up!, San Francisco, CA 1979-1989, UCB
Communities, Louisa, VA, 1972- , UMI
Con Safos, Los Angeles, CA, 1968-1969, LM
Counter-Spy, Washington, DC, 1973-1984, UMI
CovertAction Information Bulletin, Washington, DC, 1978- , UMI
CRH [Council on Religion and the Homosexual] Newsletter, San Francisco, CA, 1967, UCB
Critical Sociology, Eugene, OR, 1988- , UMI
Cruise News and World Report, San Francisco, CA, 1965-1967, UCB
Cuba Resource Center Newsletter, New York, NY, 1972-1973, LM
Cuban Review, New York, NY, 1974-1979, LM
Daughters of Bilitis, San Francisco, CA, 1959-1978, UCB
Detroit Sun, Detroit, MI, 1976, UMI
Dissent, New York, NY, 1954- , UMI
D.N.A. Newsletter, Window Rock, AZ, 1973-1975, CW
Dollars and Sense, Somerville, MA, 1974- , UMI
Dykes and Gorgons, Berkeley, CA, 1973, UCB
East Bay Gay Men's Newsletter, Oakland, CA, 1973, UCB
East Village Other, New York, NY, 1965-1972, UMI
East-West: The Chinese-American Journal, San Francisco, CA, 1967- , LM
East West Journal, Brookline, MA, 1978- , UMI
Ecology Center Newsletter, Berkeley, CA, 1971- , UMI

Effeminist, The, Berkeley, CA, 1971, UCB
Environmental Action, Washington, DC, 1970- , UMI
Fag Rag, Cambridge, MA, 1971- , NYP
Feminist Studies, College Park, MD, 1972- , UMI
Fifth Estate, Detroit, MI, 1965- , UMI
Food Monitor (later, Why: Changing Hunger and Poverty), New York, NY, 1977- , UMI
Free Particle, San Francisco, CA, 1969, UCB
GAA [Gay Activist Alliance] Lifeline, San Francisco, CA, 1971, UCB
Gallo, El, Denver, CO, 1968-1969, LM
Gay Bay Newsletter, San Francisco, CA, 1970, UCB
Gay Community News, Boston, MA, 1973- , NYP; GCN
Gay Flames, New York, NY, 1970-1971, NYP
Gay Flames Pamphlet, New York, NY, 19??, NYP
Gay Liberation Front Bulletin, New York, NY, 1969-1970, NYP
Gay Liberator [Detroit Gay Liberator], Detroit, MI, 1970-1976, NYP; 1970- ?, UWM
Gay People's Newsletter, Berkeley, CA, 1970, UCB
Gay Power, New York, NY, 196?, NYP
Gay Pride Crusader, San Francisco, CA, 1972-1981, UCB
Gay Radical Rag, San Francisco, CA, 1970, UCB
Gay Students' Union, Berkeley, CA, 1970, UCB
Gay Sunshine, San Francisco, CA, 1970-1982, NYP; 1970-1980, CMS; 1970-1971, UCB
Gay Switchboard, Berkeley, CA, 1970, UCB
Gay Voice, Sacramento, CA, 1971, UCB
Gaylife, Chicago, IL, 1975-1986, MML
GaysWeek, New York, NY, 1977-1979, NYP
Gayzette, Philadelphia, PA, 1974-1975, FLP
Gayzette, Salt Lake City, UT, 1975, KCP
Genesis Two, Cambridge, MA, 1970- , UMI
Gidra, Los Angeles, CA, 1971-1974, NYP
GLF [Gay Liberation Front] News, New York, NY, 1970, NYP
Gotham, New York, NY, 1979-1980, NYP
Gotham, a Ledger of the Gay Community, New York, NY, 1976, NYP
Great Speckled Bird, The, Atlanta, GA, 1968-1985, UMI
Green Revolution, York, PA, etc., 1963- , UMI
GSU Newsletter, Berkeley, CA, 1971, UCB
Guardian, New York, NY, 1948- , UMI
Haight Ashbury Free Press, San Francisco, CA, 1967, UCB
Health PAC Bulletin, New York, NY, 1968- , UMI
Hundred Flowers, Minneapolis, MN, 1970-1972, MHS
I Am, San Francisco, CA, 1971, UCB
In These Times, Chicago, IL, 1976- , UMI; 1977-1984, LM
Indian Historian, San Francisco, CA, 1964-1979, 3MC

Indian Truth, Philadelphia, PA, 1924- , CW; UMI; KTO

Industrial Worker, Chicago, IL, 1916- , UMI

Insurgent Socialist, Eugene, OR, 1972-1982

International Socialist, Highland Park, CA, 1969-1975, LM

Interracial Books for Children Bulletin, New York, NY, 1976- , UMI

Isis, Philadelphia, PA, 1913- , UMI

Issues in Radical Therapy & Cooperative Power, Berkeley, CA, 1973-1979, UMI

ITTC [Inter Tribal Council of California] Newsletter, Sacramento, CA, 1968-1969, CW

Journal of Palestine Studies, Washington, DC, 1971-, UMI

Jump Cut, Berkeley, CA, 1974- , UMI

Kalendar, San Francisco, CA, 1972-1978, UCB

Kinesis, Carbondale, IL, 1968- , UMI

Labor History, New York, NY, 1960- , UMI

Ladder, The, San Francisco, CA, 1956-1972, UCB

Latin American Perspectives, Riverside, CA 1974-, UMI

Lavender Letter, San Francisco, CA, 1971, UCB

LCE [League for Civil Education] News (later, The News and Citizens News), San Francisco, CA, 1961-1967, UCB

Lesbian Tide, The, Los Angeles, CA, 1971-1980, NYP

Lesbian Voices, Campbell, CA, 1974-1981, UCB

Longest Revolution, The, San Diego, CA, 1977-1983, CMS; 1977-1981- , LM

Los Angeles Free Press, Los Angeles, CA, 1956, 1966-1978, LM

Los Angeles Reader, Los Angeles, CA, 1978-1984, LM

Majority Report, New York, NY, 1971-1979, NYP

Malcriadito, El, Los Angeles, CA, 1975-1976, LM

Matchbox, New York, NY, 1978-1983, CMS; 1978-1979, LM

Mattachine Review, San Francisco, CA, 1955-1966, UCB

Maverick, San Francisco, CA, 1967, UCB

Medical Self-Care, Inverness, CA, 1976- , UMI

Michigan Free Press, Ann Arbor, MI, 1974-1978, UMI, SHWS

Middle East Research & Information Project (later, MERIP Report), Washington, DC, 1971- , UMI

Militant, The, New York, NY, 1937-1964, 1968-1972, SHSW; 1947-1951, NYP; 1968-1981, PUL; 1972- , UMI

Mom...Guess What...!, Sacramento, CA, 1978- , NYP

Monthly Review, New York, NY, 1949- , UMI

Mother, Stanford, CA, 1971-1972, UCB

Mother Jones, San Francisco, CA, 1976- , UMI

Mothering, Santa Fe, NM, 1976- , UMI

Muhammed Speaks, Chicago, IL, 1971-1975, LM

Mundo, El, Oakland, CA, 1971-1977, 1979, LM

Mundo Hispano, San Francisco, CA, 1970, LM

NACLA Newsletter, New York, NY, 1967-1969, LM; 1967-1971, UMI

NACLA Report on the Americas, New York, NY, 1977- , UMI

NACLA's Latin America & Empire Report, New York, NY, 1971-1977 incomplete, UMI

Nation, The, New York, NY, 1865- , UMI

National NOW Times, Washington, DC, 1968- , UMI

National Reporter, Washington, DC, 1985- , UMI

Navajo Times, Window Rock, AZ, 1976-1984, LM

New Age Journal, Brighton, MI, 1974- , UMI

New Directions for Women, Westwood, NJ, 1975- , UMI

New Politics, New York, NY, 1961-1978, UMI

New Women's Times, Rochester, NY, 1979-1983; CMS; LM

New World Review, New York, NY, 1932-1985, UMI

News and Letters, Detroit, MI, 1976-1981, LM

NLIS [National Lesbian Information Service] Newsletter, San Francisco, CA, 1972, UCB

Notes from Underground, Long Island City, NY, 1970- , UMI

off our backs, Washington, DC, 1970- , SHSW, NYP; 1971-1984, LM

One, Los Angeles, CA, 1953-1958, NYP

Oracle, The, San Francisco, CA, 1966-1969, LM

Pacific Citizen, Los Angeles, CA, 1929- , LM

Palante, New York, NY, 1971-1974, NYP

Papel de la Gente, El, Riverside, CA, 1976-1977, LM

Paperbag, Los Angeles, CA, 1968, NYP

Peace & Freedom, Philadelphia, PA, 1941- , UMI

Peacemaker, Garberville, CA, 1949- , UMI

Penal Digest International, The, Iowa City, IA, 1971-1972, NYP

People & Taxes, Washington, DC, 1976, 1979-1982, CMS

People's World, Berkeley, CA, 1943- , LM; 1938-1986, UMI.

Philadelphia Gay News (Gay News), Philadelphia, PA, 1971- , FLP

Plexus, Berkeley, CA, 19??- , LM

Political Affairs, New, York, NY, 1924- , UMI

Prensa, La, Los Angeles, CA, 1967-1970, LM

Progressive, The, Madison, WI, 1929- , UMI

Radical America, Somerville, MA, 1967- , UMI

Radical Homosexual Rag, Berkeley, CA, 1970, UCB

Ramparts, Berkeley, CA, 1962-1975, UMI

Rayas, Albuquerque, NM, 1978-1979, LM

Re Vision, Cambridge, MA, 1978- , UMI

Realist, The, New York, NY, 1958-1974 incomplete, UMI

Review of Radical Political Economy, New York, NY, 1969- , UMI

RFD, Wolf Creek, OR, etc., 1974- , UWM
Rising up Angry, Buffalo, NY, 1973-1974, MSC
Rubyfruit Readher, Santa Cruz, CA, 1976-1978, UCB
Salt Lick, The, Salt Lake City, UT, 1976, KCP
San Francisco Bay Guardian, San Francisco, CA, 1966- , UMI
San Francisco Free Press, San Francisco, CA, 1969-1970, UCB
San Francisco Gay Free Press, San Francisco, CA, 1970, UCB
San Francisco Mattachine Newsletter, San Francisco, CA, 1953-1963, UCB
San Francisco Sentinel, San Francisco, CA, 1974-1989, UCB
San Jose Gay Liberation, San Jose, CA, 1970, UCB
Sapphire, San Francisco, CA, 1973, UCB
Science & Society, New York, NY, 1936- , UMI
Science for the People, Cambridge, MA, 1969- , UMI
Seattle Gay News, Seattle, WA, 197?- , UWL
Sebastian Quill, San Francisco, CA, 1970-1972, UCB
Semana, La, Riverside, CA, 1976-1977, LM
Seven Days, New York, NY, 1975-1980, UMI
Sisters, San Francisco, CA, 1970-1975, UCB
Social Policy, New York, NY, 1970- , UMI
Socialist Review, Oakland, CA, 1978- , UMI
Sojourners, Washington, DC, 1976- , UMI
Sonoma County Gay Alliance News, Santa Rosa, CA, 1978-1980, UCB
Southern Exposure, Chapel Hill, NC, 1973- , UMI
Space City, Houston, TX, 1971-1972 incomplete, NYP
Stony Hills, Newburyport, MA, 1977- , HUL
Straightqueer, San Francisco, CA, 1972, UCB
Tecolote, El, San Francisco, CA, 1970- , LM
Town Talk, San Francisco, CA, 1964-1966, UCB
Tribal Spokesmen, The, Sacramento, CA, 1969- , CW; 196?-1977, SHSW
Tricontinental News Service, Chicago, IL, 1972-1974, LM
Tucson's Mountain Newsreal, Tucson, AZ, 1977-1981, SHSW
Tundra Times, Fairbanks, AK, 1962-1975, UWL
Underground Press Directory, Stevens Point, WI, 1969, NYP
University Press, Irvine, CA, 1979-1979, CMS
Uranian Mirror, San Francisco, CA, 1971, UCB
Vanguard, San Francisco, CA, 1966-1970, UCB
Vector, San Francisco, CA, 1964-1976, UCB
Village Voice, New York, NY, 1955- , UMI
Voice, San Francisco, CA, 1979-1983, UCB
Voz Mestiza, La, Irvine, CA, 1979-1989, CMS
Warpath, The, San Francisco, CA, 1968-1973, LM
Wassaja, San Francisco, CA, 1973-1979, LM; MSU; 1980, KTO
Weekly News Bulletin, Miami, FL, 1977-1978, NYP

Weekly Philadelphia Gayzette, Philadelphia, PA, 1974-1977, FLP
Whole Life Times, Newton, MA, 1979- , NYP
Women's Equality Action Ledger, 1971-1979, LM
Women's Rights Law Reporter, New Brunswick, NJ 1971- , UMI
Women's Studies International Forum, Elmsford, NY, 1978- , UMI
Worker's Power, Highland Park, MI, 1970-1975, LM
Yipster Times, New York, NY, 1972-1978, NYU
Young Socialist, New York, NY, 1957-1970, AMS

Note: Most titles are available on 35-mm roll microfilm; coverage may be incomplete; several titles may appear on one roll. Copies may not be available for sale for certain titles because of copyright restrictions. See also Appendixes E-G.

Preservation Source Codes:

AMS: AMS Press [New York City]
CMS: Custom Microfilm Systems [Riverside, CA]
CW: Clearwater [New York]
FLP: Free Library of Phildelphia
GCN: Gay Community News [Boston]
HUL: Harvard University Library [Boston]
KCP: Kalvar Corporation [Salt Lake City]
KTO: Kraus-Thomson [Millwood, NY]
LM: Library Microfilms [Sunnyvale, CA]; see also Appendix F
MHS: Minnesota Historical Society [Minneapolis]
MML: McLaren Micropublishing, Ltd [Toronto, ON]
MSC: Microform Systems of Connecticut [New Haven]
MSU: Mankato State University [MN]
NYP: New York Public Library [New York City]
NYU: New York University Libraries [New York City]
PUL: Princeton University Library [NJ]
SHSW: State Historical Society of Wisconsin [Madison]; see also Appendix B
3MC: 3M Company International Microfilm Press [St. Paul, MN]
UCB: University of California, Berkeley, Library
USC: University of Southern California Library
UMI: University Microfilms International [Ann Arbor, MI]
UWL: University of Washington Library [Seattle]
UWM: University of Wisconsin, Madison, Memorial Library

Sources: Micropublishers, OCLC, RLIN, GLADIS, *Microform Review* 15, no. 4 (Fall 1986): 206, *Library Microfilms Annual 1989-1990, Guide to Microforms in Print 1990, 1990 Serials in Microform, Lesbian and Gay Periodicals of Northern California* (forthcoming).